DISABILITY, CULTUR
Alfredo J. Artiles and Elizabeth B. Kozleski, *Series Editors*

After the "At-Risk" Label: Reorienting Educational Policy and Practice
KEFFRELYN D. BROWN

DisCrit—Disability Studies and Critical Race Theory in Education
DAVID J. CONNOR, BETH A. FERRI, & SUBINI A. ANNAMMA, EDS.

Closing the School Discipline Gap:
Equitable Remedies for Excessive Exclusion
DANIEL J. LOSEN, ED.

(Un)Learning Disability:
Recognizing and Changing Restrictive Views of Student Ability
ANNMARIE D. BAINES

Ability, Equity, and Culture:
Sustaining Inclusive Urban Education Reform
ELIZABETH B. KOZLESKI & KATHLEEN KING THORIUS, EDS.

Condition Critical—Key Principles for Equitable and Inclusive Education
DIANA LAWRENCE-BROWN & MARA SAPON-SHEVIN

After the "At-Risk" Label

REORIENTING EDUCATIONAL POLICY AND PRACTICE

KEFFRELYN D. BROWN

TEACHERS COLLEGE PRESS

TEACHERS COLLEGE | COLUMBIA UNIVERSITY
NEW YORK AND LONDON

Published by Teachers College Press, 1234 Amsterdam Avenue, New York, NY 10027

Cover design by Patricia Palao. Photo by FotografiaBasica / iStock by Getty Images.

Library of Congress Cataloging-in-Publication Data is available at loc.gov

ISBN 978-0-8077-5701-7 (paper)
ISBN 978-0-8077-7412-0 (ebook)

Printed on acid-free paper
Manufactured in the United States of America

23 22 21 20 19 18 17 16   8 7 6 5 4 3 2 1

Contents

Acknowledgments

I want to acknowledge the support I received to do this work from the Wisconsin-Spencer Training Program at the Univeristy of Wisconsin–Madison, the Ford Foundation Dissertation Fellowship and the Dean's Fellowship in the College of Education at The University of Texas at Austin. Special appreciation goes to several people who offered advice and support on earlier drafts of this work: Carl Grant, Gloria Ladson-Billings, Tom Popkewitz, Stacey Lee, Jerlando Jackson, Maria Hernandez, Jackie Nguyen and Jeffrey Lewis. Thanks to Alfredo Artiles, Elizabeth Kozleski, Brian Ellerbeck, Jennifer Baker, and the entire TC Press editorial staff. Thanks Ferman Carpenter for the lesson on the Samaritan woman. And as always thanks to Herman and Linda Brown, Cheri, William, Jaelyn and Jyle Hamilton, and the glue that keeps me together: Anthony, Kanaan and Kythe Brown. Much love and appreciation to you all.

CHAPTER 1

Introduction

Why Should We Interrogate Risk?

In the Judeo-Christian tradition (John 4:1–26) there is a popular story told about an interaction Jesus had with an unnamed Samaritan woman while visiting a well. As the story goes, Jesus was tired and taking a rest when a Samaritan woman came nearby to draw water. The Samaritans were viewed as an unclean people of mixed ethnic heritage, both Jewish and Babylonian. They were also enemies to the Jews. This particular Samaritan woman bore an additional mark of social stigma due to the number of marriages she had and her purported sexual promiscuity. The story unfolds with Jesus offering to share with the woman his knowledge of a spiritual source, more powerful than water, that can provide her with all she needs or may, in fact, seek. She is happy to learn of this source and to hear Jesus say that in the days to come all people, no matter their background or experiences, will have direct access to and relationship with the sovereign God. When this story is told, it often is used to illuminate the differences between the carnal and spiritual, and the perpetual nonfulfillment that people experience when trying to satisfy their longing needs with materiality. The antidote to this is Jesus, the intercessor to a life everlasting for those who choose to follow him and his ways.

Yet, I want to consider another important aspect of this story, also poignant and illustrative of how education might better address schooling for all students, particularly those positioned as potentially underachieving. I want to think about this story in relation to *risk*, an idea that is endemic and pervasive to schooling. In the story the teacher Jesus (Burbules, 2004; Burke & Segall, 2015; Keller, 1998) makes a bold move. He approaches a woman who is positioned as a social outcast. He does not label her. He talks to her, listens to her, and seeks to help her from a place of full openness and acceptance. He knows who she is and how she is positioned in the larger society. He understands power and the role it plays in structuring inequitable, oppressive societal relations, including the woman's own categorization and stigmatization as outcast. Yet he does not prejudge her because of her race, gender, or social status. In fact, he does not address any of these issues during this interaction, except to tell the woman that he knows she is living with a man who is not her husband.

1

He does not share this information to ostracize her. He wants her to know that he knows things about her that far exceed information he could have gathered from their interaction. As a teacher he wants her to realize the power of the moment and to take seriously the knowledge that he wants to share with her. He does not talk down to her, nor does he place himself above her. Rather, he entreats her into a relationship with him in order to share knowledge that she might find serviceable in her everyday life. Their interaction is brief but powerful. It highlights fundamental ingredients found in a humanizing pedagogical moment: a teaching orientation based on teacher humility, recognition, love, and the possession of and respect for the power of knowledge.

Contrast this approach with the assumptions embedded in how schools and teachers approach students positioned similarly to the Samaritan woman: the student labeled and categorized as "at-risk" for low academic achievement. At-risk students occupy the place of academic outcast. Whether used formally or loosely in conversation, the at-risk moniker is a distinguishing marker meant to identify and demarcate students positioned as less likely than their peers to achieve academically. Similar to the Samaritan woman, these markers are mired in stereotypes that link to race, class, and gender. The academically at-risk student is often of color—Black or Latino/a—lives in a low-income or working-class household, receives special services for learning and/or behavioral (dis)abilities, and/or speaks English as a second language. Students recognized as academically at-risk in official district, state, or federal education policy also might be homeless, live in neighborhoods that are considered unsafe or dangerous, or live in a single-parent, generally female-headed household (McWhirter, McWhirter, McWhirter, & McWhirter, 2012). Notwithstanding the uncertainty of the teaching enterprise itself, the academically at-risk student is particularly singled out for possible academic failure because of presumed close proximity to factors that make underachievement a more likely outcome. Taking a closer look, we also recognize that by virtue of receiving the label at-risk—either formally or informally—the student is already the target of normalizing judgment (Ferguson, 2001) by those charged with the responsibility of helping the student. To be constructed as at-risk signals difference and deficit, a partitioning outside of the normal.

In *After the "At-Risk" Label: Reorienting Educational Policy and Practice*, I explore the knowledge that informs how three education sites—policy, practicing teachers, and those preparing to become teachers—talk about, make sense of, and act in relation to potential risk and student academic achievement across national and local contexts. The impetus to write this book came from the realization that more attention was needed in order to understand how risk figures in education policy and practice,

Research
Q

most often in the use of the at-risk category and label. How does risk play out in education policies that influence the work of schooling? How do teachers understand and draw from risk in their everyday practices? What might we learn about more effectively and equitably meeting the needs of all students by attending closely to risk? This book takes up these important questions.

Risk hovers around education, lurking in conversations about student achievement and the dismal failure of schools to meet the needs of all their students. Risk is also a part of those systems put in place to work with students, most often those officially categorized and given distinguishing (and stigmatizing) labels as part of the process. Here, and throughout the book, I recognize the connection to and difference between a category and a label. A label is what we name a person or thing. A category, according to Tilly (1998), "consists of a set of actors who share a boundary distinguishing all of them from and relating all of them to at least one set of actors visibly excluded by that boundary" (p. 62). The at-risk category and label, then, serve to name *and* create specific people that are recognized as at-risk for experiencing some negative outcome. By virtue of being at-risk, this category of person is viewed as more likely than those falling outside of the category to experience the outcome.

In this book, I argue that these, and other enactments of practice around the construct of risk, reflect more than simply the everyday work of educators concerned with academic achievement. At the core of these practices resides knowledge. This knowledge comprises an accumulated set of ideas and beliefs around students, teaching, and curriculum. It also reflects dominant societal perspectives held about risk in education that are grounded in the social, political, economic, and cultural histories and contexts of the United States. I refer to this as sociocultural knowledge, and it is embedded in the work of schooling and teaching. It is important to recognize this sociocultural knowledge and, in this case, the sociocultural knowledge of risk, as it tells us a lot about what educators know, value, and privilege in their work around concerns with academic achievement.

What I take up in this book is more than simply theoretical pontification of ideas, disconnected from the everyday, sociocultural work and practices of schooling. What I aim to show is how deeply, and often problematically, the construct of risk and the practices of categorizing and labeling students as at-risk are integrally connected to sociocultural knowledge that informs policy, teachers, and the practices of teaching. The magnitude of risk knowledge in education is daunting, nationally and globally.[1] As this book will show, risk knowledge speaks not only to how students are understood and constructed, but also to how teachers envision their role and work in the classroom.

RISKY KNOWLEDGE AND TEACHING

A perennial concern in teacher education is how to best prepare teachers to teach all students effectively and equitably (Cochran-Smith & Zeichner, 2005; Darling-Hammond & Bransford, 2005). In response to this goal, teacher educators and faculty at schools of education introduce students to approaches to schooling and teaching that fall under a myriad of descriptors, including *critical pedagogy* (Duncan-Andrade & Morrell, 2008; Milner, 2003), *multicultural education* (Banks, 1993; Sleeter & Grant, 2006), *teaching for social justice* (Picower, 2012), *equity pedagogy* (Banks & Banks, 1995), and *culturally relevant/responsive teaching* (Gay, 2010; Ladson-Billings, 2009; Villegas & Lucas, 2001). While these approaches differ in goals and emphasis, what is common across them is the assumption that teachers must believe that all students, regardless of background or circumstance, are capable learners who can achieve at high levels. Each of them also recognizes the power that knowledge plays in the teaching and learning process. Given these concerns, it makes sense to ask: *What sociocultural knowledge do teachers need to possess about learning and academic achievement that will make it possible for them to provide all students with an effective and equitable schooling experience?*

In my experiences as a learner, teacher, school administrator, and now researcher and teacher educator, I have found it common to hear people discuss and even feel confident in their ability to decide what makes one student less or more likely than another to perform well academically. This is a curious undertaking because often the idea of risk—or the assumption that some students face the possibility of not learning—is fundamental to these discussions. In this study I am particularly interested in how perspectives of risk, that is, uncertainty, potential damage, and loss of something of value (Lupton, 1999a)—specifically the loss of academic learning or success—serve to open or close off the possibilities of learning for all students.

One of the enduring and most perplexing concerns in education is ensuring that all students achieve academically. In this context, academic achievement refers to students' success in relation to the expectations and learning experiences they encounter in school. In the existing neoliberal policy climate characterized by individualism, market competition, and privatization (Baldridge, 2014), the extent to which students learn is often connected to the educational opportunities they are afforded (or they fail to receive) in schools (Brown & Goldstein, 2013; Ladson-Billings, 2006; Lipman, 2011). Underserved students, including those of color, those from low-income families, those whose first language is not English, and those identified as having special needs, experience a pattern of inequitable opportunities to learn in their schooling. As a result, differences exist across various measures of achievement and school performance between these student populations and those who are White, middle class, native English speakers, and not identified as needing special education. These outcomes speak to what Ladson-Billings (2006) called an "education debt" that fuels dominant economic and political interests, while maintaining the oppressive, inequitable conditions faced historically by people of color and other underserved groups. In education, this impacts material resources directly related to schooling, including school funding; access to rigorous, relevant curriculum; and quality teachers. This dilemma highlights the risk underserved student populations face with regard to receiving a quality, equitable education. It consequently establishes the impetus to improve school practice.

During the 1980s, the term *at-risk* emerged as a moniker to describe students presumed more likely than their peers to experience low achievement and other similarly detrimental school-based outcomes (Martinez & Rury, 2012; Swadener, 1995). The rationale behind this practice was simple and aligned historically with the practices of school systems: figure out which students possibly will not do well and offer them the support needed to preemptively circumvent their failure (Cuban, 1989; Franklin, 1994). This approach to risk management (Lupton, 1999b) continues to inform how education stakeholders and policymakers address schooling. While many believe this is *necessary* in order to meet these students' needs, an outcome of this categorizing practice is that these students, by virtue of their often non-normative race, social class, language, and/ or ability identification, get positioned as deficient and in need of specialized treatment. Over time, the sociocultural markers of race, social class, gender, language, and ability have become inextricably linked to at-risk status, regardless of any particular student's actual proximity to or experience of academic risk. This rendering of risk also is recognized as *dangerous*, particularly because of its durability in mainstream societal and educational discourse, in spite of the scrutiny and criticism it has faced. Whether invoked in policy, the popular media, or simultaneously in districts and schools, the term *at-risk student* often is deployed in unquestioned, taken-for-granted ways.

WHAT DO WE ALREADY KNOW ABOUT RISK AND THE CATEGORY AND LABEL OF THE AT-RISK STUDENT?

We know from the existing literature on the at-risk student that the construct is historically situated, pervasive, and socially produced in ways that problematically invoke race, social class, and gender. Since the 1970s (Rist, 1970) and into the present (Gadsden, Davis, & Artiles, 2009), the literature in equity, schooling, and teaching argues that sociocultural factors, including race, social class, and dis/ability, play a decisive role in school and teacher decisionmaking in the United States. Gadsden and colleagues

(2009) pointed out that decisionmaking at both the individual and policy levels curtails students' opportunities to learn in both school and classroom contexts. The advent of mandatory standardized testing, along with the concomitant surveillance it encouraged, placed not only students, but also teachers, schools, and entire school systems (especially those that served historically underserved students), at threat for possible risk identification. As a result, schools, school districts, and teacher education programs face increased challenge of helping educators navigate effectively in the context of these risks, since knowing how to navigate this process is vital to ensuring that all students receive a high-quality education.

The specific use of the term *risk* was transported to the field of education from psychopathology, psychiatry, and developmental psychopathology (Rutter, 1979). The term *at-risk* gained popularity in educational parlance after the publication of *A Nation at Risk* in 1983 (Land & Legters, 2002; Placier, 1996). This popularity drew attention to the contention and lack of consensus across social science and education literature regarding the origins of risk, the causes of academic risk, or how school personnel, teacher educators, and policymakers should address students presumed in danger of academic risk (Boykin, 2000; Cuban, 1989; Natriello, McDill, & Pallas, 1990; Pianta & Walsh, 1996; Stringfield & Land, 2002; Swadener, 1995).

A proliferation of work dealing specifically with the category and label of the at-risk student has emerged since the late 1980s, with much of this literature focused on: (1) *identifying/reviewing the factors that make some students more likely than others to experience academic failure* (e.g., low academic performance, dropping out of school) or *some other unintended social outcome* (e.g., engagement in perceived dangerous, high-risk behaviors such as alcohol or drug usage, promiscuous and unprotected sex) (Dryfoos, 1990; Gleason & Dynarski, 2002; Land & Legters, 2002; Natriello et al., 1990; Presseisen, 1988; Sameroff, Seifer, Baldwin, & Baldwin, 1993); (2) *promoting and/or reviewing successful interventions for addressing the needs of at-risk students* (Stringfield & Land, 2002); (3) *evaluating interventions used to address the needs of at-risk students* (Bermak, Chung, & Siroskey-Sabdo, 2005; Savage & Carless, 2005; Slavin et al., 1996); or (4) *examining or theorizing how various educational sites understand, or make meaning of, the at-risk label and category* (Cuban, 1989; Edwards, Danridge, & Pleasants, 2000; Franklin, 1994; Lubeck & Garrett, 1990; Placier, 1993; Richardson, Casanova, Placier, & Guilfoyle, 1989; Swadener, 1995).

Across the 1990s and into the new millennium, a foundational body of education scholarship examined meanings of the at-risk category and label. This scholarship pointed out that-risk had a long history in the way education stakeholders understand and talk about students and their learning, as well as being a socially constructed term based on historically raced, classed, and gendered notions of normality. This scholarship generally examined risk in a single education site, including state education policy, an educational research database, state law, a school, and a classroom (e.g., Casanova, 1990; Edwards et al., 2000; Frost, 1994; Frymier & Gansneder, 1989; Placier, 1993, 1996; Richardson et al., 1989).

Scholarship also has focused specifically on discourses of risk, exploring how the sociocultural factors of race, social class, and gender historically have operated in the use of the at-risk construct (Fine, 1993; Swadener, 1995). Additional examples of this work looked at how the at-risk label constructs Black male students (James, 2011) and operates in the schooling experiences (McGee, 2013) of Black boys and in the uncertain work of schools and teaching (Gershon, 2012; Ginsberg, 2012). In some cases, authors note the necessity to reframe and embrace risk, particularly in the context of urban education where authentic teaching and learning remains under threat (Ginsberg, 2012). Collectively this work drew from an interpretivist lens that examined how vested stakeholders made meaning of the at-risk construct. In some cases, a critical perspective was adopted to account for the raced, classed, and gendered ways the construct has operated in the United States.

Due to its longevity and continued relevance in describing students, some might question the necessity for examining risk and the category and label at-risk. In my case, this issue presented as three questions I encountered when initiating my research. I took these questions seriously. They were not blanket inquiries. They presented arguments that called into question the significance and relevance of my study. I share them here because they bear consideration, speaking not only to the contentious nature of the at-risk moniker, but, more important, to the normative, common-sense (Apple, 2014) acceptances people too often afford to the use of the term itself. Below I outline the three key queries and their corresponding arguments I encountered when beginning this study:

"Don't we know what people mean by at-risk?"

The "we" in this sentence generally referred to scholars and researchers. When posing this question, those asking were certain they knew what people meant when using the term, thus leaving nothing else of value worth exploring. The question suggested the existing research provided a body of substantive, well-documented, and clearly elucidated knowledge on the meanings and use of the category and label at-risk.

"Why do you want to study that—don't we already know what at-risk is all about?"

This question similarly presumed that knowledge about the term at-risk was already known. It also indicated skepticism, of both the term and its use. This question, then, served to give pause, interrogating what of any value such an inquiry might yield. This is why the first question was followed by the second: It placed me on notice for daring to ask the question in the first place. The question foregrounded the idea that *at-risk* was a term rooted in stereotypes and biases that called attention to certain raced, classed, and gendered bodies.

Yet also embedded in the question was the assumption that the term existed without tension, contentiousness, or complexity, or that these were fully accounted for in the extant literature. It also assumed that "what we already know" remained relevant to contemporary education contexts. Fundamentally, both questions foreclosed the opportunity to interrogate further the meaning of a term that clearly remained relevant in education policy and practice.

"Isn't the term *at-risk* used only in the academy?"

The third response took a different angle, suggesting *at-risk* was, at best, a term found only in academic and not popular or everyday education discourse, or was, at worst, simply passé. For example, when asked this, I sometimes gave a follow-up question: "Does anyone even use the term *at-risk* anymore?" This question highlighted the growing number of alternative terms and phrases that have cropped up in education discourse since the introduction of *at-risk* to categorize and label students. Examples included *at-promise, resilient, placed at-risk*, and *vulnerable*, terms sometimes positioned as moving away from the deficit-oriented framing of the at-risk label that placed conditions of risk-ness and riskiness on the student. These terms recognized that while students were at-risk due to their close proximity to risk factors, in some instances students could mitigate these risks when drawing from the internal and/or external support mechanisms located in their environment. Regardless of the label used to reframe risk, each of these alternative terms remained enclosed in a framework of risk whereby some bodies were categorized as uniquely risky, even if that-risk had yet to (or never would) fully manifest. This question also failed to acknowledge how the category of the at-risk student continued to serve as an official designation for students in federal, state, and district policies across the United States.

WHY WE NEED A BOOK ON MEANINGS OF RISK AND THE AT-RISK CATEGORY AND LABEL

Since the existing scholarship points to the contentious nature of the construct of risk, what is there left to know? Well, actually considerably more. To date, what has not been examined, and what this book explores, is the knowledge that informs how policy, practicing teachers, and those preparing to become teachers talk about, make sense of, and act in relation to academic risk and the at-risk label and category across national and local contexts. This inquiry extends what the extant literature tells us about risk: that it is employed in socially constructed, yet inequitable ways regarding race, class, and gender. While this is vitally important, this does not tell us what education stakeholders know about risk, or how they enact it—either through policy or in practice—in the everyday context of education. It does not tell us whether this knowledge is complex or contains contradictions that make it difficult to disrupt in the everyday work of schooling and teaching. Thus, if there is any hope for transforming the potentially myopic, dangerous ways that-risk is used in education practice, we need to understand just what we think we know about risk and how it is applied and used in the at-risk category and label.

For instance, in addition to the lack of research on the knowledge that informs how risk and the category and label of the at-risk student are picked up across education sites, the existing literature does not account for the varying orientations that-risk might take up in education policy and practice (Lupton, 1999a, 1999b). Accounting for these differences enables a more complex reading of risk that simultaneously acknowledges the materiality of risk (i.e., the everyday effects associated with societal and school conditions) and points out the culturally sanctioned practices that position certain people and behaviors as "risky" (i.e., how some students and behaviors become synonymous with potential risk for academic failure).

An example of this would be the diminished opportunities for quality education afforded presumably at-risk students who attend schools in high-poverty areas and school systems. These opportunities wane as a result of the challenging conditions (i.e., risk factors) associated with schooling in these areas, such as inequitable funding, high teacher turnover, and high student mobility. In this instance, it is difficult to isolate risk as a discretely material or culturally sanctioned phenomenon, as risk is attached to both (1) the material conditions that potentially result from attending schools in underresourced areas (e.g., poorer teacher quality, fewer curricular options, diminished opportunities for access to higher education), as well as (2) the social practices and ways of thinking that make it possible for inequitable conditions to emerge over time.

The degree to which multiple education sites acknowledge and assume that-risk operates as a static or fluid notion is important in this study. Is risk posited as objectively real and of measurable quality? Or is risk positioned as a socially constructed concept that loses its power outside of such constructions? What are the implications for practice of holding either or both of these orientations? This book explores the messy relationships, interconnections, and ambiguities that lurk in the sociocultural knowledge of risk and the at-risk category and label. This knowledge is of particular interest to policymakers, school districts, schools, and teacher preparation programs charged with providing an equitable schooling experience that meets the academic needs of all, not only some, students.

In this book I draw from data generated in a multi-sited ethnographic case study (Marcus, 1995; Stake, 1995) that explored how three education sites—U.S. federal policy from 1965–present, preservice teachers and inservice teachers—employ and make meaning of risk. My initial entry into this work began as a personal puzzle: I wanted to know what meanings education stakeholders held about risk and the at-risk student. I framed these meanings in the context of concerns with academic achievement because much of the school-based literature focused on students who were presumed at-risk of failing to achieve academically. Drawing from a framework that accounted for multiple orientations to risk (Lupton, 1999a, 1999b), my initial inquiry lead me to examine how the constructs of risk and the at-risk student were framed and discussed in federal education policy documents by both preservice and inservice teachers. In the case of the elementary preservice and inservice teachers, I talked with them about their understandings of risk and the at-risk student. I was specifically interested in how both recognized the ways risk might or did operate in their everyday practices. Across each of the three sites I examined, I used Lupton's (1999a, 1999b) orientations of risk as a heuristic to consider if and how policies, preservice teachers and inservice teachers talked about, located and proposed to remedy or redress risk. Lupton (1999a, 1999b) argued that each of these perspectives target fundamental issues around which constructs of risk operate theoretically.

My inquiry yielded many important findings that spoke to the existing literature. These findings supported and extended this scholarship. While risk operated contextually, both in dangerous and deficit-oriented ways, it also challenged these perspectives. In addition, risk served a key pedagogical function that paradoxically was tied to the desire to more equitably meet students' educational needs. Risk was integrally connected to how teachers viewed their professional role and responsibility. Yet only some of the participants recognized the possible dangers associated with drawing from the at-risk category and label in their present and future work as teachers.

In this book I show how the complexities of the at-risk discourse exist in the social practices of education in the United States. I also illuminate how the twin dilemmas of risk, as both a necessary and a dangerous practice, frame its deployment. Rather than focusing my argument at either end of these poles, I move between them, arguing that if we are to imagine and enact a more equitable education for all students, in light of the enduring role that-risk holds in societal ways of thinking and acting, we need to contest and ultimately reorient how risk is used in education discourse and practice. I propose that this approach, with its focus on academic achievement, complicates what we presume to know about risk, schooling, and teaching. It also asks that we both transform how we think about academic risk and prepare teachers to teach in more equitable and socially just ways.

CONCEPTUAL FRAMING

In taking up the sociocultural knowledge of risk as a focus of inquiry, this study was guided by specific ways of thinking and knowing that informed how I approached risk and the at-risk category and label. These frames did not serve as the primary analytical heuristic to read data, but rather operated in my own theoretical commitments that affect how I make sense of the social world. I entered into this work holding a critical standpoint, with a particular understanding of the endemic, lasting legacy of race in the organization and inequitable social relations of the United States. I similarly recognized the inequitable ways in which power frames the production and legitimation of knowledge. Thus, I privileged the space of knowledge and valuation systems. Here I focused particularly on their production and relationship to sociocultural practices, both historically and in the present. This stance created a space to critically interrogate the fundamental sources of knowledge found in social enactments of risk both in policy and in the talk and practices of teachers.

Cultural Analysis

McDermott, Goldman, and Varenne (2006) theorized cultural analysis as a process where the researcher examines the sociocultural contexts that frame and bring into relief enactments of practice. Researchers have used a cultural analysis approach to examine various constructs, including the construction of learning disability (McDermott et al., 2006); school achievement patterns (Pollock, 2008); discourses on at-risk Black male students (James, 2011); and discourses on the academic achievement gap (Carey, 2014). Cultural analysis recognizes that individual actions, inclusive of those found in a given official federal policy or in the everyday talk and practices of teachers, involve cultural ways of knowing and doing. These operate in normative systems that continually validate the legitimacy of the at-risk label and category. A cultural analysis, then, takes seriously the construct under inquiry, not as a single or individual instantiation but as "arrangements among persons, ideas, opportunities, constraints, and interpretations . . . that allow or even require that certain facts be searched for, discovered, measured, recorded and made consequential as label relevant" (McDermott et al., 2006, p. 13). For this study, a cultural analysis approach informed my making the at-risk student visible as a result of culturally discursive practices that allowed for and buttressed its existence in education policy and practice.

Production of Knowledge

Critical and poststructural theories of knowledge production (Foucault, 1983; Hacking, 2002; Popkewitz, 1998; Wynter, 2005) speak to the durability and legitimation of knowledge. What counts as valid knowledge exists in power relations that shift across time and space. This points to the complexity of knowledge—both its stability and possibility for transformation. Knowledge is legitimated through an amalgamation of histories, practices, economies, strategies, and technologies that involve power and subjectivity that emerge in relation to discourse. Discourses shape both knowledge and social practices, and in so doing provide a frame to think about and act on oneself and others in the social world. Drawing from a Foucauldian perspective, Kaplan (2006) defined discourse as "a culturally and historically contingent domain of knowledge and practice that establishes truth claims about self, other, and the world" (p. 21). Discourse, then, is understood as a deciphering tool to make sense of the world and to construct both people and ideas (Hacking, 2002). Informed by these theoretical ideas, in this study I draw from this perspective in recognizing and privileging the production of knowledge as a critical lens for making sense of risk and the at-risk construct in education policy and practice. I focus on the various kinds of knowledge found in education policy (Ball, 1993) and in the talk and practice of preparing and practicing teachers.

Critical Theory

Recognizing that neither schooling nor knowledge is neutral, my work also is informed by the theoretical insights of critical theory. Here, I acknowledge that inequitable power relations characterize the history and contemporary conditions of schooling and thus require praxis, or critical reflection and goal-directed action. U.S. schooling historically has operated in the context of unequal, hegemonic social relations at both macro and micro levels. In spite of these conditions, marginalized communities, including teachers, (can) engage in agency and resistance (Apple, 2014; Freire, 2000; Picower, 2012). Indeed, knowledge surrounding the use of risk and achievement operates in the context of historical social relations marred by power and inequity. It also offers a space for critical disruption and transformation.

Critical Race Theory (in Education)

In the vein of critical theory but with an acknowledgment of race, my work also is informed by critical race theory (in education) (Ladson-Billings & Tate, 1995; Dixson & Rousseau, 2006). Critical race theory (CRT) provides a lens to understand the endemic nature of racism (Bell, 1992). It recognizes race as a social construct that has meaningful material benefits that bolster and sustain Whiteness and White privilege. CRT emerged as a response to criticisms of critical legal studies, a theoretical approach that while concerned with how law itself helped to maintain societal inequity, failed to address how the construct of race and the practice of racism operated in these same processes. Through various theoretical precepts, such as interest convergence (Bell, 1979, 1992; Donnor, 2005), Whiteness as property (Harris, 1993; Ladson-Billings & Tate, 1995), and counter-story-telling (Solórzano & Yosso, 2001), the goal of CRT and specifically CRT in education is to excavate how race operates in society and in schooling, at both the structural and the local, everyday levels. It also seeks to inspire hope in the midst of the struggle for racial redress and equity.

Critical Lockean Value Theory

Drawing from the intellectual thought of philosopher Alain Locke (1989) around values, this study recognized the vital role that value theory plays in how people in a culturally diverse society interact. Locke believed "values informed how people understood themselves, others and the social world" (Grant, Brown, & Brown, 2016, p. 124). Locke challenged an essentialist view on values that approached them as universal across different temporal and spatial contexts. He recognized values as cultural constructions that changed over time. Locke argued the need for culturally pluralistic societies to have a more inclusive, less normative approach to valuation systems. In addition, he fully realized that in such societies, a hegemonic, dominant set of values generally exists that serves as a normalizing filter to judge and discipline the advent of divergent value systems. In the case of the United States, race features prominently in the valuation process. Those values aligned with hegemonic White interests frame people, knowledge, and ways of knowing and acting as correct and normal, while other values frame those who hold them as abnormal and deficient. The normalizing practices of valuation speak directly to the problematic ways that-risk and the at-risk category and label function in concerns around student achievement. These reflect values on what and who constitute risk.

GOALS OF THE BOOK

I seek to meet two ambitious aims. The first is to illuminate how the sociocultural knowledge of risk exists in and operates across three education sites concerned with academic achievement in the United States. A second, related aim is to illuminate the powerful role of knowledge and, in this case, the sociocultural knowledge of risk. Critical to understanding this knowledge is to acknowledge the construct of risk. In discussing this construct I approach risk as a signifier and not a stable or essentialized idea. This means that the construct of risk—what it means, who and what it defines and amplifies—may shift in relation to how individuals understand its meaning and use it over time and across different spaces (Derrida, 1976). The study I present in this book took seriously the idea that-risk knowledge operated in how education stakeholders made sense of and acted in relation to academic achievement.

In the realm of education, it is reasonable to consider risk and the at-risk category and label from the standpoint of practice. In using the word *practice*, I do not limit attention solely to how ideas about risk get enacted through specific actions or behaviors. Rather I view practice as a realm of actionable possibilities that exist in the everyday enactments of social life (Wortham, 2006). Taking the sites in this study as examples, practice would entail unearthing the knowledge that informed how federal education policy, preservice teachers, and inservice teachers approached risk.

Thus, the sociocultural knowledge of risk is not indicative of simply abstract or theoretical ideas that stand distant and apart from practice. Knowledge operates in the everyday dealings of the world, and no less is true for the sociocultural knowledge of risk. We can access it by attending to what we find in social practice. This includes interrogating popular social categories we use (I. Perry, 2011; Pollock, 2009), such as the category and label *at-risk*. Enacted practices of risk knowledge in education have implications for who and what gets recognized as risk, where risk resides, and ultimately whether and how one chooses to address risk.

Risk touches all aspects of life and social relations because there is nothing certain in life except that all living beings eventually will die. In light of this assurance, life itself comprises a dizzying array of experiences into the unknown. Since we never know beforehand whether an intended action will lead to a particular end, this uncertainty often leads people to seek out knowledge that will make them feel less vulnerable and helpless. The process of schooling and teaching, more specifically, is recognized as an uncertain enterprise (Britzman, 2003; Gershon, 2012; Ginsberg,

2012). There is no way of knowing that students will meet the intended outcomes set for schooling or will meet predetermined learning objectives established for classroom instruction. Quite often they do not. As Chapter 2 will show, the construct of risk historically evolved as a way to harness danger in order to move more comfortably across the uncertainties of life. Risk, then, as a modernist invention of calculability and probability, was imagined as a safety mechanism.[2] It was a technology fashioned to offer a nominal degree of confidence that made uncertainty more tolerable. Over time, the construct of risk has become a cornerstone in how education policy and practice approach education. That it equally operates in disparate, inequitable ways lends further support for its critical reconsideration.

ORGANIZATION OF THE BOOK

Given the paucity of book-length treatments that move between the theoretical, empirical, and praxis-oriented knowledge that informs the risk–achievement nexus in education, *After the "At-Risk" Label* addresses each of these important areas. It also includes tools to help readers explore more deeply the ideas presented in each chapter and their connection to education practice. Each chapter concludes with a set of questions, key terms, and optional activities that allow for extended exploration and critical reflection.

In Chapter 2 I set the context for studying how the construct of risk has played and continues to play a pivotal role in education. I discuss the material consequences associated with the use of the category and label *at-risk* to identify students. I then discuss the historical traditions and theoretical orientations associated with risk, considering what made it possible to view risk as a viable way to make sense of achievement concerns. From this discussion I advance my argument that when addressing risk and achievement in education, existing discourses place risk alternatively as either a necessary or a dangerous education discourse.

Chapter 3 examines how U.S. federal education policy has situated the discourse of risk from 1965 to the present, paying close attention to how these perspectives envision education institutions intervene in presumed and potential academic risk. For this discussion I look specifically at the Elementary and Secondary Education Act of 1965, *A Nation at Risk*, America 2000, Goals 2000, the No Child Left Behind Act of 2001, Race to the Top, and the Every Student Succeeds Act. I illustrate how policy shapes the discussion on risk, including how risk operates as both a necessary and a dangerous concept in need of attention.

In Chapters 4 and 5, respectively, I discuss how a group of preservice teachers preparing to work in a "diverse" school setting and a group of inservice teachers working in a school that received Title I funding understand

and make meaning of risk and academic achievement. Findings illustrated that both sets of teachers subscribed to the belief that teachers needed to engage in what I call *risk discourse*, the practice of identifying students presumed more likely than their peers to experience low academic achievement. However, only the preservice teachers wrestled with the potential biases associated with race and class that might occur in the teacher identification process. This discussion highlights the value of contesting and making more complex how risk is conceptualized and presented in teacher education and education discourse.

Chapter 6 concludes by considering how this research extends previous discussions of education risk and academic achievement as necessary or dangerous discourse. It also considers how the education community might reorient itself to a more equitable discourse and construct of educational risk. Given the sociocultural landscape of schools and deep inequities that mark longstanding social arrangements in U.S. society, I argue that the use of a concept of risk remains viable but requires critical intervention. I propose that similar to the endemic nature of race in the United States that critical race theorists alerted us to (Bell, 1992; Ladson-Billings & Tate, 1995), risk also occupies an enduring place. Risk, as a modernist invention, is deeply entrenched in how people think about and act in the social world, thus making it difficult to completely eradicate. Additionally, it offers a way to recognize structural problems and inequities in schooling (and society) that need redress. The problem with risk, and specifically the at-risk category and label in education, is its essentialized relegation to only certain people and conditions. These people and conditions become framed as problems (as opposed to people with problems—Du Bois, 1994; Gordon, 2006) because they fall outside of the popular values and norms accepted by a dominant, White, middle-class cultural subjectivity. I argue that a viable concept of risk requires reorientation. This concept would take into account but expand the existing necessary and dangerous discourse on the risk construct. I offer and outline a framework for making sense of and acting in response to a critical reorientation of risk that approaches risk self-reflexively and in a nonessentializing manner, with attention to both the individual and the institutional. It is also deeply contextual, expansive, and flexible in its application and use.

Recognizing that in order to make these shifts in how one approaches the concept of risk, I propose that educators adopt what I call a *critical risk standpoint*. This allows for a more critical and reflexive practice around academic risk that makes a *critical reorientation to risk* both necessary and viable. I discuss what constitutes this knowledge and offer practical strategies that one can acquire and use critically in the everyday work of teacher education and teaching. In doing this, I ask readers to move away from viewing risk as something that is inside people and groups, and instead recognize it as a warning sign that leads to critical appraisal of how systems (i.e., schools, policy, etc.), and the individuals working within them that seek to remedy the risk, must stay on guard not to be complicit in perpetuating, exacerbating, or recreating the very conditions that lead to a continuance of risk itself.

You can locate the methodology as supplementary appendixes on www.tcpress.com.

TOOLS FOR CRITICAL REFLECTION AND PRACTICE

Key Terms to Consider

- Sociocultural knowledge
- Normalizing judgment
- Discourse
- Signifier

Questions

1. Do you think it is important to examine how education stakeholders make meaning of risk and the at-risk student? Why or why not? How do these ideas impact students' opportunities to learn?

2. In what contexts have you encountered the term *at-risk*? How was it used? To whom did it apply?

3. At-risk operates as both a category and label. What are the differences between these two? Why are these differences important in the work of schooling and teaching?

Extended Activity

Reflect on the various ways that you observe risk playing out in the everyday world. Spend 30 minutes either critically examining social media (e.g., Facebook feeds, blogs, etc.) or listening to or reading the news (e.g., television, print). Select and critically analyze an example. What does risk mean in these contexts? What are the assumptions that inform how people enact or draw from risk?

CHAPTER 2

Historicizing Risk in Education Discourse and Practice

In this chapter I set the context for examining how the discourse of risk and the category and label of the at-risk student has functioned in education parlance and practice. I do this by interrogating the history of discourse on risk and achievement. Positioning this history as a site of inquiry, I take seriously what this examination tells us about the sociocultural knowledge of risk. I begin with a discussion of the material realities related to drawing from risk and using the category and label *at-risk* to identify students. I then explore both the historical and theoretical traditions associated with the deployment of risk. I consider what made it possible to view risk as a viable way to make sense of education and achievement concerns. Here I focus on both the modernist turn to risk and the competing theoretical orientations to risk that have emerged since this time. From this discussion I review how the trajectory of ideas on risk and achievement in the United States shifted across the 20th century, providing insight into how risk was imagined as a technology to address students and their achievement potential. This inquiry reveals how the history of discourse on risk and achievement operates across a continuum, with these ideas positioned as both necessary and dangerous to attend to when considering students' needs.

MATERIAL REALITIES OF EDUCATIONAL RISK AND THE CATEGORY AND LABEL OF THE AT-RISK STUDENT

Since the early 20th century, public schools have struggled to effectively educate all students. Whether focusing on "city," "urban," "suburban," or "rural" schools, these concerns sought to address learners normatively positioned as different, potentially underachieving, and in need of specialized/targeted support/assistance.

The primary approach used to meet these students' needs focuses on risk management. This entails first identifying and then effectively intervening for specific students positioned as more likely than their peers to experience problems in school. Historians Barry Franklin (1994) and Larry Cuban (1989) argued that since the early 20th century, discourses of risk have led to the creation of specialized categories and labels meant to assist education stakeholders in identifying and intervening on students believed to have special academic needs.

Numerous categories have emerged since that time to define and categorize potentially low-achieving students. These terms include *backward children* (Richman, 1906), *educationally retarded* (M. Perry, 1914), *culturally deprived* (Riessman, 1962), *educationally deprived* (Clark et al., 1972), and *educationally disadvantaged* (Committee on Labor and Public Welfare, 1965). Since the publication of *A Nation at Risk* in 1983, the term *at-risk* has served as the most recent category of use. It is used both officially and informally in practice to describe students assumed more likely than others to experience low academic achievement. However, the underlying construct of risk informing the term, as well as the methods used to categorize and label students as at-risk, has existed since the earliest stages of compulsory public schooling in the United States (Deschenes, Tyack, & Cuban, 2001).

In the 21st century, the at-risk category and label remain a popular way to recognize students. A Google search of the term *at-risk student* generated over 214,000,000 hits. A search on Google Scholar and the Web of Science database yielded 3,500,000 and 17,524 results, respectively. At-risk student reflects an official category of student in federal education policy, as well as in policy at the district and state levels around the country. For example, the most recent national education policies, Race to the Top and the Every Student Succeeds Act, use "at-risk" to describe specific student populations who require targeted attention through resource allocation. School districts across the country recognize at-risk as an official category to describe students viewed as more likely than their peers to experience unintended outcomes such as low scores on standardized tests, grade retention, truancy, and dropping out. The term also describes students who have experienced other negatively positioned social outcomes, such as homelessness, physical abuse, substance abuse, and other health risk behaviors. An example of this is found in how a large urban school district in Texas officially defines the at-risk student. This definition is grounded in the larger statutory definition provided by the Texas Educational Agency—the state agency for primary and secondary education in Texas. Below I offer the district's full definition at length.

> **"At-Risk" Student**—A student is identified as at-risk of dropping out of school based on state-defined criteria. The statutory criteria (Texas Education Code, section 29.081) for at-risk status include each student who is under 21 years of age and who:

- was not advanced from one grade level to the next for one or more school years;
- is in grades 7, 8, 9, 10, 11, or 12 and did not maintain an average equivalent to 70 on a scale of 100 in two or more subjects in the foundation curriculum during a semester in the preceding or current school year or is not maintaining such an average in two or more subjects in the foundation curriculum in the current semester;
- did not perform satisfactorily on an assessment instrument administered to the student under TEC Subchapter B, Chapter 39, and who has not in the previous or current school year subsequently performed on that instrument or another appropriate instrument at a level equal to at least 110% of the level of satisfactory performance on that instrument;
- is in prekindergarten, kindergarten or grades 1, 2, or 3 and did not perform satisfactorily on a readiness test or assessment instrument administered during the current school year;
- is pregnant or is a parent;
- has been placed in an alternative education program in accordance with Section 37.006 during the preceding or current school year;
- has been expelled in accordance with Section 37.007 during the preceding or current school year;
- is currently on parole, probation, deferred prosecution, or other conditional release;
- was previously reported through the PEIMS to have dropped out of school;
- is a student of limited English proficiency, as defined by Section 29.052;
- is in the custody or care of the Department of Protective and Regulatory Services or has, during the current school year, been referred to the department by a school official, officer of the juvenile court, or law enforcement official;
- is homeless, as defined by 42 U.S.C. Section 11302 and its subsequent amendments; or
- resided in the preceding school year or resides in the current school year in a residential placement facility in the district, including a detention facility, substance abuse treatment facility, emergency shelter, psychiatric hospital, halfway house, or foster group home.

Clearly impacted by the neoliberal context of high-stakes testing and accountability (Lipman, 2011) in this district (and state) definition of the at-risk student, one notes the normative raced, gendered, classed, and cultured ways the term operates. The at-risk student is one with below-level performance on school readiness measures, statewide assessments, or classroom learning objectives. These students span a wide age range, from the youngest school-aged children in kindergarten to those in 12th grade. At-risk students are viewed as at-risk for what they presumably do not know and cannot do (e.g., state-sanctioned content knowledge and skills, English proficiency), for the conditions in which they live (e.g., homelessness, foster/group home placement, poverty), and for the outcomes of social behaviors deemed non-normative to school life (e.g., dropping out of school; parenting while a teen, regardless of the context in which it occurred; history of disciplinary/legal infractions).

These official identifying factors are raced, gendered, and classed, given their disproportionate impact on female students and students of color. Both of these groups often constitute a larger proportion of their respective total school population for living in poverty, speaking a first language other than English, and receiving disciplinary action by a school/legal entity. Larger societal factors, the centuries-long practices of both economic and political divestment of communities of color in the United States (Marable, 2000), are not accounted for in these at-risk student criteria. Nor are the entrenched dehumanizing discourses and inequitable social practices that characterize the treatment of historically marginalized people of color (Fanon, 2007), including those who are Black (Brown, 2012; Dumas, 2015), Latina/o (San Miguel & Valencia, 1998; Villenas, 2012), and Indigenous (Tuck & Yang, 2012). The material effects of risk are on full display as the presumed at-risk student stands alone, an individual full of risk that requires identification, management, and remediation.

AT-RISK DISCOURSE: SOURCES OF
CONTENTION AND CONTROVERSY IN THE RISK TERMINOLOGY

Educational risk is a primary issue of contention for those education stakeholders that wish to provide an equitable and socially just school experience for all students (Gadsden et al., 2009). This contention often concerns the variable way the category and label *at-risk* are used in policy and practice, specifically when discussing how and when risk status is assigned to a student.

When looking at literature on risk and prevention studies, five activities play a key role in meeting the needs of potentially at-risk students, including: (1) identifying the specific populations that experience some negative outcome more than other populations; (2) isolating, in the population that experiences the negative outcome, the specific factors related to the occurrence of that negative outcome; (3) categorizing those populations deemed more likely than other populations to experience the negative outcome as at-risk; ④ designing and implementing interventions to eliminate or buffer the possible effects of the risk factors; and ⑤ evaluating how effective the risk intervention was in countering the effects of the risk factors (Pianta & Walsh, 1996). The underlying premise is that by first identifying the specific factors associated with undesired outcomes, one can more efficiently locate student populations in closest proximity to these factors, as well as potentially safeguard against the possible effects of those factors (Vacha & McLaughlin, 1992). This process also allows the researcher to locate protective factors that may keep members of at-risk populations from actually experiencing a negative outcome (Garmezy, 1983).

Interestingly, this entire frame is built upon the assumption of *possibility*, not certainty, that some student populations have a higher likelihood than others of experiencing an unintended outcome (Pianta & Walsh, 1996). Notwithstanding the normative ways in which certain conditions are recognized as risky in this approach, close proximity to presumed risk factors does not necessarily *lead* to negative or undesired outcomes. Rather, risk factors reflect *potential* factors that increase the likelihood that some negative outcome may occur. Thus, those individuals in close proximity to these factors may benefit from targeted intervention to mitigate the risk. In this approach to risk identification and management, the question is not whether risk objectively exists. This is accepted *a priori*. What is asked, however, is: What is the risk? In what location does risk exist? What is the underlying cause of risk? How should one most effectively address risk (Lupton, 1999a, 1999b)?

Pianta and Walsh (1996) argued that-risk research has been useful as a tool of inquiry into "the etiology of the problem of interest, the prediction of disorder, the identification of 'protective factors' and the translation of this information into early intervention and prevention programs" (pp. 20–21). They also noted that education practice and popular discourse often fail to use the terminology of risk in ways that speak to its designed intention. In the case of U.S. public education in general, it often is presumed without question that poor students and particular student populations of color (e.g., African American, Latino, Native American, South Asian, Pacific Islander) will experience low academic achievement and educational attainment. Why is this the case?

Some authors have argued that these student populations possess or come more closely in contact with specific risk factors related to low academic achievement and educational attainment.[1] During the 1980s, risk factors traditionally were placed at the level of the child and her family (Natriello et al., 1990). Since the 1990s, authors have directly critiqued this view, pointing to how schools, and the risk factors associated with them (e.g., school-level poverty, tracking practices, school and teacher expectations) *places* students at-risk (Boykin, 2000; Cuban, 1989; Jagers &

Carroll, 2002; Land & Legters, 2002; Swadener & Lubeck, 1995). When suggesting that students get placed at-risk, these authors challenge the perspective that-risk is the result of deficiencies located in students or their families and/or communities. These authors critique the deficit thinking (Valencia, 2010) found in the discourse and category of at-risk, highlighting that-risk inevitably emerges within a sociopolitical context that relies on fully raced, classed, and gendered notions of normality (Swadener, 1995; Swadener & Lubeck, 1995). If a student experiences risk, it is a condition placed on the child and not one that emanates from the child or the child's family/community.

This discussion highlights the tensions and ambiguities that exist in how education stakeholders understand and conceptualize risk and the category of the at-risk student. Yet to fully appreciate these issues it is necessary to consider how risk, as a construct and way of looking at, making meaning of, and acting on the social world, became possible. For this, one must turn attention to modernist Western European thought that emerged during the Middle Ages (Lohmann & Mayer, 2009).

MAKING RISK A POSSIBILITY

The construct of risk has experienced shifts in meaning over the centuries (Ewald, 1991; Luhmann, 1993; Lupton, 1999a). It enjoys interdisciplinary appeal, speaking to disciplines as far-reaching as sociology, anthropology, psychology, business, social work, and education. In education, concerns with risk, and specifically the use of the at-risk category and label, have flourished since the 1980s. A growing international body of scholarship across Australia (Hughes, 2011; Riele, 2006), Canada, and several European countries including England (Hughes, 2011; Turnbull & Spence, 2011), Germany (Betz, 2014; Lohmann & Mayer, 2009), Belgium (Roets, Rutten, Roose, Vandekinderen, & Soetaert, 2015), and the Netherlands (Dekker, 2009) has focused attention on the meanings and use of "at-risk" across education and social welfare policy domains. At-risk, as an education construct, has global appeal.

While acknowledging that the etymology of the word *risk* is unknown (Luhmann, 1993), authors typically agree that during the Middle Ages in Europe, the term had significant application in the navigation and trade fields (Ewald, 1991; Luhmann, 1993). Lupton (1999a) asserted that during the Middle Ages, magic and Christianity "served as the belief system by which threats and dangers were dealt with conceptually and behaviorally, allowing people to feel as if they had some control over their world" (p. 2). The existence of a supernatural that incorporated both a vengeful God and an evil Satan was a commonly accepted belief, and systems of superstition were used to deal with evil and the unknown. Risk often was associated with natural events, such as storms, floods, or epidemics, and was characterized as a danger related to acts of God, rather than the direct result of human fault. In these cases, it was presumed that humans could do virtually nothing to avoid risk (Lupton, 1999a).

Then, as well as now, risk evokes the idea of uncertainty and potential damage, particularly in relation to something of value, whether loss of property or life. It was not until the 18th and 19th centuries that modern European and American societies began to view risk as something to be actively avoided or at least managed, except during those times when the potential benefits of some risky action outweighed the possible dangers or costs (Barnes, 2003; Lupton & Tulloch, 2002; Rose, 1999; Simon, 2002). Here, one could denote risk as having either "good" or "bad" qualities (Lupton, 1999a). Not surprisingly, risk was integrally connected to the transition into modernity. This both impacted the growth of the insurance field, as well as accompanied the rise of capitalism (Bialostok & Whitman, 2012).

What accounted for the shift in how risk was imagined during the Middle Ages and how it is discussed and understood in the present? Hacking (1990) considered this question when tracing the connections between the eroding views of the natural world as determinant and the formation of laws of probability that were applied to the characteristics of people. Hacking noted that prior to the 1900s, probability, or what he termed the "doctrine of chances," was viewed as "defective but necessary tools of people who know too little" (p. 1). Here, rational thinking prevailed, with the assumption that probability reflected too closely the notions of "chance, superstition, vulgarity, unreason" (p. 1). It was not until the late 1800s that the use of statistics and probability became "an alternative to strictly causal laws" (p. 1). As a result, the introduction of normalcy and deviance as scientifically calculable concepts became a possibility. While these new laws of probability implicitly relied upon laws of nature, they were uniquely outfitted for calculating people—both their behaviors and their human nature. Hacking stated:

> Such social and personal laws were to be a matter of probabilities, of chances. Statistical in nature, these laws were nonetheless inexorable; they could even be self-regulating. People are normal if they conform to the central tendency of such laws, while those at the extremes are pathological. Few of us fancy being pathological, so "most of us" try to make ourselves normal, which in turn affects what is normal. (p. 2)

In this sense, normalcy is based on certain socially and scientifically acceptable beliefs about probability that, prior to the 19th century, western European scholars did not acknowledge as possible, rational, or useful. What is normal (or deviant) emerges not from some inherently static or deterministic category of people, behaviors, or things, but rather reflects specific practices and beliefs, culturally sanctioned as both scientific and necessary (Foucault, 1980; Hacking, 1990, 2002; Rose, 1999). That some people, behaviors, and things come to embody particularly deviant or risky natures is one result of these practices. Indeed, the system of identifying and attempting to manage risk could not have emerged if not for the advent of particular styles of reasoning (Hacking, 1990, 2002) that

> had everything to do with life: living people. Not living people regarded as vital organic unities, but rather regarded as social atoms subject to social laws. These laws turned out to be statistical in character. They could be seen as statistical only when there were, literally statistics. There could only be statistics when people wanted to count themselves and had the means to do so. (1990, p. 15)

In this way, it seems, humans were granted both the ability and responsibility for managing the future in relation to what they presumed to know about the present.

The growth of risk studies across a variety of academic and social fields constitutes what Fox (1999) called a science of risk. This is associated with practices of risk calculation, risk assessment, and risk evaluation that are "emblematic of modernism and its commitment to progress through rationalization" (p. 12). In this calculus, risk becomes something capable of rational observation, measurement, and analysis, ultimately allowing those concerned with risk to develop strategic methods for gaining a sense of control over an unwieldy, uncertain, and potentially dangerous future.

These new technologies and particular ways of thinking about risk (Rose, 1999) made inroads for the child as risk discourse emerged in Western Europe and traveled to the United States and beyond. Lohmann and Mayer (2009) contended that-risk was a uniquely European invention that transformed the nature of the child into a model of normal childhood that was statistically constituted and derived. This view relied on an amalgamation of practices, technologies, and rationalities that helped to expand the emphasis on the child as a subject of surveillance, calculability, and rescue. Situating his analysis in the sociohistorical context of France, Dekker (2009) linked the expansion for the child as risk discourse to the growth of discursive practices in child science, child research, child policy, and intervention of the state. This expanding emphasis existed in the paradox of seeking to protect children by diminishing the number of at-risk children, while simultaneously increasing the number of children diagnosed as such. An end result was the growth of institutions and experts charged with identifying and calculating risks for the purposes of managing and minimizing the impact of childhood risk on the larger society. These practices were not unique to France. Similar efforts, informed by discursive practices that traveled across Europe and into the United States, set the stage for viewing children and youth as potentially troubled, risky, and in need of targeted intervention (Lohmann & Mayer, 2009). Other scholars have noted that on the heels of global economic shifts that celebrate a neoliberal logic, intensified risks have elevated how countries situate risk and place responsibility on individuals to identify and manage their own risks (Turnbull & Spence, 2011).

The shifting way that-risk has operated across modernity as a system of calculable identification and management speaks keenly to underlying logics that inform how risk is theorized to operate. These logics concern both epistemic (i.e., ways of knowing) and ontological (i.e., ways of being) assumptions about the nature and role of risk. In the discussion that follows, I outline four popular orientations of risk that offer insight into how the sociocultural knowledge of risk operates in education.

THEORIZING RISK IN SOCIAL PRACTICE

No discussion of educational risk and the label and category of the at-risk student can occur without first taking seriously what-risk means theoretically as an organized body of knowledge. Looking across multiple subject areas in the literature on risk, social theorist Deborah Lupton (1999a, 1999b) identified four general orientations around which theories of risk have organized. Lupton argued that these risk orientations constituted an interdisciplinary body of theories on risk, situated across the academic fields of psychology, sociology, and anthropology. Lupton's conceptual typologies of risk offer a lens to account for the multiple and even competing ways risk as a construct operates in social practice. This is an important consideration when examining how risk—as a construct and as a specific label and category of student—plays out across education sites.

Each of Lupton's four risk orientations reflects particular epistemic and ontological assumptions regarding (1) how a site conceptualizes risk; (2) where a site locates risk and its origins; and (3) what suggestions a site offers for resolving particular problems associated with risk. For instance, in some orientations, socializing and cultural factors form the basis for who/what is considered risky, while for others, risk is advanced as a real, objective threat that is noncontingent on the context of a given setting. The next section outlines the four key orientations of risk: technico-scientific, risk society, cultural symbolic, and governmentality.

Technico-scientific Orientations

Lupton (1999a) characterized these approaches to risk as "the problem of conflict between scientific, industrial and government organizations and the public" (p. 18). Work in this area often falls within the cognitive sciences, where various psychological models of human behavior are used to identify how people respond behaviorally and cognitively to risk. These responses are then compared with expert, or presumably more objective, measures of how people would be expected to respond to risk (Lupton, 1999a).

Another approach taken in the cognitive sciences is to identify patterns in the way that people assess and respond to risk. This often is accomplished through a psychometric perspective where researchers identify how the influence of different cognitive factors assists in shaping a "layperson" response (Lupton, 1999a). Lupton (1999a) also discussed the "health belief model," another prevalent model within this orientation, which is based on work done in the fields of health promotion and health education. Lupton (1999a) noted, "This model relies upon an understanding of the human actor in which there is a linear relationship between knowledge of a risk, developing the attitude that one is at-risk and adopting a practice to prevent the risk from happening to oneself [or others]" (p. 21). While this approach focuses mainly on how the individual responds to risk, I would argue that the technico-scientific model, particularly the health belief model, extends to how particular individuals, groups, or institutions perceive, assess, and respond to alleviate or contain risk. This perspective aligns clearly with approaches used in education to address risk.

Lupton (1999a) stated that technico-scientific orientations of risk assume that-risk is an objective hazard, threat, or danger that exists and can be measured empirically. This particular orientation places a heavy emphasis on the application of rationality and science to understand and address risk. Thus, while acknowledging that social and cultural frameworks of interpretation can lead to distortions or biases, technico-scientific perspectives often portray risk as a concept that can be understood independently of sociocultural processes. Not surprisingly, Lupton (1999a) pointed out that while most practitioners working in settings that apply a technico-scientific approach to risk would acknowledge that their work is not absolutely value-free, the specific calculations produced as a result of this work often are approached as objective truth. Lupton (1999a) also noted that technico-scientific perspectives of risk typically address the following key questions: (a) What-risks exist? (b) How should risk be managed? and (c) How do people respond cognitively to risk? Although work in this field often falls in the areas of risk management (i.e., How can risk be located, assessed, intervened upon, and evaluated?), the discourses associated with the cognitive sciences also have tended to focus on risk perception (i.e., To what degree do individuals "accurately" perceive risk?) and risk-taking (i.e., What leads certain people to engage in risky behaviors?). In the context of looking at-risk in schooling, a technico-scientific approach to risk would privilege the use of science as a means to identify, manage, and remediate the risks that certain students possess.

Risk Society Orientations

Rooted in the sociological tradition, risk society orientations were popularized through Ulrech Beck's *Risk Society: Towards a New Modernity*, published in English in 1992 (Green, 2009). Lupton (1999a) summarized risk society orientations solely in relation to this work and other pieces by both Ulrech Beck and Anthony Giddens. According to Lupton (1999b), "risk society theorists have chosen to focus their analyses largely on macrostructural factors influencing what they see to be an intensification of concern in late modern societies about risks" (p. 3). These theorists suggested that the new concerns with risk have emerged as result of the changing global conditions of living in late modernity. As a result, risks have become more difficult to calculate and manage. Rather than viewing expert knowledge as the solution for handling risk, this orientation suggests that people in these societies view institutions, such as government, industry, and science, as the main producers of risk (Lupton, 1999a, 1999b). According to Lupton (1999a), both the poor and the affluent are subjected to the threats of risk society. And while the poor have fewer means with which to circumvent risky situations, both groups, ultimately, according to Beck, fall victim to certain risks "because they are so widespread and 'invisible' in their manifestation" (Lupton, 1999a, pp. 68–69). These particular risks deal primarily with health and environmental issues such as radiation, smog, toxic chemicals in food, and water pollution (Lupton, 1999a).[2] They also might include education and schooling, particularly in the context of neoliberal anxieties around individual choice, accountability, and responsibility.

As with technico-scientific orientations, risk society orientations assume that-risk exists as an objective hazard, threat, or danger. Yet in this case, risk is mediated through social and cultural processes and cannot be identified or understood in isolation from these factors. As a result, a risk society orientation focuses on how modernity and the institutions associated with modernity "create" risk. It is assumed that good citizens will take responsibility for managing the risks they face in life. By linking individual responsibility and risk in this way "individuals become defined by, and responsible for, their own choices as risks are navigated through 'reflexive biographies'" (Turnbull & Spence, 2011, p. 939). Additionally, Lupton (1999a) noted that-risk society orientations consider the following question: What is the relationship of risk to the structures and processes of late modernity? In the context of schooling and risk, a risk society orientation would seek to understand how individuals—teachers, school leaders, students, families, and so on—increasingly are expected to manage the growing risks found in their social reality.

Cultural Symbolic Orientations

Lupton (1999a) distinguished cultural symbolic orientations of risk as focused on establishing and maintaining conceptual boundaries between the self and other. According to Lupton (1999a), the work of cultural anthropologist Mary Douglas played a pivotal role in shaping cultural symbolic orientations to risk, in which "Douglas' approach to risk is best understood as part of a trajectory of theorizing on the body, selfhood and the regulation of contamination and danger that [the author] . . . began three decades ago" (p. 36). The human body is used symbolically/ metaphorically in discourses and practices around risk, with "a 'risky' Other . . . pos[ing] a threat to the integrity of one's own physical body or to the symbolic body of the community or society to which one belongs" (Lupton, 1999b, p. 3). Much of this work has considered why some things become identified as risks while other things do not, with risk conveyed as a "locus of blame, in which 'risky' groups or institutions are singled out as dangerous" (p. 3).

Culture figures prominently in discussions of risk, at the levels of both risk identification and risk response. Primary explanations concerning risk propose that social groups, societies, and organizations utilize discourses of risk to "maintain boundaries between self and Other, deal with social deviance and achieve social order" (Lupton, 1999a, p. 36). Work in this area often questions the degree to which technico-scientific approaches can adequately capture how risk operates, particularly the importance placed on examining the "individual" rather than the "cultural."

Similar to risk society orientations, cultural symbolic orientations assume that-risk exists as an objective hazard, threat, or danger. However, risk is mediated through social and cultural processes and cannot be identified or understood in isolation from these factors. Lupton (1999a) suggested that cultural symbolic orientations often focus on the following questions: (a) Why are some dangers selected as risk and others not? (b) How does risk operate as a symbolic boundary measure? (c) What are the psychodynamics of our risk responses? and (d) What is the situated context of risk? A cultural symbolic orientation of risk in schooling would highlight the ways that-risk is recognized as operating as a social boundary demarcating the lines between those who are presumed to come in close proximity to risk (i.e., at-risk) and those who do not.

Governmentality orientations

Lupton (1999a, 1999b) argued that governmentality orientations toward risk rely upon the idea of discursive construction of reality as found in the work of philosopher Michel Foucault. The notion of discursivity suggests the melding together of discourses, strategies, practices, and institutions to produce particular "truths" (Lupton, 1999a) and, in this case, create ways for thinking about and ultimately acting upon risk. Governmentality orientations question the role of governmentality as a form of power characterized by an "ensemble formed by institutions, procedures, analyses, and reflections" (Foucault, 1991, p. 102) that define, redefine, and make possible certain ways of thinking and behaving.

According to Lupton (1999b), governmentality orientations understand risk as just one of the many, heterogeneous governmental strategies of disciplinary power used to manage and monitor populations. This is accomplished primarily through normalization, or

> the method by which norms of behavior or health status are identified in populations and by which individuals are then compared to determine how best they fit the norm. . . . Those who are determined to deviate from the norm significantly are typically identified as being "at-risk." To be designated as "at risk," therefore is to be positioned within a network of factors drawn from the observations of others. The implication of this rationalized discourse [techniques of normalization] again is that-risk is ultimately controllable, as long as expert knowledge can be properly brought to bear upon it. (Lupton, 1999b, pp. 4–5)

Expert knowledge plays an important role in the method of governmentality, as it provides "the specific guidelines and advice by which populations of people are surveyed, compared against norms, trained to conform with norms and rendered productive" (Lupton, 1999a, p. 87). Thus, governmentality orientations advance the idea that nothing is a risk in itself. Rather, risk is a product of historically, socially, and politically contingent ways of seeing and thinking about risk (Lupton, 1999a). A key question that emerges in this perspective is: How do the discourses and practices around risk operate in the construction of subjectivity and social life? When considering risk and schooling, a governmentality approach would recognize risk as a fundamentally created construct that exists outside the boundaries of an objective hazard or danger. Here, risk is understood only in relation to the larger system of practices, technologies, and knowledges that make it possible to observe, calculate, manage, and remedy risk in the first place.

As noted in Chapter 1, the four orientations to risk as outlined by Lupton (1999a, 1999b) allow for a deeper accounting of how risk operates in educational concerns around student achievement. These orientations require one to attend to core assumptions held about risk when examining how it operates in social practice. Fundamental to these assumptions, then, is a knowledge base that highlights what knowledge is privileged and valued regarding risk and achievement. The extent to which risk is understood as real and timeless, or socially constructed and possessing the potential to change, offers insight into what-risk means and how it is used in education policy and practice. These understandings can illuminate larger patterns in how societal discourses fashioned risk as a viable grammar for reading students and their achievement. In the section that follows, I consider the discourses of achievement and risk that circulated across the 20th century. This history points to the contentious nature of knowledge about risk and achievement, illustrating how its recognition has precariously straddled between necessary and dangerous to the education and lives of the students it sought to assist.

DISCOURSES OF ACHIEVEMENT AND RISK IN THE UNITED STATES: A HISTORICAL TRAJECTORY

Previously in this chapter it was noted that while the at-risk terminology became popular with the passage of *A Nation at Risk*, concerns with risk and schooling have existed since the late 19th and early 20th centuries in the United States. Since that time, school administrators and teachers have identified students who were positioned as presenting challenges to the teaching and learning process. Franklin (1994) stated that "the children who we are labeling as being at-risk have been, it seems, a perennial concern of American educators" (p. 5). Issues associated with "the presence in schools of children who for a host of reasons [were] difficult to teach and often troublesome to manage" (p. 5) were addressed in the educational discourses of the early 20th century. This was particularly the case in urban schools. School leaders and teachers were unprepared for the changes in work conditions brought about by increasing student enrollment of newly arriving European immigrants, the passage of compulsory school attendance laws, and an increasing number of students with physical dis/abilities.

For example, during the late 1800s, schools began to challenge the common school notion that all students should receive, or were capable of receiving, the same education. Educators argued that such a policy, while good in an ideal sense, did not address the individual challenges posed by students who did not typify the ideal, or "normal" student (Osgood, 1997). These students often were characterized as overage, or too old for the particular academic and intellectual grade level in which they were placed. In some cases, they possessed a physical or mental dis/ability believed to place an impediment on their overall intellectual ability to learn and function "normally" in the classroom (Franklin, 1994). During this time, urban public school systems, such as the one located in densely populated New York City, began to push for differentiated curriculum. This signaled a shift away from the ungraded school model (Richman, 1906; Tyack & Cuban, 1995). Given the unprecedented levels of immigration from southern European countries, teachers also worked in overcrowded classrooms. Many of the newly arrived students did not speak English or speak it well. Many also were considered overage and underprepared for academic work, having had little to no access to schooling in their former homeland.

Late 19th and Early 20th Centuries

During the late 19th and early 20th centuries there were two ways to explain the intellectual capability of students positioned as "different" and deviant from mainstream society. The first explanation argued that students of a Black heritage, as well as immigrants from southern and eastern European backgrounds, and those of Indigenous and Chinese descent, were incapable of high intellectual achievement because of innate, *genetic deficiencies* (Degler, 1991; Valencia, 1997). With the advent of IQ testing, Latino students also were positioned as genetically inferior (Gonzáles, 1999; San Miguel & Valencia, 1998). Voluminous research was undertaken on the study of race differences in intelligence. This work started from the assumption that intelligence was transmitted to individuals through genetic heredity (Valencia, 1997). It also was posited that in spite of increasing educational opportunities, some races were incapable of reaching the intellectual level of others, with White, Anglo Saxon populations serving as the norm. Degler (1991) noted sociologist Franklin Giddings' (cited in Degler, 1991) apprehension in these matters when quoting Giddings as stating:

> "They [Chinese and Amerindians] have been in existence . . . much longer than the European race, and have accomplished immeasurably less. We are, therefore warranted," he concluded, "in saying that they have not the same inherent abilities." And when lower and higher races come into contact with one another, he insisted, there is no reason to believe they will improve significantly. "The same amount of educational effort does not yield equal results when applied to different stocks," [Giddings] explained. (p. 17)

In another instance, sociologist William Elwang suggested in 1904 (cited in Degler, 1991) that Black people could not achieve at the level of Whites, even with an education. Degler (1991) stated:

> "The trouble with the negro is not merely that he is ignorant," Elwang explained. Better schools would remedy that. "The difficulty is more radical and lies embedded in the racial character, in the very conditions of existence. The negro race," Elwang asserted, "lacks those elements of strength that enable the Caucasian to hold its own, and win its way and bring things to pass. Negroes cannot create civilization," he simply concluded. His explanation was almost straight out of Darwin. "Theirs is a child-race, left behind in the struggle for existence because of original unfavorable inheritance of physical and mental conditions that foredoom to failure their competition on equal terms with other races." (p. 16)

Similarly, psychologist H. H. Goddard, who was responsible for both importing and revising the Binet intelligence scales for use in the United States, suggested in his well-known investigation of the Kallikak family in 1914 that improvements in neither education nor environment could modify an individual's feebleminded condition (Gould, 1996). These explanations for race disparity in intelligence were located in both sociological and psychological literatures. They approached risk as a biological, deterministic attribute incapable of modification or development. These theories influenced national policy on immigration and provided support for the eugenics movement and social interventions, including mandatory sterilization. In this context, educational risk was identifiable and manageable yet innately determined and static. The necessity to recognize this risk was important, not because one could intervene and disrupt its nature, but in order to control and contain it from causing possible future danger.

These perspectives on race and genetic deficiency did not emerge simply with the advent of IQ testing in the early 20th century. Authors pointed out that explanations of differences between people on the basis of physical characteristics have existed for many centuries (Degler, 1991; Menchaca, 1997). These beliefs, however, were propelled into prominence by the work of evolutionary theorist Charles Darwin. Darwin's work offered a socially convincing explanation of how plants and animals in the natural world emerged in their current biological form through the process of reproduction and natural selection. To the extent that the "environment changed or if new organisms entered the habitat of established organisms . . . those organisms that best adapted to the changed situation would gradually outbreed those less well adapted" (Degler, 1991, p. 6). The melding of biological evolutionary theory with explanations of how the social world operated and should operate found its way into the work of Herbert Spencer and Francis Galton, proponents of social Darwinism and eugenics, respectively. It was a number of events, scholarly developments, and works such as these that combined "to help heredity become entrenched as a powerful explanatory base of human behavior in the nature–nurture controversy" (Valencia, 1997, p. 43).

A second explanation of intellectual capacity emerged during the 1910s and 1920s. This work was located in the sociological and anthropological tradition and challenged the idea of a firmly entrenched intellectual capacity on the basis of heredity and race (Valencia, 1997). Degler (1991) offered that an early trace of this work was situated in a pre-Darwinian theory of evolution proposed by the early-19th-century French philosopher Jean-Baptiste Lamarck. Lamarck stated that "evolutionary change occurred as a consequence of an organism's effort to improve its situation in its habitat" (Degler, 1991, p. 20). Implicit in this idea was the role that will, or personal intention, might play in modifying an individual's situation in life. It also was assumed that an offspring was likely to inherit his/her parents' behavioral patterns. This made it vital to change the environmental and social conditions of individuals living in adverse settings.

These ideas resonated in the U.S. social sciences context with the emergence of the culture construct and the work of anthropologist Franz Boas. Boas sought to dismiss the idea of biology and race as a determining factor in intellectual ability (Clark et al., 1972). Degler (1991) stated:

> Boas' rejection of the traditional view [biology and race as determinate in intellectual ability] was truly radical; it simply denied the existence of any significant innate differences between savage, colored people and civilized, white people. The differences in physical appearance, in short, did not lead to any significant difference in mental or social function. That there were observable social differences was undeniable, but the explanation for those differences, Boas maintained, was that they were the product of different histories, not different biological experiences. (p. 62)

The dehumanizing construction of Black and other people of color was not questioned, even as studies used culture to highlight how environmental factors and societal opportunity impacted intellectual and academic ability. However, scholars recognized the contributions of Franz Boas and Otto Klineberg in shifting attention to the power of social influences on human potential (Clark et al., 1972; Degler, 1991; Valencia, 1997). This new perspective highlighted that the conditions of poverty and urban life, rather than one's genetic disposition, made it difficult for students to achieve intellectually and live a moral life. The solution was to provide a better environment and more suitable opportunities for success.

There is a longstanding tradition in education and the social sciences of positioning urban life, specifically for those living in poverty, as uniquely maladaptive and problematic (O'Connor, 2001). The desire to eliminate, or at least control, the negative influence these potentially at-risk people might have on the larger society justified actions taken by researchers, social welfare agents, and school officials to better understand how to meet these students' needs. Prior to 1850, city schools, such as those found in New York City, were highly populated by poor, immigrant children. These students, who generally came from southern and eastern European countries, often were described as problems, capable of "poison[ing] society all around them" (Kaestle, 1973, p. 77). To address these concerns, a number of charitable organizations sought to improve the lives of the poor and indigent. Public schooling was viewed as one potential cure for bad moral character (Kaestle, 1973; Tyack, 1974), particularly when students from both rich and poor backgrounds were educated together. The Free School Society's *Annual Report of 1825* stated:

> Our free schools have conferred the blessing of education upon a large number of the children of the poor, but still it is to be lamented that a description of public school is wanting amongst us, where the rich and poor may meet together; where the wall of partition, which now seems to be raised between them may be removed; where kindlier feelings between the children of these respective classes may be begotten; where the indigent may be excited to emulate the cleanliness, decorum and mental improvement of those in better circumstances; and where the children of our wealthiest citizens will have an opportunity of witnessing and sympathizing, more than they now do, with the wants and privations of their fellows of the same age. (Kaestle, 1973, p. 85)

These ideas about the poor city children continued after the 1850s and into the turn of the 20th century, when they often were depicted as "useful idlers" and "truants" believed to inhabit "incorrigible character" (Tyack & Berkowitz, 1977) because both they and their parents were "perfectly indifferent to school" (p. 38).

A number of organizations and programs were developed to address the growing concern for the "child of the slum" (Riis, 1895). These children were described as dirty, unkempt, and ragged. It was argued that what they needed most was removal from the conditions of crowded tenement housing. Clubs such as the Boys' Clubs in New York were started as a way to keep boys off the street and out of trouble. These boys were characterized as low in mind and expression, unwashed, and having come from home influences that were of the worst kind (Wendell, 1895). The Fresh Air Fund, a project that raised money to send poor city children for

2 weeks to a host-family home in a rural setting, also was initiated. While organizers for this program believed such children could benefit from fresh air, nutritious food, and the experience of decent family living, these organizers also hoped the participating students would later teach their families what they had learned during the experience (Parsons, 1895).

Other philanthropic organizations, including women's clubs and settlement houses (Addams, 1911; Rouse, 1984), believed more was needed to ameliorate the effects of poverty, immigration, Black migration from the South to the North, and other social conditions thought to impact the intellectual and moral growth of children in the public schools. The growing concern about educating immigrants and their children (Richman, 1906), along with increasing attention to the children of recent Black migrants from the U.S. South (Blascoer, 1915), become vitally important at this time.

In 1915, Francis Blascoer published *Colored School Children in New York*, a report that specifically addressed perceived challenges with schooling Black children in New York public schools. This report was one of the first comprehensive studies that situated Black students as problems in the public school system. The report suggested the need to improve race relations in the workplace, provide Black mothers with more appropriate, middle-class parenting models, increase social outlet opportunities for Black children in their neighborhoods, and provide more White "traveling teachers" (social workers) at the school level. Fundamentally, these students were viewed as problems that made the work of the teacher, and ultimately the school and school district, more difficult. Rousmaniere (1997) pointed out that during this time, challenges posed to traditional curriculum gave way to curriculum reform in which teachers were expected to "educate both academic principles and social skills" (p. 55). This "dual emphasis on the instruction of children's minds and the socialization of their behaviors was encapsulated in the term *social efficiency*" (p. 55). Doing this required that teachers "expand their role from pedagogue to social servant, from purveyor of knowledge to a more creative advisor on health, behavior, civics, and culture" (p. 55). It is not surprising that the use of intelligence testing in schools emerged as a scientific method for efficiently identifying and categorizing students on the basis of their presumed intellectual capability (Deschenes et al., 2001). This process was thought to offer students the access needed to prepare them for their "proper place" in society.

Mid-20th Century

During the mid-1940s, and well into the 1960s, there was another wave of Black and Afro-Caribbean migration into large urban centers in the midwestern, northeastern, and western regions of the United States. Simultaneously, immigrants from Spanish-speaking countries in the Caribbean and Mexico moved into crowded urban enclaves. Sociologists attributed these moves to several factors, including the mechanization of southern agriculture, the burgeoning industrialization of urban cities, and the intense political and physical oppression and repression found in the South toward African Americans. According to Kantor and Brenzel (1992), nearly 80% of the nation's Black population still lived in the South and 63% lived in rural areas during the 1940s. During this time, 1.6 million African Americans migrated to northern and western cities, and another 1.5 million followed in the 1950s. By 1970, 47% of all African Americans lived outside the South and three-quarters lived in metropolitan areas (Kantor & Brenzel, 1992).

Increased migration to large cities coupled with the flight of White Americans to the suburbs led to a decrease in jobs and resources in urban cities. The result was a high concentration of poor and working-class people, primarily Black and Latino, within the largest U.S. locales. While African American migration slowed during the 1970s, a growing number of immigrants arrived in major American cities from Mexico, Central America, and the Caribbean (especially Puerto Rico) (Kantor & Brenzel, 1992). For many, northern migration did not represent the milk-and-honey dreams some had imagined. Inadequate housing and health care, unemployment, and crowded and run-down schools often characterized urban centers. These conditions helped widen the gap between poor people of color and their White counterparts along various social, economic, and academic indicators (Kantor & Brenzel, 1992). According to the *Kerner Report*, released by President Lyndon Johnson's National Advisory Commission on Civil Disorders (U.S. National Advisory Commission on Civil Disorders & Kerner, 1968), these factors also paved the way for growing civil unrest, particularly in the form of race riots in large, urban cities around the country. In the aftermath, there was a pressing need to understand and rectify the social, political, and economic disparities believed to plague such communities. Education played an ever-expanding role in this mission.

To address these concerns, the federal government assumed a more prominent role in tackling poverty and its effects on U.S. life through President Johnson's War on Poverty programs. One result, the Elementary and Secondary Education Act of 1965 (ESEA, 1965), ushered in a proliferation of K–12 education research that sought answers to why low-income students and students of color, primarily African American, Mexican American/Chicano, and Puerto Rican, experienced lower academic achievement than their middle-class, White counterparts across the United States. Researchers also began to investigate what schools, teachers, and students needed to do in order to increase the academic performance of poor students of color in urban areas. While some scholars recycled theories from the early 20th century that presumed innate, genetic deficiencies accounted for students' lower academic achievement (Jensen, 1969; Shuey, 1966), others argued that the environment and cultural practices played a pivotal role in potential academic performance (Clark & Plotkin, 1972; Deutsch, 1967; Loretan & Umans, 1966; Riessman, 1962). Proponents of the latter view believed poor students and students of color in both urban and rural schools, as well as their families and communities, lacked the necessary skills, perspectives, and cultural understandings to successfully navigate within mainstream school environments.

The idea of *cultural deficit/deprivation* was situated within the field of psychology (Martinez & Rury, 2012; Pearl, 1997) and assumed that differences in academic achievement between poor students and students of color, and their counterparts from White, middle-class backgrounds originated from deficient environmental conditions rather than from one's genetic code. Pearl (1997) states that this model "singled out the family unit as the transmitter of deficiencies" (p. 133). While a proposed lack of culture was pivotal to this work, "the family unit—mother, father, home environment— was pegged as the carrier of the pathology" (p. 133). Much of the work in the cultural deprivation paradigm focused on the cognitive and linguistic implications of parenting strategies used with children of color and those living in poverty. There was an assumption that the home environment of the poor neglected to provide the sensory stimulation necessary for child development. Drawing from his culture of poverty theory, anthropologist Oscar Lewis (1963) provided additional support for this idea. Lewis argued that living in poverty created maladaptive cultural practices that families passed down generationally. These cultural practices were to blame for students' curtailed achievement and societal advancement.

As a result, the education system and schools specifically were positioned to help poor students and students of color overcome their culturally deprived backgrounds through compensatory education. Banks (2004) stated:

> Cultural deprivation theorists, unlike geneticists, believe that low-income students can attain high levels of academic achievement, but socialization experiences in their homes and communities do not enable them to attain the knowledge, skills, and attitudes that middle-class children acquire and that are essential for academic success. (p. 18)

Compensatory programs, including Head Start, Follow Through, and Title I, were federally funded through ESEA 1965. They were designed to provide students the skills and experiences needed to successfully navigate school systems that viewed White, middle-class values and lifestyles as the ideal. A foundational tenet of these programs was the belief that poor students and students of color had the capacity to achieve, in spite of their economic, social, and cultural impediments.

This history illuminates an obvious point. It was dangerous to position poor children of color as genetically deprived, for it locked them into a place of intellectual degeneracy and hopelessness. A more astute identification of risk was necessary, one that accounted for both the capability of students and the cultural conditions that made it difficult for the culturally deficient student to flourish. The underlying logic of risk identification and management did not change; rather, the *what* and *why* of risk transformed. To alleviate risk, the culturally deprived student needed distance away from the constraints of a limited and problematic culture. This required a disavowal of one's self, family, culture, and community, and the adoption of a more culturally normative set of values, knowledge, and ways of being associated with Whiteness. Risk, then, in this context, was recognized as objectively real, yet also malleable for risk identification and management.

By the 1970s researchers seriously challenged theories that positioned students, their families, and the cultural groups to which they belonged as culturally deprived. These researchers disagreed with deprivation perspectives, challenging their underlying deficit assumptions about poor students and students of color (Baratz & Baratz, 1970; Martinez & Rury, 2012). What cultural deprivation theorists saw as deficiencies and generally regarded as socialization problems related to socioeconomic status and cultural inadequacy, cultural difference theorists viewed as a cultural mismatch. The inability of education systems and schools to bridge these cultural gaps leads to academic failure.

Scholars also pointed to the underlying racist assumptions associated with cultural deprivation theories (Baratz & Baratz, 1970; Clark, 1965). They argued these paradigms tacitly accepted and utilized White, middle-class skills, perspectives, and cultural understandings as the standard criteria for comparison. These critics also suggested that the cause for low achievement in poor students and students of color was more likely the result of *cultural differences* that existed between the cultural values of the school and those found in the child, her family, and the community in which she lived. Proponents of this perspective argued that these students came to school with distinct perspectives and beliefs about the world and education that often conflicted with the cultural values affirmed in the school and larger society. Thus, in this context, if student achievement is to occur, schools must find ways to adapt to the perspectives and values of the student, rather than try to fit the student within the existing, normative structure.

Cultural difference perspectives highlighted problems with the institution of schooling. Attention was given to organizational practices, the shortage of multicultural curriculum and inclusive instructional strategies (Gay, 1979; Grant, 1979; Grant & Sleeter, 1986), and low teacher expectations for student learning (Gouldner, 1978; Rist, 1970).[3] To address cultural mismatch, work in the cultural difference paradigm focused on understanding learning styles, teaching styles, and the role of language in the teaching and learning process. (Delpit & Dowdy, 2002; Heath, 1983; Smitherman, 1977). Some of this work also attempted to outline the cultural features of how particular groups of students learned (Banks, 1988; Boykin, 1978; Hale-Benson, 1982; Shade, 1982). Other work illustrated the power of teachers drawing from community and familial ways of knowing, or funds of knowledge, to enhance classroom teaching and curriculum (Moll, Armanti, Neff, & Gonzales, 1992).

Recognizing how cultural differences operated in teaching, along with issues of power and injustice, scholars theorized the effective pedagogical practices used with students of color (Gay, 2010; Irvine, 1990; Ladson-Billings, 2009; Villegas, 1991). This work has grown, moving across different content/subject areas and with an expanding focus on teacher education (Villegas & Lucas, 2001) and school reform (Lipman, 1995). In the critically oriented cultural difference paradigm, risk was culturally situated and dependent on normative rules of Whiteness for who and what was viewed as risk. In this context, risk retained a real, objective quality. Yet the danger that these critical difference perspectives pointed to was a lack of recognition that what traditionally counted as risk relied on normatively valued knowledge that was both racist and classist. This created the necessity for more culturally expansive approaches to teaching and curriculum that disrupted unquestioned assumptions about student ability and potential academic risk.

While cultural difference perspectives recognized the inability of schools as institutions to meet the needs of non-normatively positioned students, other perspectives focused on larger societal issues, with *structural/institutional inequality* as the problem of schools. These critiques paid attention to how macro-level conditions of inequality operated in everyday schooling to adversely impact the achievement of historically marginalized student populations. Scholars suggested that schooling was far from a neutral, apolitical process, and instead served to reinforce and help maintain existing political and economic structures (Apple, 2004; Bourdieu & Passeron, 1977; Bowles & Gintis, 1976; Emoungu, 1979). A key aspect of this work addressed curriculum concerns, with the understanding that curriculum encompassed both the formal and informal knowledge/skills learned in classrooms (Anyon, 1980; Apple, 2004) and the organization of course offerings (Oakes, 2005). It was theorized that the curriculum was differentially provided to students, impacting the curriculum that students received. It also spoke to the intended and unintended knowledge students gained while in school. Consequently, this work suggested that the existing structures and arrangements of schools reinforced the achievement of some students, while creating conditions for others to fail.

Researchers also examined the inequitable and differential resources that schools across different communities possess. This work proposed that differences in resources (e.g., school funding, quality and choice of curriculum, teacher quality) make it more challenging to provide low-income and/or students of color with an optimal educational experience. It was not uncommon for such viewpoints to cite racism as an underlying cause for these conditions (Baratz & Baratz, 1970; Ladson-Billings & Tate, 1995).

Structural/institutional inequality explanations also sought to understand the relationship between larger societal arrangements, patterns, and practices, and the local, micro-level actions of students around achievement. For example, stereotype threat (Steele, 2011) illuminated how the situational achievement of individuals is adversely impacted when they are asked to perform a task associated with a negative societal stereotype held about a certain group.

Seeking to bridge issues of culture and structure with the individual agency of students, researchers also posited that students struggled academically due to their resistance to school. Ogbu (1978) called this a Black oppositional culture to schooling. Extending this argument, Fordham and Ogbu (1986) argued that Black student achievement is compromised due to negotiations around the burden of acting White. It was theorized that culturally Black children are ridiculed for choosing to engage in school, a cultural domain presumably associated with Whiteness. In spite of their continued popularity in policy and everyday discourse, these theories have received considerable critique as culturally deficient, as well as ahistorical and incomplete in explaining how Black students navigate school and achievement (Carter, 2006; K. M. Foster, 2004; Fryer & Torelli, 2010).

Similar to cultural difference paradigms, structural/institutional equality approaches recognized risk as an objective reality in achievement. Risk, in this case, was connected to historical and structured patterns of inequality that operated institutionally and individually in students' lives. Danger rested on how such risk was found in the variable, inequitable opportunities afforded students based on their social location and on how it was addressed in the everyday work of schooling and internalized by students. This necessitated making connections between larger structural arrangements and the everyday realities of schooling and achievement implicated by these risks.

Late 20th and Early 21st Centuries

The passage of *A Nation at Risk* in 1983 represented the second prominent wave of federal attention placed on the effectiveness of U.S. education and schools. This policy pointed to the impending dangers facing the United States with regard to existing mediocre standards for academic achievement. It sought to renew the nation's commitment to K–12 and higher education. Unlike ESEA 1965, *A Nation at Risk* did not specifically address concerns with educating students from "disadvantaged" backgrounds. However, policymakers, researchers, and educators picked up the language of risk, specifically as they evoked fears about the continuing strength and future economic vitality of the United States. The nation had a responsibility to identify and mitigate the risks posed to it.

Throughout the 1980s, this language shifted in focus from a nation at-risk to one that viewed particular students as at-risk. The category eventually served as a replacement for earlier terms (e.g., culturally deprived/disadvantaged) used to identify students presumed to face unique academic challenges. *At-risk* became the term of choice to discuss students believed more likely than their peers to experience low academic achievement and educational attainment (Martinez & Rury, 2012; Swadener, 1995). The underlying goal of classifying certain students and student populations as at-risk was to identify, at the level of the individual student, the specific risk factors and their origins that made low academic achievement and educational attainment more likely to occur. By doing this it was believed that school systems, teachers, psychologists, and other providers could offer the necessary remediation and intervention. The research that had accumulated over the past 4 decades, examining the relationship between individual, familial, and social characteristics, and one's resultant achievement, IQ, and social competence, was used to identify the risk factors associated with low achievement.

While there was (and continues to be) no definitive agreement on the risk factors that place a student at-risk, Natriello et al. (1990) identified the following most frequently cited and researched individual/family-level risk factors associated with the at-risk student: (1) poverty; (2) race/ethnicity; (3) limited English proficiency; (4) parents' educational attainment; and (5) single-parent family homes. This approach to understanding issues of risk followed an epidemiological perspective (Swadener, 1995) that attempted to locate the causes and factors that ultimately lead to an undesired, pathological state. As noted previously, a student characterized as at-risk technically is one who is part of a population of people who either have come or have a high likelihood of coming into contact with risk factors associated with the occurrence of some negative outcome (Pianta & Walsh, 1996).

Since the 1990s, the term *at-risk* has taken on a life of its own, becoming a descriptor that generally, and often problematically, represents students of color, those who are poor, dis/abled, or for whom English is a second language. Scholars criticized these perspectives of risk, specifically as they related to schooling, for their adherence to culturally deficient models of thinking (Fine, 1993; Swadener, 1995). These critiques recognized risk as a social construct that depended on normalized, dominant perspectives about what it means to be a "normal" student. These constructions of risk resulted from longstanding social constructions that positioned students of color and their families, as well as those living in poverty and those with particular kinds of special needs, as abnormal and potentially deviant. Researchers interested in the socially constructed nature of risk as it played out in school systems and classrooms noted the flexible ways that the concept was utilized in schools and by teachers to construct students as at-risk for low academic achievement (Richardson et al., 1989).

During this time, however, research continued to explore the links between genetic predisposition, environmental conditions, and cognitive ability (Kagan, 1998; Plomin, 1989; Plomin, DeFries, Knopik, & Neiderheiser, 2013; Plomin & Rutter, 1998), including the widely criticized and controversial book, *The Bell Curve* (Herrnstein & Murray, 1994). More recently, this work has focused less on IQ, arguing that a relationship exists between environmental conditions, specifically socioeconomic status and a child's executive function (Hackman, Farah, & Meaney, 2010; Sarsour et al., 2011). In light of this, since the 1990s two predominant perspectives have emerged in the educational literature to discuss students positioned as at-risk. Both perspectives acknowledge the socially constructed view of risk and challenge the negative undertones associated with categorizing students as simply at-risk.

One school of thought advocated the need to shift the terms used to refer to students presumed at higher probability of low achievement (e.g., *at-promise, placed at-risk, vulnerable*) rather than using simply *at-risk* (Boykin, 2000; Swadener, 1995). This move was thought to decrease the stigma students might encounter when labeled at-risk. This change also emphasized that the responsibility for meeting the needs of students who faced challenging life circumstances should shift from students and families to school systems. For example, in the 2002 National Society for the Study of Education publication, *Educating At-Risk Students*, Deborah Land and Nettie Legters cite the following school-level factors associated with placing students at-risk: (1) school-level poverty; (2) class size; (3) school size; (4) urbanicity; (5) expectations; (6) school violence; (7) tracking; (8) special education; (9) retention; and (10) suspensions and expulsions. By identifying the school factors that place students at-risk, Land and Legters (2002) sought to identify the protective factors that buffer or, in some cases, ameliorate the negative effects school risk factors play in these students' lives. This is done in the hope of creating effective intervention and prevention programs for students facing such conditions.

The second perspective, popularized during the 1990s and used to discuss the at-risk student, also drew from the notion of identifying protective factors. The notion of protective factors spans back to the late 1960s and was situated within the fields of psychopathology, psychiatry, and newly emerging developmental psychopathology (Rutter, 1979). This work drew from previous literature in the field that focused on mental illness and that denoted "risk" as

> a statistical concept, indicating that a child of a parent with a major psychiatric disorder (e.g., manic-depressive illness or schizophrenia) has a greater probability of subsequently developing mental disorder than the child of a well parent. (Musick, Stott, Spencer, Goldman, & Cohler, 1987, p. 230)

Utilizing an integrative framework, these newer approaches to risk thought it relevant to examine why some individuals, in spite of close proximity to the risk factors associated with mental illness, did not become mentally ill (Cicchetti, 1990; Garmezy, 1983; Luthar, Cicchetti, & Becker, 2000; Smith & Carlson, 1997; Smokowski, 1998; Werner & Smith, 1982). These individuals were characterized as invulnerable (Anthony & Cohler, 1987) or resilient. Luthar, Cicchetti, and Becker (2000) defined resilience as "a construct connoting the maintenance of positive adaptation by individuals despite experiences of significant adversity" (p. 543). Across the multiple fields in which it was found (e.g., psychiatry, developmental psychopathology, psychology, education, social work), resilience connoted the existence of protective mechanisms that assist in buffering the stressors, or risk factors, associated with presumably vulnerable populations (Garmezy, 1983; Smokowski, 1998). For example, Smokowski (1998) offered an explanation of protective processes, quoted here at length:

> In this model, a protective effect is present if an attribute enhances functioning for high-risk individuals but makes no difference for their low-risk counterparts. Protection is also at play when high levels of a variable mediate stress, and yet when low levels of the variable are present, an individual's competence decreases. . . . Exactly how they [protective mechanisms] work is not well understood, but it is hypothesized that these mechanisms may intercede by reducing risk's effects, reducing negative chain reactions, establishing and maintaining self-esteem and self-efficacy, or opening opportunities. . . . [L]evels of risk, resilience, and protection are hypothesized to fluctuate (in some domains more than in others) across developmental periods, to vary by gender, and to show variations by race or ethnicity. (p. 339)

When discussing resilience in relation to schools and educational outcomes, Howard, Dryden, and Johnson (1999) suggested that the concept of resilience was a move away from previous risk-based deficit models that did not focus on "the assets in individuals and systems" (p. 309). Compared with the term *at-risk*, there is less empirical consensus about the notion of resilience, particularly the factors and cumulative processes that inevitably lead to resilience as well as the types of interventions that help promote it (Howard & Johnson, 2000; Luthar et al., 2000). The ambiguity around operationalizing the resilience construct continues into the new millennium. This is the case even as calls are made for researchers to adopt a constructivist stance that challenges resilience as a predetermined or normative set of conditions (Ungar, 2011).

Drawing from the research of Masten and Garmezy (Luthar, 2000) and Werner and Smith (1982, 1992), Luthar and colleagues (2000) listed the following set of early factors believed to be at play in the development of resilience: (1) attributes of the children themselves; (2) aspects of the children's families; and (3) characteristics of the children's wider social environments. They argued that "the focus of empirical work in resiliency has shifted away from identifying protective factors to understanding underlying protective processes" (p. 544). Just as earlier researchers pointed to the role multiple risk factors played in increasing the likelihood of negative outcomes, it currently is argued that cumulative protective factors lead to increased resilience. Accordingly, Luthar, Cicchetti, and Becker advocated using resilience as a construct to help augment the understanding of processes affecting at-risk students. Smokowski (1998) agreed with this statement, but went further when advocating for an "interface between resilience research and applied prevention programs" (p. 359) that benefit from a multicomponent design that affects both children and families. Such efforts are underway in school settings (Nettles & Robinson, 1998; Waxman, Gray, & Padrón, 2002). What is perhaps most interesting about this discourse is the way that it seemingly moves beyond a deficit notion of risk, while simultaneously relying on this idea to make and validate its claims. The notion of a constructivist orientation to resilience hints at the possibility of approaching the construct as socially negotiated and culturally situated (Ungar, 2011). Yet in the end, the resilient person—regardless to how the condition of resilience is defined—remains enclosed in a frame as always and perpetually at-risk (Rutter, 1987) by virtue of being identified as resilient in the first place.

The at-risk approach to risk and achievement placed a premium on identifying, managing, and ameliorating risk. This approach valued science and systematic inquiry into understanding how risk operated, in order to create optimal strategies for intervention. The existence of risk itself was not questioned; risk was an objective quality capable of identification and remedy. What remained open was how one should orient to the construct of risk. Was it an individual-level construct, or something understood only in sociopolitical, economic, and historical context? What were the criteria one should use to judge and assess risk? Was it capable of shifting from set qualities that resided in people, families, groups, and communities, to something that was constituted by various factors unrecognizable outside of the context in which it was housed? The contentiousness of the at-risk approach pointed to the *danger* implicit when using the at-risk construct to describe people and groups as potentially underachieving. Ironically, then, while there was a *necessity* to more accurately identify, talk about, and meet the needs of students positioned as at-risk, regardless of the actual label used (e.g., placed at-risk, at-promise, resilient, vulnerable), this process remained fraught with *dangers* of its own.

RISK KNOWLEDGE AND ACHIEVEMENT: NECESSARY, DANGEROUS, OR *BOTH*

Reviewing the historical trajectory of discourses on risk and achievement points to the pervasive way that certain people become constructed as at-risk for low achievement. These practices span the history of public schooling in the United States and continue into the present. While explanations have shifted for why and how to account for the condition of low achievement, what remains consistent is how groups positioned as antithetical to normative Whiteness were uniquely identified as risky and in need of intervention or containment. These discourses also have straddled between arguments that viewed this knowledge as necessary and those that viewed it as dangerous to consider in the context of schooling and achievement. This knowledge was recognized as necessary to engage with when scholars asserted the need to better identify or even critique the existing ways that risk was understood and used in practice. Conversely, this knowledge was seen as dangerous when it failed to adequately identify real risk, most often because of the normative ways it aligned with Whiteness. The danger was that those whose knowledge, values, and ways of being departed from dominant White standards were already consigned to possible risk.

Orientations to risk shifted over time, with some discourses recognizing risk as innate and unchanging, due to perceived beliefs about genetic disposition and one's riskiness. Harkening to *technico-scientific* approaches to risk (Lupton, 1999a, 1999b), technologies for making this risk calculable informed popular methods of risk identification and management. Yet in the end for advocates of the genetic approach, such methods could not offer any hope for risk remediation. Containment of the risk—often advocated for in the context of finding the right place for the risky body— was viewed as a necessary end result.

Genetic explanations for achievement were contentious and widely challenged. This response came as a result of the emergence of the culture construct. While still recognizing risk as real and objective, culture allowed risk to shift from something innate, static, and contained genetically within the body, to something that was contextual and malleable. *Cultural deficit/ deprived* explanations recognized risk as deeply connected to the larger social milieu. This approach was more hopeful than its predecessor regarding risk. One was not relegated to remain a victim to the risky body inherited from a culturally damaged family or group. Federal programs emerged as key sites of intervention. Yet in spite of the changes in how risk was understood, the basic logic of risk identification and management did not change. Normative constructions of the normal and risky body were not questioned; they were assumed *a priori*. Mechanisms for identifying risk remained important, as did the tools for managing it as well. However, fundamental to shedding risk from a *cultural deficit* paradigm was a disavowal of the self in order to refill the body with highly valued, yet culturally normative knowledge.

Challenging these perspectives, *cultural difference* and mismatch explanations also recognized risk as having a real, objective quality. Yet what the different explanations illuminated was the dangerous nature of *culturally deficient* orientations to knowledge about achievement. This spoke clearly to a *cultural symbolic* approach to risk (Lupton, 1999a, 1999b). It was posited that deficit orientations operated in normative ways when accounting for achievement and risk, relying on taken-for-granted logics that were both racist and classist. Thus, while risk in the difference paradigm remained culturally situated, it simultaneously was recognized as deeply problematic and divisive. These conditions underscored the necessity to advocate for more culturally expansive teaching and curriculum to disrupt unquestioned assumptions about student ability and potential academic risk.

Structural/institutional equality approaches viewed risk as an objective reality as well. Risk was connected to longstanding, entrenched patterns of inequities. These concerned both the past and present. They also implicated the everyday lives of students. A key danger regarding risk in this approach was the variable, inequitable opportunities afforded students based on their social location. Another danger was the possibility that students might internalize the negative dominant messages they received about their inability to achieve due to entrenched inequities in society. The necessity was for students and educators to understand these risky conditions, while simultaneously working to transgress, rather than re-inscribe, their effects. *Structural/institutional equality* approaches, then, recognized risk as a signpost to remain vigilant to how risk operated in raced, classed, and gendered ways.

The *at-risk* approach adhered primarily to a *technico-scientific* approach to risk, with its necessity to find more effective ways to identify and meet the needs of potentially underachieving students. Risk was real and objective, even as it had the capacity to transform as ideas around what leads to at-riskness shifted. These shifts, however, were slight, with most of them centering on whether risk was viewed from the perspective of risk itself or of resilience in spite of risk. These distinctions have not produced a more certain science around risk, nor have they mitigated the dangers still present in normalized constructions of who/what counts as risk or what constitutes the conditions of resilience. Continued debate on the lack of clarity around terms and conditions of the risk/resilience relationship make it certain that the quest to find risk will continue into the future.

TOOLS FOR CRITICAL REFLECTION AND PRACTICE

Key Terms to Consider

- Approaches to academic achievement
    - ✓ Genetic perspectives
    - ✓ Cultural deficit perspectives
    - ✓ Cultural mismatch/difference perspectives
    - ✓ Structural/institutional perspectives
    - ✓ At-risk perspectives
- Theoretical approaches to risk (Lupton, 1999a, 1999b)
    - ✓ Technico-scientific
    - ✓ Risk society
    - ✓ Cultural symbolic
    - ✓ Governmentality

Questions

1. What does it mean that-risk and the at-risk label and category have material consequences for people in the everyday world? Do you agree or disagree with this idea?

2. Risk-ness is based on the possibility, not the actuality, of some unwanted outcome. What are the implications of this for schooling and teaching? Why do education stakeholders need to understand about this in the context of policy and practice?

3. Discuss how the practices of risk identification and management existed in the earliest stages of compulsory, public schooling in the United States. Do you think this legacy continues in the present? Why or why not?

4. How does the history of risk in education operate as a necessary and dangerous discourse?

Extended Activity

Write a critical reflection that considers the popular discourses around risk and academic achievement that you have heard across your life experiences. How did people discuss and account for academic achievement in the schools you attended/worked in? In the communities where you lived? In the media? What explanations did you not hear across these spaces?

CHAPTER 3

Federal Education Policy

Examining Risk and the Category and Label of the At-Risk Student

This chapter presents the findings from my sojourn into the world of U.S. federal education policy. During my journey, I examined how risk and the category and label of the at-risk student played out in federal education policy from 1965 to the present. Drawing from the tradition of multisited ethnography, I moved within and across different policy locations when trying to make sense of what-risk and the category and label of the at-risk student meant over time. This movement introduced me to diverse bodies of knowledge, all of which I found during explorations through textual documents (e.g., theoretical, historical, policy) and during my interaction with people in the field.

I begin with a discussion of how authors have approached the study of federal education policy. I focus specifically on how and to what extent this work impacts education practice. Yet in order to understand how policy operates in practice, it is also important to first interrogate what actually is meant by "policy." I do this in the second section by briefly discussing the two approaches I used to read and make sense of how policy operated across education discourse and practice over time (Ball, 1993).

Recognizing that policies emerge in the context of multiple interconnected factors (Ball, 1993), in the third section I provide a selective outline of the historical role federal education policy has played in the United States. This discussion contradicts a popular assumption that the federal government did not play a prominent role in education until the mid-1960s. It also offers a context to understand how individuals working closely with U.S. federal education policy, as well as policy documents themselves, employed risk and the category and label of the at-risk student over time.

The next section of the chapter presents the findings generated from my examination of seven federal education policies enacted since 1965 in the United States: the Elementary and Secondary Education Act of 1965 (President Lyndon Baines Johnson); *A Nation at Risk* (President Ronald

Reagan, 1983); America 2000 (President George H. W. Bush, 1991); Goals 2000 (President William Clinton,1994/1996); the No Child Left Behind Act of 2001 (President George W. Bush); Race to the Top (President Barack Obama); and the Every Student Succeeds Act (President Barack Obama). When I conducted the initial study, No Child Left Behind was the federal education policy to which states adhered. Since that time and while I was completing this manuscript, the Race to the Top program was initiated and the Every Student Succeeds Act passed. I decided to examine and include these policies in order to offer a more comprehensive picture of U.S. federal education policy around risk and achievement. In the discussion that follows I explore how federal education policies have addressed concerns with academic risk over time.

WHAT CAN FEDERAL POLICY TELL US ABOUT RISK?

One of the enduring concerns in education policy scholarship is the extent to which "policy matters," or actually exerts an impact on the way education and schooling manifest in practice. This concern leads authors to explore whether a policy or given set of policies leads to significant or lasting change (Clark & Astuto, 1986; Elmore & McLaughlin, 1983), or, in some cases, reflects a new, fresh approach to some longstanding educational problem (Cross, 2004; DeBray, 2006; Kaestle & Smith, 1982; McDonnell, 2005; Tyack & Cuban, 1995). It is not uncommon for authors to consider whether federal education policies—both their goals and the extent to which they are effectively implemented in school settings—simply continue in the tradition of previous policies or serve as radical departures from their predecessors. For example, in the case of NCLB, McDonnell (2005), along with Cross (2004), suggested that in spite of popular rhetoric that it reflected revolutionary transformation in federal approaches to education policy, this policy was simply an extension of and outgrowth from previous policy attempts.

Thus, the idea that policies do not get created in a vacuum, where previous assumptions about and approaches to solving education problems do not exert influence, provides a productive perspective to examine how federal policy addresses risk and the category and label of the at-risk student. In the article "What Is Policy? Texts, Trajectories and Toolboxes," Stephen Ball (1993) argued that to understand policy, one first must recognize and account for two conceptualizations of policy that acknowledge the complex relationship between agency and constraint.[1] The first perspective—policy as text—viewed

policies as representations which are encoded in complex ways (via struggles, compromises, authoritative public interpretations and reinterpretations) and *interpreted / discourse*

decoded in complex ways (via actors' interpretations and meanings in relation to their history, experiences, skills, resources and context). (p. 11)

This approach suggested that policy was both contested and changing, always in a state of "'becoming,' of 'was' and 'never was' and 'not quite'; for any text a plurality of readers must necessarily produce a plurality of reading" (Ball, 1993, p. 11). From this perspective, policies do not contain a definitive or deterministic way in which stakeholders can understand and implement them. In this instance, policy as "the enactment of texts relies on things like commitment, understanding, capability, resources, practical limitations, cooperation and (importantly) intertextual compatibility" (p. 11). As pointed out by Ball, policies, and those who support or critique them, are likely to interact and compete with one another, effectively placing constraints on how and to what extent vested stakeholders actually can enact any given policy of choice. Ball (1993) noted that while policies often contain parameters for interpretation and action, they "do not normally tell you what to do" (p. 12). In this vein, there was an assumption that policy necessarily filters into localized contexts where

many people many results interpretation

> given constraints, circumstances and practicalities, the translation of the crude, abstract simplicities of policy texts into interactive and sustainable practices of some sort involves productive thought, invention and adaptation. (p. 12)

Policy necessarily includes room for interpretation, maneuverability, and enactment on the part of vested stakeholders.

Ball's (1993) complex view of policy as text suggested that stakeholders possess some agency and movement in how they make sense of and act in relation to policy in the local context. However, this view does not negate the limits that exist on what is possible to see and do regarding policy in a localized setting. These concerns focus on a second conceptualization of policy—*policy as discourse* (Ball, 1993). Here, policy served as the embodiment and construction of "certain possibilities of thought" in which "words are ordered and combined in particular ways and other combinations are displaced or excluded" (p. 14).

This approach to policy draws from the work of Michel Foucault. It illustrates that policy as discourse exists within and helps to create a frame for what is possible to imagine when "reading" a policy in the first place. This notion of boundaries and limitations is different from the previous discussion of policy as text, where Ball (1993) proposed that because of their unique standpoints, viewpoints, and/or agendas, stakeholders can selectively attend (or not) to policy. Policy as discourse, rather, pointed out the very limitations contained within policy construction. This is evidenced by what gets framed as a "problem" worthy of remediation, as well as the fact that only certain kinds of responses to the problem get picked up as reasonable and appropriate to undertake. Ball stated, "We may only be able to conceive of the possibilities of response in and through the language, concepts and vocabulary which the discourse makes available to us" (pp. 14–15). Drawing from the work of Foucault, Ball noted that discourse does not refer simply to language, words, or text, but rather they operate as "practices that systematically form the objects in which they speak. . . . Discourses are not about objects; they do not identify objects, they constitute them and in the practice of doing so conceal their own invention" (p. 14).

Following from this, I offer that any given discourse inevitably must account for historical factors and localized contexts that over time and space fasten in place how people make sense of and act in the world. This means that while at times policy might operate as a textual artifact where people struggle over its meaning and implementation, it is much more than simply this. Policy is a product of power relations that simultaneously, and even contradictorily, allow for movement and struggle that are always contained within limited boundaries of possibility and interpretation.

LOOKING BACK TO THE PAST:
FEDERAL EDUCATION POLICY IN THE UNITED STATES

On January 8, 1964, in his State of the Union Address, President Lyndon Baines Johnson proclaimed his intent to end poverty in the United States. He had been in office for only a month following the assassination of his predecessor and former running mate, John F. Kennedy, on November 22, 1963. In the address, President Johnson declared "unconditional war on poverty in America" and warned this undertaking "will not be a short or easy struggle" as "no single weapon or strategy will suffice" (Janda, n.d.). One of the primary strategies selected by President Johnson to remedy poverty was to target education. ESEA 1965 was born out of this concern and commitment.   ? Every Student Succeed Act

While it is common to discuss ESEA 1965 as an unprecedented attempt on the part of the U.S. federal government to take a decisive role in K–12 schooling, such efforts did not begin in the mid-1960s. The federal government had taken an active and financial interest in matters related to education since the late 18th and early 19th centuries.[2] In 1787 Congress passed the Northwest Ordinance, which required townships in the former Northwest Territory to set aside land for sale from which the proceeds would go to the creation of educational institutions (Cross, 2004; Kaestle & Smith, 1982; Snyder, Tan, & Hoffman, 2004). In 1802, legislation passed that established the first U.S. Military Academy. The first Morrill Act, passed in 1862, authorized land grants to states for the creation of agricultural and mechanical colleges. The second Morrill Act followed in 1890, providing financial grants targeted to instructional support in agricultural and mechanical colleges (Snyder et al., 2004).

Although many other legislative acts related to education were passed throughout the late 1800s and early 1900s, it was the passage of the Smith–Hughes Act in 1917 that perhaps had the most significant impact on K–12 education prior to the passage of ESEA 1965 (Cross, 2004; Kaestle & Smith, 1982). According to Kaestle and Smith (1982), the Smith–Hughes Act was "unprecedented, and for a long time it was unique" (p. 388). The authors pointed out that this act provided categorical aid to secondary public schools that focused on the creation of vocational educational programs. Cross (2004) asserted that the political impetus behind this act was both the increasing enrollment of 14- to 17-year-old students in public schools, as well as the concern that growing numbers of illiterate inductees were enrolling in military service. Wanting to have more efficiently run schools, educators at various levels looked to adopt educational programs that would target students for whom they believed an elite, or college-preparatory, program was not intended. The Smith–Hughes Act continued to receive funding well into the 1960s (Kaestle & Smith, 1982).[3]

ESEA 1965 was introduced and passed during the Johnson Administration. It was a part of the Great Society programs that sought to "increase attention on the character of American life" (Committee on Labor and Public Welfare, 1965, p. 4).[4] This program, specifically the aspects associated with education, was viewed as pivotal in the pursuit to end poverty. This approach placed considerable responsibility on federal policy to provide all children (e.g., poor students and/or students of color) with a quality, pre-K–12 educational experience. This was due in part to the presumed "relationship between achievement and income level," as well as the recursive character of "poverty and ignorance." "Just as ignorance breeds poverty, poverty all too often breeds ignorance in the next generation" (p. 14).

ESEA 1965 authorized the federal government to allocate $1 billion to address education concerns at the preschool, elementary, secondary, and college/university levels (Lagemann, 2000). These concerns focused on earmarking funds for the creation of preschool programs (e.g., Head Start) and state and local funds for schools that served low-income student populations; creating supplemental educational centers and regional educational labs to improve curriculum, train teachers, and provide support for economically and culturally deprived students; and strengthening state educational agencies by offering funding to colleges/universities and scholarships for promising and needy students (Committee on Labor and Public Welfare, 1965).

President Johnson and those that worked closely with him in the creation of ESEA 1965 were not the first to believe that national policy should and could help to remedy poverty and its concomitant effects. As pointed out in Chapter 2, it was the convergence of many factors, including traditional concerns with the poor, and the growing belief in the early 20th century that societies were capable of addressing the presumed effects of poverty through the application of scientific methods. Then, as well as during the War on Poverty, these beliefs were based on longstanding assumptions about the need for and capability of specialized knowledge and scientific inquiry to resolve social problems. In a study that examined the history of social scientific ideas about poverty in the United States and the role this knowledge played in social policy, O'Connor (2001) supported this claim.

> The idea that scientific knowledge holds the key to solving social problems has long been an article of faith in American liberalism. Nowhere is this more apparent than when it comes to solving the "poverty problem." For well over a century, liberal social investigators have scrutinized poor people in the hopes of creating a knowledge base for informed social action. Their studies have generated massive amounts of data and a widening array of research techniques, from the community-based social surveys of the Progressive Era, to the ethnographic neighborhood studies conducted by Chicago-school social scientists in the 1920s, to the technically sophisticated econometric analysis that forms the basis of the poverty research industry today. Although its origins can be traced to what historian Daniel Rodgers calls the transatlantic "borrowings" of late nineteenth- and early twentieth-century progressives, contemporary poverty research is very much an American invention, with a degree of specialization and an institutional apparatus that is unmatched in other parts of the world. (p. 3)

What O'Connor (2001) powerfully illustrated is that while poverty, as a topic of scientific inquiry, has enjoyed a long tradition in the United States and perhaps even possessed some unique defining characteristics, these perspectives owe much to ideas that emerged about poverty across different temporal and spatial contexts. Historical forces, such as immigration, urbanization, and the concomitant ways of thinking about life, traveled across geographic sites and over time made it possible for a distinct body of knowledge related to poverty to emerge and become recognized as a target of intervention in the United States. One of the fascinating aspects of poverty knowledge is its ability to adapt to and even anticipate changing social conditions.

TALKING ABOUT RISK IN FEDERAL EDUCATION POLICY

Each of the seven policies examined addressed risk and achievement. They all did so in the context of a key emergent theme: losing international/

global prominence and national vitality. This theme reflects a fundamental danger: *losing future social, economic, and/or political national influence/ competitiveness*. This was found across each of the seven federal policies and helped to rationalize why the policy was needed and the potential dangers related to acting on the recommendations outlined in the policy.

Losing International/Global Prominence and National Vitality

Consider an opening statement in ESEA 1965:

> Nothing matters more to the future of this our country: not our military preparedness, for armed might is worthless if we lack the brain power to build a world of peace; not our productive economy, for we cannot sustain growth without trained manpower; not our democratic system of government, for freedom is fragile if citizens are ignorant. (Committee on Labor and Public Welfare, 1965, p. 12)

Here, there was an assumption that the United States can remain a vital and free power only if its citizens receive knowledge and skills that come from having direct access to a strong education system.

This belief also was found in *A Nation at Risk* (*NAR*), released in 1983 during the Reagan Administration. Similar to its 1965 predecessor ESEA, *NAR* suggested that the United States was "at-risk" of losing its international preeminence if steps were not taken to improve mediocre standards for academic achievement. The loss of international preeminence was an important concern. *NAR* asserted that such a loss would lead to a decline in American prosperity, security, and a free democratic society. The document began:

> Our nation is at-risk. Our once unchallenged preeminence in commerce, industry, science, and technological innovation is being overtaken by competitors throughout the world. This report is concerned with only one of the many causes and dimension of the problem, but it is the one that undergirds American prosperity, security and civility. We report to the American people that while we can take justifiable pride in what our schools and colleges have historically accomplished and contributed to the United States and the well-being of its people, the educational foundations of our society are presently being eroded by a rising tide of mediocrity that threatens our very future as a Nation and a people. What was unimaginable a generation ago has begun to occur—others are matching and surpassing our educational attainments. (p. 1)

Similarly America 2000, proposed in 1991 during the Bush I Administration, also drew from the rhetoric of declining international preeminence. The primary rationale offered for this policy was based on concerns that the United States was falling behind its international competitors and trading partners.

> As a nation, we now invest more in education than in defense. But the results have not improved, and we're not coming close to our potential or what is needed. Nor is the rest of the world sitting idly by, waiting for America to catch up. Serious efforts at education improvement are under way by most of our international competitors and trading partners. Yet while we spend as much per student as almost any country in the world, American students are at or near the back of the pack in international comparisons. If we don't make radical changes, that is where they are going to stay. (U.S. Department of Education, 1991, p. 5)

Additionally, America 2000 pointed out that while the federal government "spen[t] more in education than in defense," U.S. "employers cannot hire enough qualified workers," thus requiring "companies [to] export skilled work" (U.S. Department of Education, 1991, p. 5).

Goals 2000, the federal education policy passed in 1994 and amended in 1996 during the Clinton Administration, cited as important goals for reforming schools, the need to (1) provide students with internationally competitive content, student performance, and opportunity-to-learn standards, as well as (2) promote initiatives that would provide equal educational opportunity for all students to meet high academic and occupational skill standards and to succeed in the world of employment and civic participation (Goals 2000: Educate America Act, Sec. 2, Purpose, 1994, p. 1). These concerns implied that, in common with previous policies, Goals 2000 was concerned with international competition and ensuring that U.S. students became successful participants in the national economic and civic arenas.

NCLB, passed in 2001 under the Bush II Administration, also pointed to the presumed growing gap between U.S. students and their international counterparts. The policy stated:

> ESEA was enacted in 1965. Yet despite hundreds of programs and hundreds of billions of dollars invested during the last generation, American students still lag behind many of their fellow foreign students and the academic achievement gap in this country between rich and poor, white and minority students, remains wide. (U.S. Department of Education, Office of Elementary and Secondary Education, 2002, p. 9)

NCLB critiqued the inability of federal policy to close the gaps in achievement between different populations of students. More than previous policies, NCLB highlighted that little improvement in academic achievement had occurred for student groups historically positioned as underachieving. This recognition offered additional justification to support NCLB. Both Race to the Top (Race) and the Every Student Succeeds Act (ESSA) cited the need for a stronger education system to ensure the global competitiveness of the United States. For example, ESSA stated, "We have some of the best schools and best universities in the world—but too often our students are not prepared to compete in the global economy" (Executive Office of the President, 2015, p. 2). Improving K–12 schools to equip students with the skills needed for college or career entry is positioned as integral in meeting this goal. — *How !*

[handwritten margin note: where is the discourse]

LOCATING RISK IN FEDERAL EDUCATION POLICY

When considering how risk was located in federal education policy, I was concerned with questions such as: What is risk? Where is risk? and Who is the risky or at-risk student? Across policies examined, each located, explicitly or implicitly, what was considered risk, where this risk was situated, and which particular entity or individual was assumed risky or at-risk. I also found that what constituted risk, where risk was located, and the things and individuals classified as "risky" often were connected to concerns with future social problems and the desire to circumvent their potential occurrence in society. Three key themes emerged across the policies regarding the location of risk: (1) risk as a threat to the risky individual and larger society; (2) families and schools as risky and the cause for low achievement; and (3) poor students and students of color as at-risk. Accordingly, *risk associated with the danger of future social problems that threaten the well-being of the risky individual and the larger society* surfaced as a way to understand how and where risk was located in federal education policy.

Threat to the Risky Individual and Larger Society

As pointed out in the previous section, risk often is discussed in relation to the vitality of the nation and its economic prowess. Across many of the seven policies, risk was fundamentally tied to concerns with the viability, growth, security, and well-being of the nation. For example, in ESEA 1965, *NAR*, and America 2000, the primary risk under consideration was that without some form of federal intervention in educational matters, the United States would lose its ability to compete economically and politically in an international context, as well as to retain a strong national presence and position. Outside of these concerns, however, three of the policies cited additional risks that warrant mention.

In *NAR*, there was an assumption that the risk of losing international preeminence would lead to a loss in U.S. prosperity, security, civility, and the maintenance of a free democratic society. America 2000 cited these concerns, but also acknowledged that while the U.S. government was funneling resources into K–12 education, these efforts did not lead to improved student achievement. Additionally, the policy pointed to another risk: that schools were not adequately designed to compensate for negative home life influences that impacted students' achievement. The document stated:

> And there is one more big problem: Today's young Americans spend barely 9 percent of their first eighteen years in school, on average. What of the other 91 percent, the portion spent elsewhere—at home, on playgrounds, in front of the television? For too many of our children, the family that should be their protector, advocate and moral anchor is itself in a state of deterioration. For too many of our children, such a family never existed. For too many of our children, the neighborhood is a place of menace, the street a place of violence. (U.S. Department of Education, 1991, pp. 6–7)

Here, America 2000 foreshadowed that the current configuration of school systems could not adequately address the larger factors that exerted an influence on learning and thus required immediate modification.

In Goals 2000, the danger associated with the inability of school systems to meet the academic needs of students was of vital importance. For instance, the document pointed out that for certain student populations, poor learning and teaching characterized their learning experiences. Over time, this deficiency led to the inability of schools and school systems to ensure that all students received an equitable educational opportunity and consequently performed at high levels of achievement. It was not surprising that NCLB also highlighted the danger that not all students had the opportunity to obtain a high-quality education.

The concern in education policy with failing to offer all students a high-quality education is linked to anxiety over the future strength and health of the nation. In the case of Race to the Top, the program reflected a larger effort to "stimulate the economy, support job creation, and invest in critical sectors, including education" (U.S. Department of Education, 2009, p. 2). This also was echoed in ESSA, with specific attention placed on "strengthening the middle class" (Executive Office of the President, 2015, p. 1) and bolstering the nation to "compete in the global economy" (p. 2).

Families and Schools as Risky and the Cause of Low Achievement

Diminished economic and political vitality of the nation, as well as the inability of schools and school systems to provide all students with an equitable and high-quality educational experience, characterized key risks across federal policy. What, then, do the policies tell us about where risk resides?

Beginning with ESEA 1965, the risk was located in the condition of poverty. The document noted that while "most Americans . . . enjoy a good life . . . far too many are still trapped in poverty, idleness and fear" (Committee on Labor and Public Welfare, 1965, p. 7). ESEA 1965 assumed that these conditions made it difficult for children who lived in poverty to reap the full benefits of education:

> The child from the urban or rural slum frequently misses his chance even before he begins school. Tests show that he is usually a year behind in academic attainment by the time he reaches the third grade—and up to 3 years behind if he reaches the eighth grade. By then the handicap has grown too great for many children. Their horizons have narrowed; their prospects for lifetimes of failure have hardened. A large percentage of our young people whose family incomes are less than $2,000 do not go beyond the eighth grade. (Committee on Labor and Public Welfare, 1965, p. 13)

Although poverty was cited as the primary location of risk in ESEA 1965, *NAR* situated risk in the overall structure and function of U.S. school systems. Risk was associated with insufficient time devoted to teaching, ineffective teacher training, substandard school leadership, and, perhaps most important, mediocre learning expectations. Little focus was placed on the external lives of students. Instead, more emphasis was placed on the internal functioning of K–12 schools, colleges, and universities. These concerns pinpointed non-rigorous secondary school curricula and loose requirements for both high school graduation and college matriculation as key locations of risk in U.S. education.

America 2000 and Goals 2000 also highlighted school-related factors as the primary site of risk, with the former also noting that-risk resided in unaccountable school systems and in certain families and communities where students did not receive adequate support for their learning. Both of these documents situated risk in the same location. This was likely the case because they both drew from the National Education Goals—a set of reforms adopted by the National Governors' Association in 1989. These goals were proposed first during the Bush I Administration, but failed to receive legislative support, and were proposed again during the Clinton Administration.[5] Implicit in these goals was the idea that-risk was associated with a lack of school readiness (a condition often associated with poverty and assumed to be caused by inappropriate or nonexistent family support); lowered rates of school completion; a gap in overall student achievement and development of student citizenship; inadequate preparation of teachers and ongoing mechanisms for professional development; insufficient training offered to students in mathematics and science; lowered rates of adult literacy and ongoing lifelong learning; and an increased number of schools that were unsafe, were undisciplined, and contained students who used alcohol and illegal drugs (Goals 2000: Educate America Act, National Education Goals, 1994, Sec.102; U.S. Department of Education, 1991).

NCLB also noted that-risk was found in the organization and practices of schools and school systems. In addition, the policy placed focus on schools' lack of accountability for student achievement, as well as the lack of attention paid to and implementation of educational programs that had demonstrated effectiveness with all student populations. Like its predecessor, America 2000, NCLB noted problems associated with the lack of local control and flexibility given to school systems to target the specific needs of their students. However, NCLB went further than America 2000, suggesting that academic risk was found in the condition of parents not having the choice to remove their children from schools that consistently had high rates of low student achievement. Similar to its predecessor NCLB, ESSA targeted attention to improving schools. However, ESSA took direct aim at NCLB, arguing that "it was too often a burden rather than a help" because of its one-size-fits-all solutions (Executive Office of the President, 2015, p. 2). Although ESSA did not directly position families as risky, it recognized that some communities faced substantial economic challenge that impacted effective schooling. For example, it referenced working with the Obama Administration's Promise Neighborhoods program, an effort that worked to "break the cycle of intergenerational poverty" through investment in comprehensive wrap-around support programs and the inclusion of community organizations in schools (Executive Office of the President, 2015, p. 5).

Across the policies, academic achievement generally related to the amount and kind of experiences and acquisition of knowledge/skills gained over some time period. For instance, in ESEA 1965, academic achievement was evidenced by the attainment of a high quantity and quality of education. This was measured at least partially by the use of tests. *NAR* also looked to the use of standardized tests to measure academic achievement, in addition to student grades and the number of students admitted to 4-year colleges and universities. In this case, academic achievement was discussed in relation to secondary schooling and was connected to the quantity and quality of coursework taken (i.e., knowledge and skills learned in class). In America 2000, Goals 2000, and NCLB, academic achievement was discussed in relation to standards. The focus here was that through the use of standardized tests, students showed evidence of meeting a set of standardized learning expectations (e.g., content and performance standards). While Race to the Top and ESSA recognized standards and testing as integral to assessing achievement, ESSA expressed concerns with the overemphasis placed on testing in schools. Both policies recognized additional indicators of achievement, including high school graduation rates and college-going and 2-year completion rates.

While a few differences existed in how federal education policies constituted academic achievement, was this also the case in how they accounted for failure to achieve academically? Beginning with ESEA 1965, poverty and the lack of educational opportunity presumed to accompany poverty (e.g., lack of initial school readiness) were cited as contributing factors to low academic achievement. One can assume that ineffective teaching was also a culprit or possibly a solution. The policy specifically set aside resources designed "to advance the technology of teaching and the training of teachers" (Committee on Labor and Public Welfare, 1965, p. 13). It also wanted to support "teachers who are superior, techniques of instruction that are modern, and thinking about education which places it first in all our plans and hopes" (p. 12).

With a primary focus on secondary schooling and academic achievement, *NAR* (1983) stated, "If an unfriendly foreign power had attempted to impose on America the mediocre educational performance that exists today, we might well have viewed it as an act of war" (p. 1). This statement captured one of the key concerns raised about academic achievement in *NAR*: fear that low expectations and mediocrity would multiply rapidly. Since in *NAR* academic achievement was understood as the quantity and quality of coursework mastered by students, this policy highlighted the problems associated with soft, non-rigorous content—that is, "minimum requirements" (p. 6) and low expectations held for student achievement. The report also called attention to the limited time allocated to teaching and learning in schools, as well as overarching problems with the preparation of teachers more generally.

America 2000 also outlined some of the causes of low academic achievement, pointing specifically to external factors many students were assumed to face, including the lack of family support and of early exposure to the knowledge and skills needed to learn and perform successfully in school. This policy also cited living in environments plagued with drug and alcohol abuse, random violence, adolescent pregnancy, and diseases such as AIDS as potential causes for low achievement (U.S. Department of Education, 1991). Additionally, like its predecessors, America 2000 pinpointed another important reason for low academic achievement: not requiring students to demonstrate their competency in challenging subject matter.

While the policies from Goals 2000 to the present placed less emphasis on the role factors external to school played in low academic achievement, they still acknowledged or alluded to the role families and communities played in exacerbating low academic risk. For example, Goals 2000 highlighted the lack of a coherent, clear, and coordinated system for addressing student learning. This approach focused on analyzing data gathered from student assessments to gauge which students were meeting learning goals (e.g., content and performance standards). Based on these data, school and district staff would develop intervention programs targeted specifically to students' academic needs. At the same time, inadequate parent participation was cited as contributing to academic risk.

In the case of NCLB, low achievement was associated with inadequate school practices, but here the policy addressed the limited use of pedagogical methods and instructional materials that show "scientific evidence of effectiveness" (U.S. Department of Education, Office of Elementary and Secondary Education, 2002, p. 13). There was also concern that too many students received instruction in core subject areas taught by teachers who were not highly qualified. The lack of choice offered to parents when deciding on school options for their children, presumably those that were Black, Hispanic, from low-income backgrounds, with disabilities, or with limited English proficiency, was also of concern. Similarly, Race to the Top and ESSA placed focus on school factors, while recognizing certain students as particularly vulnerable to low achievement. Race to the Top defined "high-needs students" as:

> at-risk of educational failure or otherwise in need of support, such as students who are living in poverty, who attend high-minority schools . . . are far below grade level, who have left school before receiving a regular high school diploma, who are at-risk of not graduating with a diploma on time, who are homeless, who are in foster care, who have been incarcerated, who have disabilities, or who are English language learners. (U.S. Department of Education, 2009, p. 12)

ESSA similarly used the term "high-needs" students (Executive Office of the President, 2015, p. 5) to highlight students living in distressed communities that would benefit from stronger, more comprehensive schools.

Poor Students and Students of Color as At Risk

When considering who was positioned as at-risk in U.S. federal policy, I found an overwhelming pattern of situating students who came from "disadvantaged" home environments as especially vulnerable to academic risk. While the nation and the larger citizenry clearly were positioned as at-risk in each of the policies, a combination of different populations of students also were positioned as such across these documents. For example, ESEA

1965 cited the poor child who came from either an urban or a rural slum as potentially "risky," while *NAR* pinpointed all students as at-risk, with gifted and talented students, socioeconomically disadvantaged students, minority students, language-minority students, and handicapped students noted as most at-risk.

Although America 2000 did not point to specific demographic characteristics or categorized groups of students as at-risk for low student achievement, it did provide a description of the students that fell in this category, including those who started school unready to begin learning; those who arrive at school hungry, unwashed, and frightened; and those who come in contact with drug and alcohol abuse, random violence, adolescent pregnancy, and AIDS (U.S. Department of Education, 1991). These factors generally are associated with students from poor or low-income backgrounds, as well as those of color.

Goals 2000 and NCLB noted that minority students were also at-risk, with the latter policy pointing to specific categories of students who experience higher rates of low academic achievement, including low-income students, African American students, Hispanic students, students with disabilities, and students with limited English proficiency (U.S. Department of Education, Office of Elementary and Secondary Education, 2002). Both Race to the Top and ESSA recognized students of color and those from low-income backgrounds as potentially at-risk for underachievement. This was evidenced in the focus on turning around the lowest achieving schools—schools that held Title I status. Race to the Top pointed to the need for more equitable distribution of effective teachers and principals in "high-poverty and/or high-minority schools" (U.S. Department of Education, 2009, p. 9). *[handwritten: ↳ nice thought — reality is very diff.]*

REMEDYING RISK IN FEDERAL EDUCATION POLICY

Given the seeming consistency over the past 40 years in how federal education policy talked about and located risk, it was not surprising that the solutions offered for remedying risk also shared similarities over time. While some differences surface across different documents, which some might suggest align with specific political party affiliations and their concomitant ideological commitments, even here there is very little deviation from approaches that assume potential risk can be ameliorated through more effective identification and management. One key theme emerged with regard to remedying risk: addressing risk by creating better schools and improved teaching. Relatedly, when I examined the solutions offered for remedying potential risk, *risk as associated with the danger of inadequately meeting the risky individual's academic needs* was reflected across the data.

Addressing Risk by Creating Better Schools and Improved Teaching

In the case of ESEA 1965, the primary remedy for addressing risk was to provide additional financial support for schooling poor students. This support came in the form of additional funding offered for remedial instruction; providing food, enrichment activities, and curricula and instructional materials for students; and the development, dissemination, and implementation of educational innovations. In the case of *NAR*, remedies for potential risk centered less on providing direct funding for state and local school efforts and more on identifying areas to target in secondary schools, colleges, and universities. Specific focus was placed on raising expectations for graduation and acceptance into institutions of higher learning. For example, authors suggested that high schools needed to implement more rigorous expectations for graduation and admission to college; ensure the maximum amount of time for actual classroom teaching; provide better preparation for teachers; and encourage more effective school leadership.

Improving the way schools operated was of vital concern in America 2000 and Goals 2000. America 2000 advocated for the creation of better, more accountable schools through the use of standards, the creation of exemplary community schools, as well as providing parents with more opportunities to choose where their children would attend school on the basis of student performance on national assessments. Goals 2000 placed more attention on helping school systems provide more coordinated, clear, and common approaches to teaching through the creation of standards. Additionally, America 2000 advocated freeing up bureaucratic rules for using federal funding, as well as providing higher pay for teachers and easing the requirements for alternative teacher certification.

One of the salient federal recommendations that has made an imprint on education practice in schools over the past 20 years is the use of standards and assessments.[6] The push to create large-scale academic standards and assessment systems in federal policy surfaced in America 2000 and was more deeply considered and realized in Goals 2000. For example, in America 2000, it was suggested that

> Standards will be developed, in conjunction with the national Education Goals Panel. These New World Standards—for each of the five core subjects—will represent what young Americans need to know and be able to do if they are to live and work successfully in today's world. These standards will incorporate both knowledge and skills, to ensure that, when they leave school, young Americans are prepared for further study and the work force. (U.S. Department of Education, 1991, p. 11)

Given that Goals 2000 drew from the same National Education Goals referenced in America 2000, it made sense that the former policy also addressed the need to design and implement standards for learning. However, in the case of Goals 2000, it also was assumed that both *content* and *performance* standards were necessary. Additionally, this policy suggested that assessment systems were needed to gauge students' proficiency with both sets of standards, and also encouraged schools to use the data from these assessments to plan and strategize instruction.

There was an assumption that data and results should be used to guide how education stakeholders understood and intervened in student learning. Evidence of this was found in America 2000, Goals 2000, and NCLB. Addressing student learning in this way was justified due to the achievement gap between poor students and students of color, and their middle-class, generally White and sometimes Asian counterparts (Haycock, 2001). This justification was prominent in NCLB. It was argued that performance data be "disaggregated for students by poverty levels, race, ethnicities, disabilities, and limited English proficiencies to ensure that no child—regardless of his or her background—is left behind" (U.S. Department of Education, Office of Elementary and Secondary Education, 2002, p. 9).

In what it called "a landmark in education reform," the No Child Left Behind Act was "designed to help all students meet high academic standards by requiring that states create annual assessments that measure what children know and can do in reading and math in grades 3 through 8" (U.S. Department of Education, Office of Elementary and Secondary Education, 2002, p. 9). As noted earlier, while this was not the first time that this method of measuring and keeping track of student achievement was advanced (e.g., America 2000), it was the first time that federal policy linked state and local funding with the implementation of mandatory assessment systems. Assessment systems were intimately connected with the creation and use of statewide academic standards that purported to offer clear, objective learning outcomes. Implementing these systems was one of the primary solutions advocated by federal policy to address potential risk. In addition to these remedies, NCLB suggested that schools and school systems focus on implementing instructional programs that showed evidence of scientifically based effectiveness; reducing bureaucracy and increasing flexibility of requirements at the state and local levels and holding school systems accountable for the performance of all students; and providing parents with more school choice.

Race to the Top and ESSA both acknowledged the need for better schooling as a remedy to risk, while also speaking to the backlash against the NCLB provisions related to testing. Preceding ESSA, Race to the Top advocated for more rigorous standards for college and career readiness, decreased testing, and improved strategies to recruit, train, and retain effective teachers. ESSA has continued this agenda, with a focus on providing more quality preschool, innovative approaches to teaching and learning, higher standards to prepare students for college and work, better and fewer assessments, and improvement in how schools coordinate and use student assessment data. It also recognized the need to increase equitable access to technology and to strengthen communities through building partnerships between schools and communities.

BRIDGING REMARKS: U.S. FEDERAL EDUCATION POLICY, RISK, AND THE LABEL AND CATEGORY OF THE AT-RISK STUDENT

Since the passage of ESEA 1965, federal education policy has focused on meeting the needs of students assumed disadvantaged and at-risk for low academic achievement. The students that fell in this category were generally poor and/or of color. While these criteria signaled different, but sometimes interrelated conditions (i.e., sometimes students who are poor are also students of color), it was not uncommon for the policies examined to discuss the two as existing in an already predetermined, symbiotic relationship. Given the original emphasis of ESEA 1965, it is not surprising that the focus on the needs of low-income students and/or students of color has continued over the past five decades. If anything has shifted, it is the strategies offered on how to best address these students' academic needs.

Across U.S. federal education policy, it was not uncommon to find rationales offered for addressing risk. These rationales suggested the necessity for the United States to maintain a strong, vital presence both politically and economically. Without this, it was assumed that the country ran the risk of *losing future social, economic, and /or political national influence/ competitiveness*. To address this concern, policies focused on identifying potential risks and those individuals who presumably came in close proximity to the risks. This was done to more efficiently remedy these areas. In this way, a *technico-scientific* orientation of risk (Lupton, 1999a, 199b) operated across the policies.

Concerns about the danger of losing future social, economic, and/or political national influence/competitiveness also speak to a *risk society* orientation (Lupton, 1999a, 1999b) around the intensification of risk in the context of national security concerns in the neoliberal context. In this site, most federal education policies introduced risk as a potential danger that threatened both individual citizens and the larger U.S. citizenry. More recent policy, including NCLB, made little direct mention of the potential loss of national vitality, but placed emphasis on closing the achievement gap that existed between multiple groups in the U.S. and between U.S.

students and their international counterparts. ESSA focused on gaps in achievement, as well as on opening opportunities and pathways for college attendance/completion and career readiness. In taking this approach to risk, the documents examined sought to *justify* why it was necessary for the federal government to take action toward the amelioration or, at a minimum, the management of risk in society. I argue that this approach attempted to rationalize why it was necessary to pinpoint individuals perceived as more likely than others to experience risk. The intention was to find ways to remedy risk. With its focus on identifying and seeking to remedy risk, this approach similarly drew from a *technico-scientific* orientation of risk (Lupton, 1999a, 1999b).

When considering where risk gets located across the federal education policies examined, a specific kind of risk emerges: danger associated with future social problems that threaten the well-being of both the risky individual and the larger society. Policy documents focused on defining what constituted risk, where it was found, and which individuals were at-risk for low academic achievement. Risk often was connected to concerns facing the economic and political vitality of the nation and the ability of schools to provide an adequate education for traditionally underserved student groups. Risk itself generally was located in the condition of living in poverty or in low-income families/communities. This aligned with the original purposes of ESEA 1965. Student groups positioned as at-risk generally came from populations outside of, or different from, the norm (i.e., White, middle class, average ability level). Students who were poor or who lived in low-income families, as well as those who lived in neighborhoods characterized by poverty and/or high crime, often were cited, along with students who were members of minority groups. *NAR* highlighted students presumed to possess higher than average ability levels as also vulnerable to risk. Additionally, in the policies of the 1990s and into the new millennium, risk was located in the structure, organization, and functioning of schools and, most prominently, teaching. Consequently, both cultural deficit and structural/institutional perspectives, specifically as they related to larger socioeconomic conditions and schools as institutions, were used to account for low academic achievement across the seven policies.

There was little disagreement across the seven policies on what constituted academic achievement. Academic achievement generally was understood as the amount and kind of experiences and acquisition of knowledge/skills gained by a student over time. In the earliest federal policies, achievement was associated with outcomes on standardized tests and other societal indicators such as literacy rates. Since Goals 2000, achievement was recognized as performance on standardized tests, as well as high school graduation rates and college enrollment and completion as additional indicators. When accounting for why some students experienced low academic achievement, factors related both to family and schools were pinpointed as impactful. The focus on schools specifically targeted the use of data to guide instruction, creating more innovative approaches to teaching, recruitment, development, and retention of quality teachers.

All of the policies discussed remediation of risk, as this was the general function of policy in the first place. Here, risk emerged as a danger associated with inadequately meeting the risky individual's academic needs. There was concern that without applying appropriate strategies to remedy risk, the academic needs of risky students would go unmet. As illustrated earlier, the strategies offered to remedy these students' needs shifted over time across the federal policies, with strategies ranging from providing remedial instruction and food for students to changing the requirements for graduation and improving school accountability systems. There was an interesting shift from a focus on remedying the external conditions of students (e.g., poverty) to one that targeted the organization and functioning of schools, with a growing interest in implementing stronger accountability measures and broadening schooling options for families (e.g., allowing for parental choice in selecting schools). Race to the Top advocated for more rigorous standards for college and career readiness, decreased testing, and improved strategies to recruit, train, and retain effective teachers. ESSA has continued this agenda, with a focus on providing more quality preschool, innovative approaches to teaching and learning, higher standards to prepare students for college and work, better and fewer assessments, and improvement in how schools coordinate and use student assessment data. It also recognized the need to increase equitable access to technology and strengthen communities through building partnerships between schools and communities. A trend toward waning confidence in public schools and teachers has grown in recent years across federal policy. This has opened the door to defunding schools with public monies and giving control of public education to for-profit management companies.

What this chapter has illustrated is how deeply entrenched ideas around risk and academic achievement are within the context of federal education policy. These perspectives reflect how risk discourse operates in both necessary and dangerous ways. The original ESEA 1965 was designed to address educational disparity caused by poverty. This was positioned as a necessary endeavor to ensure the vitality and strength of the nation. Undergirding this was the concomitant danger that in failing to do so, the country would compromise its power and security as a global leader. As federal education policy began placing greater emphasis on schooling as a progenitor for academic risk, the necessity to improve how schools functioned, teachers were trained, and instruction was delivered took precedence.

Indeed, what counts as risk and who is assumed to be at-risk undergird the very foundation and intention of federal education policy. But to what extent do ideas about risk play out in the context of teaching, the space perhaps closest in physical proximity to the everyday world of students and their learning? To consider this question, in the chapter that follows, we take a look at the ideas held by preservice teachers about risk and academic achievement.

TOOLS FOR CRITICAL REFLECTION AND PRACTICE

Key Term to Consider

- Poverty knowledge

Questions

1. What is the distinction between policy as text and policy as discourse? What is the importance of attending to these distinctions in education policy and practice?

2. How is the relationship between risk and the nation taken up in federal education policy? How and why does risk feature prominently in this work?

Extended Activity

Locate the latest education policy document for the state where you currently reside. How do risk and the category and label at-risk student feature in this document? Consider how the document talks about, locates, and proposes to address academic risk. Who is considered the at-risk student? How does the policy account for academic achievement?

CHAPTER 4

Preservice Teachers

Examining Risk and the Category and Label of the At-Risk Student

In this chapter I present the findings from my exploration in a preservice teacher site that is based on interview data generated with five preservice teachers who had recently completed a university-based teacher preparation program. I conducted one semi-structured interview with each teacher that lasted about 60–90 minutes. The interview focused on the teacher's background, beliefs on large educational issues, and perspectives on risk and academic achievement. I begin by providing an overview of the teacher education program at Midwest University where each of the students completed coursework for their teacher certification program. Then, I introduce each of the teachers with a discussion of their background, educational experiences and teaching goals and the perspectives they held about the responsibility of teachers and schooling in the U.S. Following this section, I discuss how the teacher candidates across the preservice teacher site talked about, understood and used the signifier of risk and the category of the at-risk student.

TEACHER EDUCATION AT MIDWEST UNIVERSITY

The five preservice teachers interviewed for this study were all enrolled in the same elementary education teacher education program where they were working toward pre-K–5 certification.[1] I recruited them through a snowball sampling procedure (Cohen, Manion, & Morrison, 2000) that included contacting supervisors that had recently worked with preservice teachers. All participants were at the end of their program. They had just completed student teaching, the final phase of their program, and were in the process of securing employment.

The teacher education program where the candidates completed their program was located at Midwest University, in the city of Lakeville. Midwest University is one of the most prestigious and well-respected public research universities in the United States. The elementary and secondary teacher education programs at Midwest consistently ranked in the top five programs as reported by *U.S. News and World Report*, and entry into the programs was very competitive. The elementary education program at Midwest offered various options where students were prepared to work at the preschool, primary, or intermediate level. At the time of the study, the elementary education program was distinguished by its two foci: multicultural education and reflection. The program was designed to educate teachers who:

- Were effective at encouraging high academic achievement in all students, particularly those students from diverse racial, cultural, linguistic, socioeconomic, gender, and ability groups.
- Recognized that their own race, culture, language, socioeconomic group, gender, and abilities shape their thinking and actions.
- Reflected on their practices and changed them to better meet student needs.
- Were aware that institutions like schools reflect both the strengths and inequities of society.
- Made a commitment to social justice and equity through their classroom practice and interactions with communities.
- Welcomed parents, caregivers, and community members to their classrooms as partners in the educational process.
- Worked within communities of educators who were professionals.
- Implemented research-based practices in their teaching.[2]

Students accepted into the program were expected to show evidence of strong academic preparation and competence, as well as possess the ability to work effectively with students from diverse backgrounds (e.g., racially, culturally, economically, linguistically, sexual orientation). Admission to the program was based on a candidate's academic competence, multicultural and interpersonal competence, and reflective competence; the latter focused on applicants' ability to reflect on and learn from their life and teacher preparation experiences.

The elementary education program consisted of four components: *liberal studies* and *general education courses* that exposed students to a broad range of academic disciplines; *minor coursework* that offered an in-depth study of one academic discipline; *education coursework* that included an examination of the schools' relationship to society and the processes by which students grow and learn; and a five-semester *professional sequence* that included teaching methods coursework and experience in schools. Students in the professional sequence took 57–60 credits in a wide range of courses that led up to student teaching, the last set of courses taken during the final semester in the program. Students could complete their student teaching in several sites. In the case of the pre-service teachers in this study, four candidates did their student teaching in Lakeville and only one person, Marisol, completed her teaching in a Millside public elementary school.[3]

WHO ARE THE PRESERVICE TEACHERS?

In the snapshots below I provide a portrait of each teacher that contextualizes their background, experiences as a student, and perspectives about teaching, learning, and schooling. Through these data and in the ethnographic tradition of thick description (Geertz, 1973), I present the preservice teacher participants as future educators grappling with multiple kinds of knowledge they hold about teaching. They were passionate and excited about becoming teachers. They also recognized the seriousness of this work. As a result, they were thoughtful and careful as they shared with me a slice of themselves—who they were, where they came from, and what they imagined themselves becoming as teachers. See Table 4.1 for an overview of the background characteristics and beliefs held about schooling, the role of the teacher, and expectations for future job placement among the five preservice teachers in this study.

Janice

Janice is a White female who grew up in a rural area in a midwestern state that sits just southwest of the state where she currently resides. In high school, her family moved to her current state of residence, settling down in Wolf Pointe, an area comprising a small cluster of communities falling in close proximity to one of the larger metropolitan areas in the state. Janice attended parochial school during her elementary and middle school years, but went to a public high school in Wolf Pointe. Janice expressed always wanting to be a teacher, a profession connected to her larger goal of wanting to help others she views as less fortunate. While she did not identify any distinct differences between or preferences for either type of school she attended, she wanted to teach in a public school that was "more urban" (Interview transcript, p. 4). When asked what she specifically meant by the term *urban* and why she felt drawn to such a school community, she did not directly answer the question. Her response, however, provided insight into what she valued, including her views on schools, her future teaching, and the way her own K–12 student experiences informed her thinking. Janice said:

> I guess at this point of my life I am not ready for inner-city urban, but it is a possibility.

[I want to teach in] more than just a metropolitan area. Suburban [schools] I feel that they're really good schools—most of them—and they have a lot of resources available to them, but . . . like I said earlier, one of the reasons why I got into teaching is to help those who don't have what I always had. I kind of grew up in a suburban type area, so I find that's kind of where I want to stay away from a little bit and expand my horizons. (Interview transcript, p. 4)

While Janice was not interested in teaching in a suburban area because she felt it was too racially homogenous and similar to the kinds of schools she attended, she did not feel ready to teach in an "inner-city urban" school context. She also wanted to work in a school that was "fully funded" (Interview transcript, p. 4) and this was something she questioned finding in an urban school setting.

Janice had ample time to consider her teaching philosophy during her teacher education program. During a time of reflection as she prepared for her first assignment, she highlighted the importance of building a strong "classroom community." This kind of environment would allow students to "feel safe that they [could] take academic risks and feel comfortable among others. That way they can work and do the best that they can" (Interview transcript, p. 1). The notion of community not only played a role in the configuration and quality of the classroom as a communal space but also was integrally connected to Janice's beliefs about the purposes of schooling. Janice expressed that schooling should "create people who are more knowledgeable and that can give back to society" (Interview transcript, p. 2).

Janice felt that teachers held an important role and responsibility in helping students meet this goal. This was something she was asked to consider in her teacher preparation program. When I asked her about this, Janice chuckled and stated:

Ah-hah. That is a question I have heard over and over. Well, I think it is to understand the students. To help them succeed and succeeding of course has various definitions depending on your background. But to help them, you know, believe in themselves, be able to take risks in life, you know, good decisionmaking and hopefully that gets them somewhere in the world where they will be satisfied with who they are and what they do. (Interview transcript, p. 2)

I was struck that Janice mentioned the term *risk* twice in the interview without any prompting from me or the interview protocol. In this and her earlier reference to risk, the term reflected an important quality that Janice felt students needed to possess in order to learn. Risk was an attribute that entailed taking a chance, a leap into the unknown in order to gain new useful and serviceable knowledge for future use.

Table 4.1. Background Characteristics of and Beliefs Held About Schooling, Teaching, and Future Job Placement Among the Preservice Teachers

Teacher	Race, Gender, and Place of Origin	Desired Teaching Position	Reason for Entering the Teaching Profession	Teaching Philosophy	Role and Responsibility of the Teacher	Beliefs About the Purpose of Schooling
Janice	White female Rural town in a midwestern state; prior to beginning high school, moved to a small community in the midwestern state where she attended the teacher education program	K–3 A diverse public school that is "fully funded" Urban (not inner city, urban) school setting, in the area where she attended the teacher education program	Always wanted to become a teacher Wants to help people	Important to build a strong classroom community where students feel safe to take learning risks	Understand students; help them believe in themselves; help them be able to take risks and make good decisions	Create people who are more knowledgeable and who can give back to society
Noah	African American male Small, urban metropolitan city in the Midwest; same city where he attended the teacher education program	K–1 A diverse public school in the same area where he grew up and attended the teacher education program	Always thought about it Comes from a family of teachers (both parents)	Important to get students actively engaged in learning and to establish good rapport with students and families	Act as a facilitator in the student learning process	Prepare students to contribute to society
Marisol	Biracial female (Latina and White) Urban metropolitan city in the Midwest about 70 miles from the city where she attended the teacher education program; moved at a young age to a suburban community outside of this city	K–2 bilingual A diverse urban school (ideal location New York City)	Always wanted to be a teacher Loves children	Important to focus on a social justice agenda that seeks to provide an equal-opportunity education system for all students and also empowers students and allows them to have a voice	Guide students in the learning process; help students recognize their own strengths and recognize what they are learning	Help students learn how to become citizens (includes gaining academic skills) and teach students how to interact socially and communicate with others

Table 4.1. Background Characteristics of and Beliefs Held About Schooling, Teaching, and Future Job Placement Among the Preservice Teachers

Teacher	Race, Gender, and Place of Origin	Desired Teaching Position	Reason for Entering the Teaching Profession	Teaching Philosophy	Role and Responsibility of the Teacher	Beliefs About the Purpose of Schooling
Samantha	White female Suburban community just north of a large urban metropolitan city in the Midwest about 70 miles from the city where she attended the teacher education program	3–5 A diverse public school that conceives of diversity in a broad way	Something that feels right to and for her Both parents were educators (father an administrator; mother a teacher)	Important to believe that all students can learn; approaches this task by recognizing the vast array of resources available to assist teachers in reaching this goal	Helping students become contributing members of society	Provide a basis for students to function in and deal with daily life
Vanessa	Mexican American female Urban metropolitan city in a large state in the southwestern region	K–2 A diverse public school in the same area where she attended the teacher education program	Has wanted to be a teacher since she began school Likes to learn new things	Important to concentrate attention on what students want and need Important to collaborate with others	Help students learn how to build community	Teach students what they need to learn in order to be ready for the social world

Janice thought that academic success was also important in schooling. She recognized success as a personal, contingent, and contextual factor. She noted:

> [Academic success] can be different depending on a person's background and experiences. What might be success for them could be another person's failure depending on their standards of themselves. And so it is knowing that person and understanding what success is for them. And then for me, success I guess is to have personal goals and to be able to meet those goals or even surpass them. You know, it is going to vary so much, depending on a person's abilities and interests. (Interview transcript, p. 3)

Hearing this response, I was reminded of how first-semester preservice teacher candidates in my own Introduction to Education course, a foundations course in the teacher education program at Midwest University, defined academic achievement. These students similarly recognized academic achievement in a variable way. They felt that no set or specific ideal should define academic achievement, as this would change depending on the student. When hearing this I would ask the students what criteria they imagined using to decide whether their students actually were achieving. Each time I posed this question, the discussion would stop. I would notice puzzled looks on the students' faces and in that silence I gathered that they had not really stopped and thought about how a concept of "variable achievement" might play out in actual classroom practice. Breaking the silence, a few brave students would chime in, rationalizing how they might assess students' achievement abilities. Yet it was clear from their responses that they assumed they would gain more effective diagnostic methods during their teacher education program and on the job from more experienced teachers. Almost none of the students recognized how this perspective on academic achievement left the door open for potential bias in teacher judgment about what students were capable of achieving. These findings were not idiosyncratic. In a study I conducted with preservice teachers who took a foundations course with me in another university teacher preparation program, students similarly viewed achievement as variable. They also did not recognize the possible biases this approach might have in practice (Brown & Goldstein, 2013).

Yet in light of Janice's belief that teachers (and schools by default) should view academic achievement as a variable and contextual construct, she felt that schools generally did not do a good job of helping all students achieve academically. This was particularly true for students of color, a group often tracked and allowed not to learn, either benignly or intentionally. Janice noted:

I think generally [schools] don't meet it for all students. From what I have seen there's always the student that slips through the cracks or gets labeled or tracked in a certain area, which is very unfortunate. And I know there is a lot of current debate, you know, there is a lot of [problems facing students who come from different] race and social backgrounds. (Interview transcript, p. 3)

Janice was especially cognizant of how students were given inequitable opportunities to learn and achieve through school practices like tracking and labeling. She also suggested that these issues were related to different values and expectations held by school staff and the students of color that failed to achieve. This difference, coupled with inequitable schooling practices, made students' academic underachievement possible.

Noah

Noah is an African American male. He was the only preservice teacher in the study from Lakeville and the only one who came to the teaching profession after having a previous career. Noah attended Lakeville Public Schools for all of his schooling and received his bachelor's degree in accounting from Midwest University. Noah "always thought about [becoming a teacher]" (Interview transcript, p. 3) but "went in other directions" because of "scholarship opportunities to pursue business-related [interests]" (Interview transcript, p. 3). His original desire to become a teacher was related to the fact that both his parents were teachers. Before coming into teaching he held a special passion for children and youth, having served as a coach for a sports league in the Lakeville area.

Noah envisioned working as a K–1 teacher in a public school setting. He wanted to work in the Lakeville Public School system because he felt "the school district does a very good job of educating students" (Interview transcript, p. 2). Fundamentally, though, his choice of school would boil down to "finding a place that meshes with my strengths" (Interview transcript, p. 2). Here, Noah was referring to his style and approach to teaching. His teaching philosophy focused on getting kids actively engaged in learning. This was important because:

If they [students] are involved and maybe even enjoying what they are doing through being active, I think as a teacher you stand a better chance of keeping their attention and getting them to learn what is deemed necessary for them to learn. (Interview transcript, p. 3)

Noah's concern with actively engaging students so they could sustain their attention on learning was connected to his own experiences as a learner and as a worker. Listening to lectures bored him, as did his previous profession because he worked at a desk all day. He felt that learning necessarily involved active engagement, something presumably far more dynamic than what he thought occurred in traditional classrooms.

Getting students actively engaged in their learning also was connected to another component of Noah's teaching philosophy: getting families connected to their child's learning. He expressed the importance of "establishing a good rapport" with families because teachers "don't always have all the answers that they need or all the information that they need in order to be able to teach every student . . . each student is different, comes to school with different backgrounds, experiences, knowledge" (Interview transcript, p. 3). Noah viewed families as especially positioned to impact the teaching and learning process, in much the same way that advocates of a culturally relevant/responsive (Gay, 2010; Ladson-Billings, 2009) and a funds of knowledge approach (Moll et al., 1992) have argued is needed. Although Noah had only a limited time to actively engage families during his student teaching, he expressed specific concern about connecting with families that did not physically visit the classroom. During student teaching, his cooperating teacher had the most difficulty forging relationships with families that came from diverse racial and socioeconomic backgrounds. While Noah did not specify what he meant by the phrase "diverse racial and socioeconomic backgrounds," I surmised from later comments that he was talking about students of color—primarily African American and Latino, as well as students who lived in poverty.

Noah's personal experiences as a student in the Lakeville Public School system offered him knowledge about the changing demographics in the city and their impact on the schools in the area. He often mentioned the "academic achievement gap" and how it likely resulted from a mismatch that existed between the values, knowledge, and expectations held by school faculty and those held by students from "diverse racial and socioeconomic backgrounds." This explanation for why certain student groups (e.g., African American, Latino, low socioeconomic status) often failed to achieve at the same level as their White (and sometimes Asian) and middle-class counterparts was new knowledge Noah acquired during his teacher education coursework at Midwest University. He stated:

> I took a class this past summer, an education policy class talking about schooling and its purpose. . . . And it got me kind of thinking about what we are told the purpose of school is for and what really is it for. . . . In the class that I had the emphasis was more on class and gender roles and things like that and how the way that school is structured doesn't necessarily make it easy for everybody to succeed. So there is a sort of contradiction there . . . the way things are . . . makes the

status quo in the future . . . versus making sure that everybody has a chance to succeed and reach whatever dreams they have. I sort of struggle with that a little bit, but my idea of what school should be is to prepare them to be successful contributors to society. (Interview transcript, p. 4)

Noah attempted to articulate the inconsistencies between the popular meritocracy view of schooling and the reality of how schools operate. The meritocracy view argues that schools serve all students equally and offers to those who avail themselves educationally, the opportunity to improve personal economic and social standing (Milner, 2010; Mueller & O'Connor, 2008). This perspective is challenged by the fact that schools historically have been organized to promote inequitable educational opportunities for students. Noah credited the course with helping him to see beyond his initially limited perspective on schools. "Up until that class . . . I really hadn't thought about it [how schooling practices promote inequitable educational opportunities]. My idea of what school was about was helping kids become adults and being successful" (Interview transcript, p. 4).

Noah was also unaware of the "academic achievement gap" prior to taking this course. When he was a student in Lakeville Public Schools, there were few minority students in the schools he attended (Interview transcript, p. 4). From his vantage point, it seemed that "everybody was pretty much doing what was expected of them and doing fairly well in school" (Interview transcript, p. 4). It was not clear whether, in saying "everybody," Noah was referring to the nonminority students and himself, or to the nonminority students as well as the few minority students in the school. However, he was sure that the changing diversity in Lakeville had played a role in the growing academic achievement gap facing the schools in his city.

When asked about the role and responsibility he believed the teacher held in the schooling process, Noah offered that the teacher should act as a facilitator who helped students develop their skills. Although these skills might span from the communication arena to interpersonal relationships and cognition, it was the teacher's responsibility to help students home in on these abilities. It was not the teacher's job to *give* students skills (Interview transcript, p. 5). He recognized a difference between giving and facilitating. He associated the former with traditional approaches to teaching where the teacher was viewed as having all of the answers (Interview transcript, p. 5). Facilitation involved operating as a "sort of guide through the process of how do you go about learning the skills and obtaining the knowledge that you need to succeed" (Interview transcript, p. 5). This meant that similar to his goal for students, teachers, too, needed to remain active learners.

Noah did not believe schools did a good job of meeting what he viewed as the purpose of schooling: preparing students to contribute to society. He cited the academic achievement gap as evidence that schools were not adequately meeting this purpose. He also felt that "schools have a tendency to favor nonminority students" (Interview transcript, p. 5). He expressed optimism that through multicultural approaches, education was shifting emphasis to meeting the needs of left-behind minority students. However, he also felt that there were "a lot of educators, schools, and districts that are still in the old mold that everybody should learn this way, and unfortunately, as we know, everyone doesn't learn the same way" (Interview transcript, p. 5).

Noah's belief that differences existed between the values and expectations for learning found in schools and those held by minority students was a recurring theme across his interview. In addition, he often pointed to the gaps in knowledge and skills that minority students came to school with—gaps that began as "disadvantages" (Interview transcript, p. 5). Here he referred directly to the arguments made around the role differentially valued capital had in structuring opportunities to learn in school (Bourdieu, 1977, 1984, 1986; Bourdieu & Passeron, 1977). According to Noah, these differences would lead to later academic deficiencies if teachers and schools "don't recognize or recognize but don't do anything to really solve the problem" (Interview transcript, p. 6). On this point, Noah did not waver. Nor did he seem aware of the normative, deficient way that minority students' capital—the knowledge and experiences they brought with them to school—was devalued and not affirmed from the very start (Brown, 2012; Yosso, 2005).

Marisol

Marisol is a biracial Latina who was born in Millside to a White mother and a Latino father. Her mother was from Millside and her father, who was from a small island in the Caribbean, came to the Midwest to attend college. Marisol's parents wanted both her brother and her to learn to speak Spanish so they attended a Spanish immersion school from kindergarten to 5th grade. Marisol had the unique experience of completing her student teaching at this same school. While she expressed that the immersion program was cool, after 5th grade she attended a suburban middle school and high school, "which was a very different experience" (Interview transcript, p. 1). This move was difficult even though Marisol had lived in a Millside suburb since a young age (Interview transcript, p. 1). So that Marisol and her brother could attend the Spanish immersion school, their parents enrolled them in the 2-20 program, "where they transfer kids from the suburbs into Millside on an exchange with Millside kids going to the suburbs" (Interview transcript, p. 2). Marisol noted that at the time of the interview, the program no longer existed.

In terms of school experiences, Marisol enjoyed school and was "always a good student and so school was never hard" (Interview transcript, p. 2). She especially loved grade school, saying, "I had friends with so many different backgrounds" (p. 2). This changed when she began attending school in the suburbs. She stated, "When you come to the suburbs it was like the first time that I had to face all of the discrimination against myself, which was really hard. You are just surrounded by people that are very different than you, [and] what I was used to" (p. 2). In spite of these social challenges, Marisol reflected that "in terms of academics, I never really struggled in either place. It was pretty easy. I liked school a lot" (p. 2). I was struck by Marisol's complex rendering of the two different kinds of schooling experiences she had during her K–12 years. While she maintained that across all of her schooling she experienced no academic trouble, she clearly felt socially isolated in the suburban context. I found myself wondering whether this provided insight into one of the key themes that emerged from Marisol's perspectives about teaching and learning: the importance of social development in the early academic lives of students.

Marisol wanted to teach early elementary grades—kindergarten or 1st grade—preferably in a bilingual setting because she felt she had the most to offer to "kids [who] struggle so much because of the language barrier" (Interview transcript, p. 2). She did not want to work in a "suburban type" school[4] and consequently did not want to teach in Lakeville. For one thing, she believed that "in the suburbs, you don't find a whole lot of bilingual students and if you do, it's just a different set of students" (Interview transcript, p. 2). She also believed that bilingual programs in these types of schools differed dramatically from similar programs in city areas. She asserted that she had more to offer students in city schools, as those students "don't really have any capabilities in English, whereas in the suburbs, they are pretty exposed and they pretty much have a grasp on it [English]" (Interview transcript, p. 3). This was not the only time that Marisol drew polar distinctions between students served in urban and suburban schools. As the interview continued I wondered about a possible connection between Marisol's experience as a student and how she later characterized students and their experiences in both kinds of school contexts. Marisol expressed wanting to teach in an urban school context where she "can make more of an impact in schools with the kids that really don't know anything and you're their only way of learning the language" (Interview transcript, p. 3). This, she thought, was a unique and rewarding experience of teaching (Interview transcript, p. 3).

Marisol's desire to teach bilingual students who, unlike her, did not have English as a first language was not the only reason she wanted to become a teacher. Her decision to teach was based on a longstanding passion she had about teaching that went back to her childhood. She said:

> I always have envisioned myself being a teacher. I had my own classroom with all my dolls. My mom was a teacher, although I have to say that I wanted to be a teacher before her. She went back to school to become a teacher when I was in high school. So I always say, I wanted to do it first. I just love kids and I hate saying that because it sounds so cheesy but it's the truth. I mean I think you have to have a passion for children and for teaching to want to become a teacher and I do. I think it's a hard profession but I think it's very rewarding. The most rewarding one that you can have. (Interview transcript, p. 3)

Teaching mattered to Marisol. Philosophically she was particularly keen to allow students to have a voice in and control over their learning. She also wanted students to "be unique and that mean[s] not everything has to be a cookie cutter way of doing things" (Interview transcript, p. 3). She thought it was okay that students did not do things exactly perfectly as they could learn from their mistakes. She acknowledged, however, that in her current student teaching context this was a difficult perspective to manage because other teachers at her school did not value her philosophy of social justice teaching.

For Marisol, social justice teaching was about making "the educational system more of an equal opportunity for all of its counterparts," which "is not happening in our country by any means" (Interview transcript, p. 4). She asserted that social justice education was not occurring presently in schools because teachers were "not making [students] feel that they're gonna make a difference in our society one day" (p. 4). Classrooms were the starting place for "help[ing] all kids feel that they are important" (p. 4). Marisol expressed that the purpose of schooling was to help students both learn how to become citizens as well as interact socially and communicate effectively with others. She acknowledged the responsibility schools played in teaching students academic knowledge, while also recognizing the necessity for schools to teach students "how to deal with their feelings." She also viewed school as a place to teach those "things . . . that kids might be learning at home" and compensate for those things "they might not be learning at home" (Interview transcript, p. 4). And while she did not believe there was only one way to be successful in the world, the responsibility of the teacher was to pass along to students "how to exist and how to make it; how to survive in the world" (Interview transcript, p. 4).

So what did this mean for the role of the teacher in the classroom and the learning and teaching process? Marisol struggled to find the right words to describe the role of the teacher in the classroom, but ultimately settled on *facilitator*. She also wanted to help students recognize "their own strengths" (Interview transcript, p. 5). With this statement, Marisol homed in on the idea she had struggled to conjure—the idea that a teacher should not seek to mold or "sculpt" the students. Rather, the teacher helps or guides them (Interview transcript, p. 5). It was curious that while Marisol believed teachers should guide students by pulling out their strengths, her earlier comments suggested that she did not view nonprivileged students, particularly those whose first language was not English, as bringing valuable knowledge to school.

Additionally, Marisol did not think schools did a good job of meeting these goals for all students. She suggested that the majority of schools did not do an adequate job at all. This was particularly true for schools in the city. Regarding these schools, she noted the following:

> I don't think a lot of teachers know how to [meet the goals she has for schools], especially in the city schools. You know, the ones that, you know, really need good teachers. They lack good teachers; all the good ones are taken up by the suburbs. The kids that, you know, [referring to the students who attend suburban schools] already have the tools, they have their parents there as guiders, as well. (Interview transcript, p. 6)

What stood out was Marisol's perspective that suburban schools categorically did a better job of educating students. This was a recurring idea across my interview with her and spoke to another generalization implicit in this statement and in previous and later statements she made. She believed that only privileged students attended and were well served by suburban and "suburban type" schools, while generally nonprivileged students attended and received inferior teaching in true urban school settings.

Samantha

Samantha is a White female who was born and raised in a small suburban city north of Millside. Samantha's hometown had a population of 30,000 and she suggested it was "not tiny, tiny, but it's sort of its own little bubble as far as everything else is concerned" (Interview transcript, p. 1).

Samantha went to public schools for her entire K–12 experience. Both of her parents were educators and worked in the same district where Samantha attended school. Her mother was a teacher and her dad worked as a curriculum coordinator in the central district office, and an elementary and middle school principal. Samantha thought this was a "unique experience" as "nine times out of ten [she] knew [her] teachers in advance from outside school experience going all the way through" elementary and middle school. Samantha noted one interesting characteristic of her high school was that it housed two high schools that were "mirror images of each other in [the] layout" (Interview transcript, p. 1). A door separated the schools, but the door did not lock. While both schools shared an auditorium, gym, and combined special classes, each school had its own separate academic classes. Students were selected for each school by a random, lottery system. However, siblings generally went to the same school.

Samantha narrowed her choice of public school to teach in down to one simple criterion: It must not use Direct Instruction.[5] She also wanted to work in a school "that's got a variety of people that work there and attend," yet she did not want to limit her notion of diversity to a specific "racial group or socioeconomic group" (Interview transcript, p. 2). She later admitted that if she was too picky about the specific kind of diversity she wanted to find in a school, she might limit herself in the job application process. Samantha wanted to become a teacher because "it's one of those things that just felt right the entire time" (Interview transcript, p. 2). She loved working in the classroom, watching students when they finally got something. She also loved the collaboration that occurred in schools, versus other work environments.

Samantha described her teaching philosophy as one that assumed "everyone can learn" (Interview transcript, p. 2). As a teacher she believed it was her responsibility to figure out how to reach all of her students. This did not mean that the teacher had sole responsibility for student achievement. She noted the necessity for "us[ing] the resources that are available" by "talk[ing] to previous teachers, contact[ing], if it is a new student . . . teachers at other schools" (Interview transcript, p. 3). Samantha imagined doing these kinds of things when she became a teacher in order to "figure out what things have and haven't worked in the past to try to reach students" (Interview transcript, p. 3). She felt that "every student is reachable . . . but definitely not in the same ways . . . it may require the help of others to get involved in the situation" because "[I] may not be able to reach every student" (Interview transcript, p. 3).

For Samantha the purpose of formal K–12 schooling was to provide a basis for students to function in and deal with daily life (Interview transcript, p. 3). Students should gain "basic skills in life" (Interview transcript, p. 3). These skills included, but were not limited to, "adding, subtracting, multiplying, and dividing" (Interview transcript, p. 3). She elaborated on this idea by sharing the following example:

> Going into the store and being able to quickly figure out whether or not . . . if you have these items and this is how much it is, and I only

have $20, am I going to be able to get all of these things? Being able to interact in society and being able to be an active member of society when they finish. Whether this means going out and getting a job right away or going on further in schooling. Or even for people that choose neither of these options. I mean if you have someone who is a stay-at-home person, or someone who just opts not to work but [is] able to be a contributing member of society in some way. (Interview transcript, p. 3)

Samantha did not go into detail on how a person who "opts not to work" can remain a "contributing member of society" (Interview transcript, p. 3). However, she asserted that teachers play an important role in helping students to become productive citizens. This was because teachers, by virtue of having "chosen a path that requires them to continue on in school after they are done with the traditional schooling, . . . have an understanding of how to [become] a contributing member of society" (p. 3). This meant teachers should help students recognize that "there are more things than just things in their house or in their school" (Interview transcript, p. 4). She also encouraged students to "look outside of yourself to see there is more than just you in the world" (p. 4).

The value Samantha placed on teachers helping students to see themselves as both members of and responsible for the larger community related to her own commitments as a U.S. citizen. While not distinguishing between U.S. citizens and those living in the United States without citizenship, she argued that living in this country offered rights and responsibilities that students need to understand, acknowledge, and respect. She stated, "They have these rights and this isn't something that's a universal. For example, voting. It's not universal [across the world] that everyone can just go to a polling place" (Interview transcript, p. 4). Although Samantha acknowledged that "even here, there are questions of how that works (ability to vote granted to all qualified U.S. citizens), she believed that schools must prepare students to participate in an active, engaged civic life.

When I asked Samantha whether she thought schools generally did a good job of meeting the goals she expressed for schooling, she asked, "For all students? No." She continued, "For the vast majority of students . . . short of you doing absolutely nothing and them just sitting doing nothing all day, they are gonna learn something" (Interview transcript, p. 4). Samantha believed that "a decent number of students do make it through and based on what they learn there, they do become contributing members of society" (p. 4). Yet in the case of some students, while they may not learn the "objective you laid out for them, based on the lesson that you do, . . . they are gonna get something from being in that setting . . . in spite of the things that go on in schools" (p. 4). This last comment is perhaps the most curious of all, as it grounded Samantha's belief that despite school or teacher intention, students in fact learn. Yet from her comments, what they learn, the quality of what they learn, and from whom they learn are less certain. What is also not clear is how she accounts for what happened to those few students whom, in her opinion, schools did not do a good job of properly schooling.

Vanessa

Vanessa was born in Mexico and grew up in Winding River before moving to Lakeville to attend college. Winding River is a mid-sized urban city in the southern/southwestern area of the United States. From grade school to high school she went to school with what she calls a "Hispanic" population (Interview transcript, p. 1). She was also the only preservice teacher in this study who acknowledged having a child.

Vanessa experienced social isolation when arriving at Midwest University. She attributed this to her limited experiences outside of the Hispanic culture (Interview transcript, p. 1). She noted that while attending Midwest University had been "a great experience, [it] had been rough because I don't think I was ready for the university work when I first came in" (p. 1). When asked whether she felt academically or socially unprepared, Vanessa pointed out each as a sore spot (p. 1). She felt that part of her personality had changed over the years. She also acknowledged that while she struggled academically, she still considered herself intelligent because she "studied lots, like three times more than the normal person would" (p. 1).

Vanessa attributed her difficulty in college to her less than adequate K–12 academic preparation, "especially in English and math" (Interview transcript, p. 2). I asked her whether she noticed any differences between the school her preschool-aged son attended in Lakeville and the classrooms where she worked as a student teacher, and what she remembered experiencing in her own schooling. She did not point to any specific differences but did believe that education in general had changed since her K–12 years, replying that "it's much more advanced now" (p. 2).

While Vanessa completed her student teaching in a kindergarten classroom, she had experience working at all elementary grade levels. She wanted to teach in an early childhood (K–2nd grade) classroom. She also wanted to work in a public school that "concentrates on teaching the children, a school that pays attention to what the children need and what the child wants, not on what the teacher wants" (Interview transcript, p. 3). She wondered aloud to me whether her preferences were somewhat "unreal" (p. 3), providing some indication that she believed many schools failed to meet this standard. She wanted to stay in Lakeville so she was looking for jobs only around the area, even though she had been told she should look elsewhere because of the intense competition for teaching jobs.

I asked Vanessa why she wanted to become a teacher and she replied, "I always have, ever since the first day I started school. And I started school in the 1st grade. And ever since, that was my dream" (Interview transcript, p. 3). Vanessa found it difficult to describe her teaching philosophy but offered that she "like[s] to . . . concentrate a lot on the children" (p. 3). She went on noting how she recognized her daily instructional plans but allowed for flexibility when the children needed or wanted something other than what she was offering them (Interview transcript, p. 4). With this in mind, she summarized her approach to teaching as focused on giving students what they want or what they need. She also added that part of her teaching philosophy acknowledged her respect for collaborative work with her peers because "it's enjoyable and I learn lots when I work with other people" (Interview transcript, p. 4).

When I asked Vanessa what she believed was the purpose of schooling, she said, "to teach a child . . . to teach whatever it is that they need to learn" (Interview transcript, p. 4). She thought that students would have gained a lot if they were "ready to be out in the social world" (p. 4). Not surprisingly, Vanessa suggested that teachers had an important role and responsibility to help students function in the social world. For example, she pointed out that teachers had a key role in helping students learn how to build community. This meant that teachers "get them [the students] to do things that'll get them to be active." She thought that "the little community is what's gonna help the children get into that social sense of getting out into the world" (p. 4). Vanessa also noted that teachers have a responsibility to teach students "academics, reading, writing, math, and all the subject areas" (Interview transcript, p. 5).

Vanessa recognized that schools do not meet these goals for all children. As she spoke, I wondered whether this belief was connected to her own K–12 schooling experiences. She went on to state, "I don't think that all teachers meet these needs and I think it's really important" (Interview transcript, p. 5). However, she was unsure why this was the case. She said:

> Why they don't [teachers meeting the goals she spoke of earlier]? I don't know. Maybe it's because of the way the teacher is, maybe I don't know. The teacher's style. I always put it back on the teacher for some reason. I just think if something goes wrong, the teacher needs to look back on, reflect on what did I do? What do I need to do to make things better? But I don't think it all falls back on the teacher. Not 100%. (Interview transcript, p. 5)

I was intrigued by Vanessa's initial insistence that teachers bear the brunt of the responsibility for students failing to meet the goals she believed all students needed to achieve in school and her later retrenchment from this position. When I asked her whether she would elaborate further, Vanessa offered:

> Well, if a child is not learning a specific material in math and the teacher looks at what's going on. I'm not doing this and this and this so I did a, b, and c and it's still not working. So then you [the teacher] go back and look at the child, what is going on, what is he doing, what is he not doing. (Interview transcript, p. 5)

From this account, I gathered that Vanessa wanted to account for factors, aside from those related solely to the teacher's instruction and curriculum, that might impact a student's learning. It was not surprising that she returned to this idea throughout the remainder of our interview.

TALKING ABOUT RISK

When interviewing the preservice teachers, I explored how they discussed risk and the category and label of the at-risk student in relation to concerns with academic achievement. Four themes emerged in how the candidates talked about risk: (1) engaging in risk discourse; (2) acknowledging *at-risk* as a familiar label for students; (3) recognizing the at-risk student as a real and viable category of person; and (4) conflicted understandings of at-risk status. This discussion highlighted an important danger related to risk that operated as an overriding concern: the danger associated with misidentifying, failing to identify, and/or holding low learning expectations for students who might face academic difficulty.

Engaging in Risk Discourse

One of the initial questions I posed to the preservice teachers around their beliefs about academic achievement was whether they believed it was necessary to identify students who seemed less likely than their peers to experience academic success. I asked this question, in precisely this manner, because it reflected the popularly accepted definition of risk in the literature. I wanted to know whether and how the teacher candidates thought about risk, without first invoking the word *risk*. In making this decision, I knew the word *risk* and more specifically the term *at-risk student* might carry politically charged undertones, biasing what the preservice teachers told me. This was of particular concern with these preservice teachers since they attended a teacher education program that challenged the use of the term because of its deficit connotations (see Chapters 1 and 2 for more about deficit perspectives).

All of the preservice teachers interviewed expressed that it was necessary to identify students who seemed less likely than their peers to experience low academic success—or students who were "at-risk" for low academic achievement. This related to the belief that the teacher had a role and responsibility to identify these students in order to meet their needs. For example, Vanessa replied to my question saying, "Oh, of course, it is very important. 'Cause then as a teacher you know what kind of support to give to those students" (Interview transcript, p. 6). Janice expressed the necessity to identify these students because

> as a teacher [I] know what I can do to help them. But it is a fine line of whether after identification then we push for these students to go in a special ed. route. That's something in my student teaching experience that I've really struggled with: Do we start evaluating these students? Do they really need that extra support or is it just kind of us struggling to bring them in? (Interview transcript, p. 5)

Janice felt that teachers should identify potentially low-achieving students in order to help them academically. She also harbored concerns that doing this might lead to the misidentification of students as having special learning needs, because of inaccurate teacher judgment.

Noah also thought it was necessary that teachers engage in risk discourse because it made them aware of students that needed specific pedagogical attention. He said:

> Well I think it is definitely important to identify them somehow. You know it sort of gets to be tricky in terms of what does that mean. Is that prejudice? Does it end up being racist? I mean there's a fine line there. I think you have to look at what the statistics show and be cognizant of those students because if you don't there is a likelihood that they could easily fall through the crack. That's not to say that students who exhibit certain characteristics or come from certain backgrounds are destined to be unsuccessful academically. As a teacher, your job is to teach every student in your classroom and so you need to know every student in your classroom. It would be irresponsible not to identify who they are. (Interview transcript, p. 7)

Noah approached this identification process as a preemptive strategy. Yet, his concern that the process might rely on prejudiced behavior was connected to the fact that students of color and/or those who live in poverty tended to achieve at lower rates than their White (and sometimes Asian) and/or middle-class peers. This disparity commonly was referred to as the "achievement gap." Noah brought this up as a concern at multiple points during the interview. What stood out was that in spite of Noah's worries that possible teacher bias might occur when using achievement gap data to help identify potentially low-achieving students, he believed these data were nonetheless valuable and useful.

Marisol, who like her peers believed it was necessary to engage in risk discourse, was the only preservice teacher to discuss this process in the context of a specific content area: literacy. She argued:

> I think that's important to an extent especially in terms of literacy since that is an underlying key to academic success, especially at this age. To be literate has to fall first because you can't really learn anything else from there. It's important in how you group the children, in terms of reading groups. You have to identify that to an extent, but I don't think it is important to draw on it, or to say, now that you have identified them, they are not going to achieve at the same level as this other group. (Interview transcript, p. 7)

For Marisol, making decisions about which students, in relation to their classroom peers, seemed to have a higher likelihood for low academic achievement, was part of the grouping process necessary for effective literacy instruction. She was adamant, however, that this approach should not lead to lowered teacher expectations for students, an occurrence she presumed took place.

Samantha also expressed that engaging in risk discourse was both a necessary and an inevitable activity for an effective teacher. She stated:

> If the teacher's paying attention to their students, I think it is next to impossible not to, at least in the back of their mind, identify these students that may not succeed as easily as the other students. But, as far as making it, giving them a label type of identifying them, or things like that, I don't think that that's a necessary part of it. And I think it's important for a teacher to at least have an idea of what students may not succeed. The stereotypical route of schools, which kind of goes back to me saying that what I believe about teaching is it's the teacher's job to figure out how to reach the students. And so I think that's an integral part. You have to be able to identify if the student is going to succeed . . . [and] if I see a student that I don't think is going to, I may take the extra time to sit down next to them and just make sure they're getting it. (Interview transcript, p. 5)

While Samantha felt teachers needed to identify students, similar to the other participants, she worried this practice might lead teachers to label students and hold low learning expectations for them, rather than help students progress academically.

Acknowledging At-Risk as a Familiar Label for Students

As discussed in Chapters 1 and 2, when risk is discussed in relation to academic concerns, it often is associated with the danger of low academic achievement. While this is not the only way that risk is talked about in the education field,[6] it is one of the primary ways the idea is understood and addressed by educators and the way I approached it in this study.

Before asking the preservice teachers whether they believed certain students were at-risk for low academic achievement, I wanted to find out whether they were familiar with the term *at-risk* as well as other popular terms used to describe these students, such as *resilient* and *at-promise*. All of the preservice teachers recognized the term *at-risk* and most were easily able to provide a definition that aligned with the common uses of the term; this was not the case for the terms *at-promise* and *resilient*. In the few cases where candidates recognized these terms, they did not offer definitions consistent with how these words are theorized in scholarly literature.

In the case of the term *at-risk*, all five candidates said they had heard of it. They said it was used in schools by staff, as well as in their education courses and in NCLB. For the preservice teachers, at-risk referred to students who (1) perform in the bottom tier academically (in relation to their peers); (2) need extra help; (3) are unsuccessful; and/or (4) face some factor likely to adversely influence their academic achievement. One person associated special education with at-risk status.

Only one preservice teacher, Samantha, had familiarity with the term *at-promise*, which she heard used in schools by staff. According to her, this term referred to

> a student who probably has those at-risk factors going on in their life but that this student doesn't fit the description of at-risk as closely because those factors are not impacting them in a negative way. At least not in their academic achievement. Or that the student has the abilities to do those things if they can overcome whatever else is going on. (Interview transcript, p. 10)

Finally, when asked about their familiarity with the term *resilient*, two candidates responded affirmatively. Both Samantha and Vanessa offered that they heard this term used in schools by staff. Samantha suggested it referred to a population similar to the at-promise student, but the resilient student was already successful academically. Vanessa, on the other hand, believed that the resilient student was a "child who wanted to do what he wanted, no matter what anyone said or did" (Interview transcript, p. 9).

Recognizing the At-Risk Student as a Real and Viable Category of Person

All of the five preservice teachers indicated that at-risk students existed in schools. While Vanessa simply responded "yes" to this question, the other candidates elaborated on why some students were at-risk for low academic achievement. Janice explained:

> That's a good question. I haven't thought about that too much. I guess you can say that, again, it goes back best with elementary students to home life too. You never know what the situations are sometimes, and depending on that, if it is a stressful environment, I think it could affect them. (Interview transcript, p. 9)

While Janice prefaced her answer by first acknowledging that she had not thought a lot about whether at-risk students existed, she went on to note that at-risk status was connected to the home lives of students.

Samantha noted that when people positioned students as at-risk, that meant the students faced "factors that [were] likely to influence their academic achievement and ability to be successful academically in school" (Interview transcript, p. 9). While she also believed that some students were at-risk, she did not believe coming into contact with risk factors inevitably led to being at-risk. For her, at-riskness was contingent on how students responded to their condition (p. 9). Noah similarly believed that some students were at-risk, stating the following:

> Yes, I do [believe risk exists]. And I think some of that-risk is just due to the idea that there are schools, there are teachers who still believe that there's one way to teach something and that's what they know how to do. And if a student isn't able to understand what is being taught in that way, then [these teachers] obviously think there is something wrong with the student. Those students are definitely at a disadvantage and at-risk of not getting the skills and knowledge that they need. (Interview transcript, pp. 10–11)

Noah broadly addressed risk in the context of school-related factors and the inability of some teachers to adapt their teaching approach to all students' learning styles.

Noah's focus on factors related to the classroom, rather than external conditions outside of the school, was similar to Marisol's perspectives on the at-risk student. Marisol, however, was the only person who expressed concern about the actual use of the label at-risk, as indicated by the exchange below:

Marisol: I think people make them at-risk. I mean, I think that is really a harsh term to associate with a child—they are at-risk for not succeeding. I think that some kids definitely have obstacles, obviously. Some kids definitely aren't where they're supposed to be academically or maybe where they should be. But, um, I don't know.

Keffrelyn: You said that some people make them at-risk and that you think the term is sort of a harsh term to use. When you say people make them at-risk, what do you mean by that?

Marisol: I think, first of all, just by giving them that title, somebody is imposing that on them. I don't think that is necessarily very fair. So I don't know. I think it's a tough question.

Keffrelyn: Do you believe that some students are at-risk of not achieving academically?

Marisol: Probably, but they are at-risk. . . . Oh that's tough.

Keffrelyn: What's tough about it, maybe that's where we should start?

Marisol: I think it's tough because I don't want to attribute those . . . I don't want to attribute all of these things by saying they are at-risk because of this or this or this or this. Because I really think that all kids are capable. I really do. I really believe in my heart that all kids are capable of learning. You have to just help them find something that interests them and something that makes them want to do it. That's what teaching is all about. That's what this is all about, you know, helping children find their niche. And helping children find the passion that they all do have. They are all capable. And I don't want to say that one child isn't because of such and such reasons. I don't think that is really fair. (Interview transcript, pp. 12–13)

Marisol felt trepidation in positioning students as at-risk. She struggled to reconcile her feelings that some students were really at-risk with understanding the problematic way students sometimes were assigned risk status and then held to lowered learning expectations.

Conflicted Understandings of At-Risk Status

Across the participants, an interesting tension emerged in how they discussed characteristics that made some students at-risk.[7] This conflict focused on the inability of the preservice teachers to outline, and/or their tentativeness in doing so, factors they believed characterized some students as at-risk. For example, Janice said:

> I think I am at a point in my career where I feel I need more experience and exposure on that specific topic because I don't want to fall into the stereotyping of specific socioeconomic backgrounds and race backgrounds. So I just don't feel like I have enough information or experience to make that opinion on my own. (Interview transcript, p. 12)

Janice hesitated to directly answer the question, suggesting that she was not experienced enough to offer a correct response. Yet what she did say provided insight into her thinking about and understanding of the category of the at-risk student. She thought that in some instances socioeconomic background and race background might serve as characteristics of at-risk students.

> *Keffrelyn:* Have you found that socioeconomic status and racial status often serve as factors, or some people believe that those are factors?
> *Janice:* I think it is more that people believe that that could be a factor. Not always the case but I think it is something to be constantly aware of. I mean that is one of the big things with our school systems today. That's a key player in the special ed. tracking so . . . [we need] to be aware of that. Is it really us not understanding the students or is it actually a real academic problem? (Interview transcript, p. 12)

While this exchange illustrated that Janice did not feel confident in delineating the factors associated with at-risk status, it also says much more. Janice was sensitive to the fact that some students were identified as "at-risk" not because of a "real" problem, but rather because of an inability of some teachers to discern whether a real problem existed. Janice struggled with this *ontological dilemma*. This dilemma was connected to her belief that White, middle-class teachers sometimes failed to accurately assess "real" academic problems because of the cultural mismatch she believed existed between many of these teachers and their students. For example, Janice stated:

> I think I am speaking from my own experiences but some schools where I have been in and growing up, it has been predominately White and predominately female and probably middle class. So when you have students coming in with a different background from that,

you have to wonder, is it a culture not understanding each other clearly, or is it an easy way out for those teachers or that staff just because they can't understand themselves and can't figure it out, so they track students? (Interview transcript, p. 12)

For Janice, cultural disconnect led teachers to hold biased perspectives about students who came from a different racial and/or socioeconomic background than the teacher's.

When I asked Marisol what factors made a student at-risk, she drew a distinction between what she thought other people might think and what she herself thought about this idea. At first glance, her response seemed to align with a statement she made previously in the interview: "people make them [students] at-risk" (Interview transcript, p. 12). However, paradoxically, the line of distinction between what she believed and what other people purportedly believed was less clear. Marisol continued:

I think other people think that students are at-risk because of something that is happening at home, they lack this at home. And to an extent I do agree with that. They might lack resources at home or they lack support at home. . . . Another reason that students are at-risk is because they are seen as being troublemakers, or kids that aren't socially . . . [adept]—that they are never going to make it because they don't even know how to communicate. (Interview transcript, p. 15)

Although Vanessa did not show the same kind of trepidation, it took her a while to actually answer the question about whether she felt some students were at-risk. When I first posed the question to her, she paused, repeated the question, and then told me, "I'm not sure" (Interview transcript, p. 11). Later, at the end of the interview when I asked her whether she had any questions for me, she said, "Maybe I can try to answer that one question that I couldn't. I'll try, but I don't know if I can answer it, though" (Interview transcript, p. 12). She then told me, "Okay, something I can think about is having an unstable home. That could definitely make a child at-risk. Because there's nothing they can go to if they have homework . . . if the home is not a proper place to do their work" (Interview transcript, p. 12).

When I asked Samantha the same question, she also focused on factors related to the student's home environment, in addition to issues related to the student and the school. She pointed to changes in a student's home life, like divorce and death, as possible risk factors. She also cited friendship and individual student learning style as possible factors. For example, she shared, "I think also that the learning style of that student, or you know if a student doesn't learn from reading from a book but that's all that's provided to them, you know they're probably going to be viewed as at-risk because they don't learn in the way that's given to them (Interview transcript, p. 12). Noah also pointed to factors related to home environment as indicative of at-risk status. He understood these concerns in relation to how they might play out within a school context. He stated:

> I think outside-of-school experiences factor in big [in] whether a student will be at-risk. Like I said before . . . there are specific things students are expected to come in already knowing. And a lot of that knowledge will come from outside of school. If a student doesn't get those opportunities or experiences and they go to the next grade, they are already behind all the other students that have had those experiences and those opportunities. And teachers tend to direct their teaching and their instruction toward the majority . . . I definitely [also] think socioeconomic status would be one [factor]. I think ethnicity would be another [factor], in terms of culture. (Interview transcript, pp. 12–13)

For Noah, the assumption that schools believe students need to possess certain kinds of knowledge in order to succeed academically is integrally connected to his belief that students who come from certain socioeconomic and cultural groups are more likely to be at-risk. When I was following up and asking Noah how he thought these factors played out, he offered that "different families have different expectations . . . and they may not be the same as what our public schools think are important and value. And so that's sort of a clash right there. If a teacher is not aware of that, that student would be at-risk." (Interview transcript, pp. 12–13)

LOCATING AND REMEDYING ACADEMIC RISK IN THE PRESERVICE TEACHER SITE

I also explored with the preservice teachers how they made sense of risk regarding its features and location in the context of academic achievement. As with the federal policy site, I was concerned with the questions: Does risk exist? What is risk? Where is risk? and Who is the "risky" or at-risk student? I asked each preservice teacher to consider where risk was situated and the entity(ies) or individuals they thought of as risky or at-risk. From these discussions, four themes emerged: (1) stable and shifting definitions of academic achievement; (2) assessing achievement using variable measures; (3) experiential and official school knowledge to understand academic achievement; and (4) family and student characteristics as key contributors to academic achievement. Two dangers emerged across these perspectives from the data. The first was the danger of misidentifying, failing to identify, and/or holding low learning expectations for students who might face academic difficulty. The second was danger associated with the belief that students were not performing where state, local, and/ or personal criteria suggest they should be.

Stable and Shifting Definitions of Academic Achievement

After asking the preservice teachers whether they believed it was necessary to identify students who seemed more likely than their peers to experience low academic achievement, I wanted to better understand their perspectives on academic achievement more specifically. The following discussion highlighted how the preservice teachers defined and addressed issues related to achievement. It also illuminated how they accounted for low academic achievement among students.

The preservice teachers overwhelmingly associated academic achievement with the mandates of federal policy and other official standardized measures. Samantha offered that academic achievement was "meeting the objectives laid out for the lesson or the unit or whatever has been laid out by the teacher" (Interview transcript, p. 4). Janice felt that academic achievement was "being able to meet the criteria or standards required for that grade level or age" (p. 4). She also pointed out that the requirements of NCLB made it "important that teachers and students meet standards" even though they were "being pushed on" schools and teachers (p. 4). Noah also thought about academic achievement in terms of standards and the NCLB policy, but recognized that achievement should go beyond simply performance on standardized tests. He said:

> I would define academic achievement in a couple of ways. As a teacher you are sort of forced to look at it in terms of test scores, No Child Left Behind, because the high-risk testing and all that you can't get around; that's here and you have to deal with that. . . . But I think there is definitely a lot more to education and achievement in terms of seeing connections between the things that you learn in school and real life. . . . I think if students are able to start seeing those connections, with help and then on their own, I think that is success as well. This is sort of an indication that they are critical thinkers, problem-solvers, are aware of their surroundings, take time to observe as opposed to just walk through life with blinders on. . . . Those are the types of individuals that stand a better chance of succeeding as adults and contributing to society. (Interview transcript, p. 6)

Marisol supported Noah's claim that academic achievement was and should be thought of as more than scores received on a test. She noted:

Well, it is definitely not passing a test. . . . Academic success . . . [at] the kindergarten level since that's what I am most familiar with . . . is a child achieving at or above. It's improvement really. I think academic success is you take a child in the beginning of the year and you kind of see where they're at. And throughout the year, their progress is going to be different than any other child in the class. But if there's improvement then they're being successful. Recognizing that for one child at the end of the year who recognized all of the letters of the alphabet may be academic success for them, where another child, reading D level books might be another. (Interview transcript, p. 6)

Marisol held what I call a *sliding scale view of achievement*. Achievement was an individualized factor, something that shifted across people and was based on the growth an individual person made in his/her learning. While Marisol's sentiment was that achievement should not operate as a static, deterministic standard of measurement across all students, it also brought into question concerns with potential teacher bias. For instance, how would a teacher decide for each student what is, or is not, adequate academic progress? This notion of achievement also was situated in what some might recognize as a "child-centered" perspective of achievement. Vanessa echoed this focus on the child, suggesting further that achievement occurred "when I see smiles [on] my kids' faces. When I see them engaged in the classroom. Once I see the children interested and we're getting everything going, I think something is going on in here." (Interview transcript, p. 5)

Assessing Achievement Using Variable Measures

The preservice teachers identified various approaches they felt were useful to identify low-achieving students. This provided insight into how the candidates made judgments about student learning. A key finding was that the participants approached the assessment of achievement in variable ways. When asked how they determined academic achievement, specifically the tools they drew from when recognizing a student as low achieving, they all pointed to the use of different forms of assessment. For example, each of the five candidates said that formal assessments, such as standardized and teacher-made tests, as well as informal assessments, including listening to students in one-on-one interactions and during class discussions and individual observations, yielded important information about how students were (or were not) progressing academically. Additionally, the preservice teachers relied on normalized expectations of where they believed students were "supposed" to be in terms of their learning. These expectations emerged in relation to (1) comparisons made between the perceived low-achieving student and his/her performance vis-à-vis other students in the class; (2)

comparisons made between the perceived low-achieving student and his/
her performance vis-à-vis local and/or state standards; and (3) comparisons
made between the perceived low-achieving student and nonspecified, generalized grade-level expectations.[8] In some instances, the teacher candidates
just took into consideration the labels previously placed on students by other staff in the school (e.g., English language learner, gifted and talented,
learning disabled).

For example, Janice made comparisons between the perceived
low-achieving student's performance and the performance of other students in the classroom, as well as between the perceived low-achieving
student's performance and nonspecified, generalized grade-level expectations (Interview transcript, pp. 7–8). Similarly, when deciding whether a
student was low achieving, Marisol compared individual student performance with the performance of other students in the classroom, with official local and state learning standards, and with nonspecified, generalized
grade-level expectations for learning. She noted:

> You know, I guess there has to be some kind of standard that you
> use. And so whether that be a sheet of paper with all of these letters,
> "can you read all of these letters to me?" The children that can't do it,
> that's how you know. You know that they are at a different level than
> the other ones. And then, pushing the kids that already know them to
> another level and seeing where they're at. There has to be some kind
> of measure that you are using with all of them in order to know which
> ones are not at the level and which ones are. So in this case, it was this
> packet that they gave us for K–5 assessment [that I used]. (Interview
> transcript, pp. 7–8)

In the case of Vanessa, she relied primarily on drawing comparisons
between the performance of the low-achieving student and nonspecified,
generalized grade-level expectations. She suggested the following as key
indicators of low academic achievement: "a lot of absentees from school,
not shy but keeping away from the crowd," as well as "being really quiet,
not participating in the classroom—not making themselves part of the
classroom" (Interview transcript, p. 9). Samantha made comparisons between the performance of students she believed were low achieving and
the performance of their peers, as well as the low-achieving student's performance in relation to other nonspecified grade-level expectations. She
was the only candidate who acknowledged—albeit ambivalently—that
she used the labels placed on students in schools. Samantha argued:

> For better or worse, I think one thing, I mean the labels that stu-
> dents are given is one way that's just sort of handed to you, saying
> that this student has difficulty in this area. But I think it's important

not to take that verbatim and just say, alright so I think that this student can't do this, but to kind of look, okay well this is something they struggle with, to what degree do they struggle with it? Just watching the students and seeing; just watching for behavioral things, watching their peers start things before they get started, or if they are sitting there not doing anything. And looking at the assessments that are in place to see what kinds of things, how that student is responding . . . if they are or are not being successful. (Interview transcript, p. 5)

Using Background, Experiential, and Official School Knowledge to Understand Academic Achievement

It was not surprising that three of the preservice teachers pointed to their own experiences as learners as one of their main sources of information about academic achievement. While four of the teachers specifically highlighted their university coursework as having an influence on their understanding in this area, it was not uncommon for the teacher candidates to make a distinction between what they learned in courses and what they experienced in field-based coursework that took place in school settings. What separated these two learning experiences was the difference between what the teacher candidates recognized as "learning about academic achievement"—which relied mainly on reading and discussion— and "observing and dealing with academic achievement"—which relied on meeting and working with actual students who presumably struggled academically in school. For instance, Janice stated:

> [In] my methods classes, it was more of reading articles about the issues and then discussing them and kind of making us aware of it [issues related to academic achievement], but it is actually in the schools where you experience it . . . it's really from my own observations within the schools and working with some of the students that I've come up with these ideas. (Interview transcript, p. 12)

Noah also made a distinction between what he called "theory and practice," with the former characterizing what he believed existed in the university setting and the latter situated in classroom teaching. In making this distinction, Noah was not dismissing what he viewed as the merits of going through the teacher education program. Noah noted that "the elementary education program at the university is very good," and while "[he] could have easily gone some other route for getting a teaching certificate, [he] specifically chose to go through the program with the idea in mind that [he] didn't want to not be prepared for teaching" (Interview transcript, pp. 13–14). One of the strengths of this program for him was that it provided instructors who "have not been professors, but they've actually been graduate students. Individuals who have just recently come from a classroom environment" (pp. 13–14). These graduate students "do a good job of telling you the theory, but then also telling you how the theory is actually played out or can be played out, by giving you personal experiences." This was important because "theory is theory, but practice very rarely goes according to theory" (pp. 13–14). Fundamentally, Noah believed that what he gained during his training were the tools "needed to make modifications as things happen [in the classroom]" (pp. 13–14). The distinction made between theory and practice is well recognized in the literature (Britzman, 2003; Lortie, 2002). It is one of the areas that teacher educators work to bridge for preservice teachers as they move through their program, by seeking to offer authentic, culturally rich and affirming field-based opportunities from which students can effectively learn and grow (Sleeter, 2008).

Recognizing the importance placed on accessing the "practice of teaching" rather than only the "theory of teaching," it made sense that three of the teacher candidates pointed to their overall field-based experiences in schools as informative, with one person specifically pointing to school staff (e.g., teachers, school psychologists, social workers) as helpful in her learning more about student academic achievement. Three teacher candidates noted that their own experiences as a student helped them gain understanding of academic achievement.

Family and Student Characteristics as Key Contributors to Academic Achievement

How, then, did the preservice teachers account for those students who experienced low academic achievement? Most of the preservice teachers identified factors related to family and individual student characteristics to account for academic achievement. In the case of Janice, she pointed to the experiences faced by students outside of school. She stated:

> That's a hard question. I think that a lot of support for academic success comes from home. For any family where parents are working a lot, or they struggle with child care, when they get home they're tired and they just don't have the time—or the energy is more like it—to spend some time, you know, working on that kind of stuff. . . . There is so much we can do during a day, but when they are not there in school, they need extra support too, I feel, at home. (Interview transcript, p. 6)

Janice suggested that achievement was integrally tied to the kind of help offered to students in their homes. What stood out was the care Janice took not to categorically dismiss as bad or uncaring those families who did not offer support to their children. She wanted to recognize the social/structural constraints that some families face, making it difficult to provide the extra assistance needed for academic achievement to occur. Implicit in this statement, though, was the belief that families were sometimes deficient in giving students what they needed and that what happened in the school was never enough to ensure that learning would occur.

Noah's perspectives on academic achievement concurred with the idea that schools—as they currently operated and were structured—did not ensure that all students would achieve academically. This was due to a mismatch between the differing expectations and values of schools and the experiences students had in their families. Noah noted the following with regard to circumstances that led to low achievement:

> Depending on the situation, some students who seem to be on their own quite a bit, in terms of lack of supervision outside of school. Going home to an empty house, things like that . . . [Another] thing that really would come to mind would be experiences outside of school. For younger kids, do they have somebody who reads books to them? Do they have somebody who has taught them letters of the alphabet, sounds of the alphabet, writing their name? Students who have opportunities to go to museums, libraries, things like that. Those are things that can put students at a disadvantage because a lot of those types of activities are drawn upon in the classroom and built upon as far as teaching. So if you have students that come in who have never experienced that, they are potentially at a disadvantage if the teacher doesn't recognize that and take steps to, sort of bridge that gap. (Interview transcript, pp. 8–9)

Noah highlighted conditions that focused on the overall environment and kinds of experiences gained in students' homes. While Janice and Noah both operated from the assumption that certain normative experiences and conditions characterized academically successful students, unlike Janice, Noah did not provide a rationale for why some families did not offer the support needed to achieve. Rather, Noah pointed to the disadvantage certain students faced from their early home experiences and the inability of some teachers to address these deficiencies.

Taking a different perspective, Marisol pointed to factors related to the organization and operation of schools, specifically at the level of the teacher. She did not want to blame teachers, but pointed out that

> it's kind of the teacher's job to find ways to draw the child into education. And they are obviously not drawn in for some reason or another because they are being too social or because they are just not interested or whatever the answer may be, they're not engaged in school. I

think that all children are capable of doing it, it's just finding the right tools to give them or to help them find and they haven't found it yet. (Interview transcript, p. 9)

Yet while Marisol believed the teacher played an important role in the academic achievement process, she went on to point out additional characteristics of low-achieving students:

[They] tend to be the children who don't do their homework. You know, who don't have the support at home, or, you know, even sitting down and reading a book with them, which in kindergarten is their homework. They don't do it and they are the ones who are talkative, outgoing in the classroom: the ones who can't sit still. The ones who are very social with their peers. The troublemakers. It's awful to say but you know it's the truth. They want attention somehow and so they go about it maybe in the wrong way. Yeah it is usually them. Or it's the other extreme and they are the very quiet ones. The ones that don't really say a whole lot and they don't really respond to you when you sit with them one-on-one. You don't really know how to reach that child because there's just really no response and so it's those kids too. But it's usually one or the other, not really the middle kids. (Interview transcript, p. 8)

Similarly, both Samantha and Vanessa cited characteristics specifically related to student behaviors as associated with low academic achievement. In Samantha's case, she was quick to note that she did not think there was a "guaranteed cause and effect (between circumstances associated with students who seemed less likely than their peers to succeed academically and actual low achievement)" (Interview transcript, p. 6). This was because she thought that "some students put in one situation will be just fine, [while] other students won't be able to handle it and respond in a very different way" (p. 6). Vanessa pointed to what she called "lots" of circumstances related to low academic achievement (Interview transcript, p. 7). She said, "It can be that the child is just a little slow and needs more time. It can be that there are a lot of issues going on outside of the school. It can be that the child just doesn't like school so he or she needs to be motivated" (Interview transcript, p. 7).

BRIDGING REMARKS: PRESERVICE TEACHERS, RISK, AND THE CATEGORY AND LABEL OF THE AT-RISK STUDENT

Preservice teachers attended the same teacher education program, they came from different places and had different experiences. While most grew up in the Midwest, some lived in rural/small community environments and others lived in small urban cities or suburban/urban fringe settings, including one who grew up in the southwesternUnited States. Collectively, the preservice teachers also reflected different racial and ethnic backgrounds and attended a variety of different kinds of schools (e.g., bilingual, public, parochial).

All of the preservice teacher candidates wanted to teach in what they personally recognized as a "diverse" school community, with the definition of diverse differing across the candidates (e.g., race, socioeconomic status, geographic location). Each indicated that they either had always wanted to become a teacher or had always considered going into the profession a possibility. These feelings, perhaps not surprisingly, coincided with the fact that three of the preservice teachers had parents who worked as teachers. The passion and excitement they all expressed about their future teaching was tempered by the conditions of teaching that they expected to experience. Several expressed a desire to teach in racially and socioeconomically diverse schools. However, they were unwilling to sacrifice their own beliefs about good teaching in order to do so, or to diminish their chances of getting a job by limiting the kind of schools they considered.

Regarding the overall purpose of schooling, the preservice teachers showed considerable similarity. They all cited preparing students for later life and productive citizenship. The preservice teacher candidates expressed different takes on their teaching philosophy to meet these goals, with some focusing on the pedagogical tools they wanted to use in the classroom (e.g., building community) and others on the outcomes they hoped to accomplish (e.g., get students engaged in learning). In the role of teacher, all of the preservice teachers recognized their responsibility to help students move forward in the learning process. This help included serving as a "facilitator," acting as a "guide," and spending time trying to better "understand" the students.

Knowledge played an important role in how the preservice teachers approached their impending teaching and how they constructed themselves as teachers and made sense of their teaching, students, and the families/communities from which the students came. When discussing achievement and risk, the participants drew from experiential and background knowledge. They also recognized knowledge they had acquired in their teacher education coursework as impactful on their thinking. Both experiential and official (university) knowledge mattered in the lives of the candidates.

Knowledge operated prominently in how the participants understood the construct of risk and the at-risk category and label. This knowledge emerged in how the preservice teachers imagined their work as teachers, even as it was both complex and conflicted. All of the preservice teachers were familiar with the term *at-risk*. However, no one recognized, or was able to provide an accurate definition for, the terms *at-promise* and *resilient,* indicating the continued popularity of the term *at-risk* to categorize and label students. While several preservice teachers acknowledged the politically charged nature of the term *at-risk,* all but one of the teachers felt certain, even when uncomfortable, that some students were indeed at-risk for low academic achievement.

A key finding was that all of the preservice teachers believed it was necessary, and a part of their role and responsibility as teacher, to identify students viewed as more likely than their peers to experience low academic achievement. I call this *engaging in risk discourse.* As pointed out in Chapters 1 and 2, this practice links to a longstanding history in the United States of using risk to make determinations about potential academic risk (Cuban, 1989; Franklin, 1994). Educators as far back as the early 20th century made judgments about student achievement and learning capability. These drew from notions of normality and deviance, and were made to help identify those students who seemed more likely than their peers to experience low academic achievement.

At the same time, most of the preservice teachers also recognized that engaging in risk discourse carried its own risks. A primary risk was misidentifying low-achieving students and engaging in biased, prejudiced thinking about students that closes off, rather than opens, the possibility of teachers providing all their students a quality and equitable learning experience. The participants also felt uncomfortable with placing labels on students. This take on risk discourse indicated that the preservice teachers held a *technico-scientific* orientation of risk (Lupton, 1999a, 1999b) that focused on identifying and remedying risk. Yet they also expressed a *cultural symbolic* orientation (Lupton, 1999a, 1999b) that recognized risk could be seen only in relation to larger social processes that position some people and things as risky. Risk was generally stable as it was not something that shifted over time, but rather was something teachers continually recognized and worked to remedy.

The preservice teachers expressed varied definitions of academic achievement. In some instances, academic achievement was grounded in criteria defined by federal, state, or district policy and by learning standards. For most, it was recognized as an individual and, more important, variable construct, or what I call a *sliding scale view of achievement.* Academic achievement, then, was understood in relation to the amount of academic growth experienced (regardless of the end point) by the individual student or the overall excitement he/she felt toward learning.

Additionally, family and student characteristics were cited as key risk factors for low academic achievement. Students who did not receive exposure to highly valued knowledge and experiences in their families, as well as students who exhibited behaviors contrary to those valued in the classroom, were identified as potentially low achieving. These factors, while overwhelmingly recognized as deficits, sometimes were discussed in relation to their difference and mismatch from the larger expectations held for students by staff. I would argue the preservice teachers drew from *cultural deficit* and *cultural difference* approaches to achievement. In those instances where *structural/institutional* approaches were invoked, it was often in the context of justifying why certain families failed to offer students the support they presumably needed in order to achieve.

Ultimately, risk was recognized as playing a role in how the preservice teachers reflected on their background experiences and perspectives on teaching, as well as their understanding of risk and achievement. Risk operated as both a necessary and a dangerous discourse. For example, when discussing her philosophy of teaching, one participant directly referenced the term *risk* twice. Risk in this context was understood as a necessary, positive quality that students needed to possess in order to fully learn. Risk, then, also was recognized as a necessary ingredient for real learning. The notion of risk and uncertainty as an entry point to personal learning and growth is acknowledged in the literature (Bialostok, 2012; Britzman, 2003; Gershon, 2012).

Yet this was not the only way that-risk emerged in the preservice teachers' experiences as learners and in their perspectives about and hopes for their future teaching. Risk generally was recognized as a possible outcome for the students who would soon come under their care. These risks all involved student outcomes—what they might fail to acquire in their learning. These risks at times were racialized and classed, with the assumption that students who were of color, lived in low-income households, or whose first language was not English were more likely to come to school lacking important knowledge and skills that teachers needed to remedy. In many instances, the factors of race, social class, or culture were not directly acknowledged. Yet they were embedded in the reasons some teachers gave for wanting to teach and were connected to the students they viewed as at-risk for low academic achievement. Some participants recognized these risks in the context of schooling, where certain knowledge, experiences, and ways of being were more highly valued and set the norm for what students were expected to bring to school.

Thus, when talking about and locating risk, the preservice teachers, while drawing from the recognized definition of *at-risk*, recognized as integral to the work of teachers the practice of identifying students who were thought less likely than their peers to achieve academically. This necessity spoke to the preservice teachers' beliefs that doing so would improve their ability to meet their students' needs. Yet this process also was potentially fraught with the possibility of engaging in biased thinking when making these judgments. An unintended outcome was that teachers would hold lowered learning expectations for these students, undermining any effort at offering a more equitable schooling experience for all students. There was a paradoxical danger, then, of students not performing in relation to where state, local, and/or personal criteria suggested they should and of misidentifying, failing to identify, and/or holding low learning expectations for students who might face academic difficulty.

What these findings illuminate is the degree to which risk exists in the concerns about academic achievement expressed by preservice teachers. This risk knowledge is complex and conflicted, both necessary and dangerous. It created tension for the preservice teachers as they negotiated what they believed about students and what they felt was their role and responsibility as teachers. Indeed, they feared that what they thought they might know about students actually might be wrong, ultimately limiting any effectiveness they might have as teachers. This provides insight into the knowledge the teacher candidates held about academic risk and would take with them into their first teaching assignments. With this in mind, in the chapter that follows, I turn attention to the knowledge practicing teachers—with varying years of teaching experience—held about risk and academic achievement.

TOOLS FOR CRITICAL REFLECTION AND PRACTICE

Key Terms to Consider

- Risk discourse
- Ontological dilemma

Questions

1. Why is it important that teachers critically reflect on their role and responsibility in the classroom? How might this shape one's perspectives on academic achievement?

2. Do you think it is necessary for teachers to engage in risk discourse? Why or why not?

3. The preservice teachers in this study felt conflicted in their ability to decide whether risk really existed. How might a person make such a determination in the everyday work of teaching? What criteria should one use to assess whether the judgment is correct?

Extended Activity

Get into small groups of three to four. Each person should share her/his perspectives on academic achievement. Individually reflect on the following questions: What is academic achievement? Why do some students achieve academically, while others do not? What informs your ideas about academic achievement? Share responses across the group. What are the similarities and differences across your responses?

CHAPTER 5

Inservice Teachers

Examining Risk and the Category
and Label of the At-Risk Student

In this chapter I discuss how inservice teachers understood, talked about, and acted on the risk and the category and label of the at-risk student. In doing so, I present the perspectives of four inservice teachers who taught in an upper elementary grade (two 4th grade and two 5th grade) classroom in the same midwestern public school. Here I draw from data collected across two semi-structured interviews (Spradley, 1979) that lasted 60 minutes each. The first addressed issues related to the teacher's background, beliefs on large educational issues (i.e., goal of schooling, role of the teacher), and perspectives on academic achievement and potential academic failure. The second interview focused on academic risk, revisiting issues around academic achievement raised in the first interview, as well as questions focused on academic risk. I begin by describing the setting where the teachers worked—the town of Resputo and, more specifically, Green Mounds Elementary School. I present a brief overview of each inservice teacher, paying particular attention to how they talk about their experiences and perspectives on teaching and schooling in general. This section offers insight into the background of the teachers in the study—highlighting the tensions, ambiguities, challenges, and fears they grapple within their role as pedagogue. The final section outlines how the inservice teachers specifically talked about, located, and remedied risk. This discussion focuses on not only how the teachers understand the risk and the category and label of the at-risk student, but also how these perspectives entwine with and implicate concerns related to academic achievement.

SETTING THE STAGE: LOOKING AT THE TOWN/CITY OF RESPUTO
AND GREEN MOUNDS ELEMENTARY SCHOOL

Town/City of Resputo

Resputo is a small town/city that sits 11 miles southwest of Lakeville. The original inhabitants of Resputo were Native American. According to 2000

small

diverse?
at-risk?

Census data, the city had a population of 7,052, with the median resident age 36.5. Demographically, 97% of the city's residents were White. Three percent were of color with African Americans, Latino/as, and Asians each making up less than one percent of the total population. The median income of Resputo residents was $65,367 and the median value of Resputo homes was $161,500. More than 94.5% of all Resputo residents over the age of 25 completed high school or some higher form of education, 39.8% held a bachelor's degree, and 14.2% attained a graduate or professional degree. Unemployment among Resputo residents was 3.2%.

According to the history of Resputo, the Winnebago tribe ceded their last rights to land in the area that was to become Resputo on August 1, 1829. By 1837, two White, Scottish settlers arrived in the newly annexed township and set up a butchering business. By 1842, 22 additional settlers had moved into the area, finding a new grist mill constructed at the southern edge of the city. Following this, several additional businesses were founded, in addition to a local post office and public house. The first school was thought to have opened in 1845. On April 20, 1850, a meeting was convened to discuss building a new schoolhouse, and within nine days a schoolteacher was hired and the school took form. Nine years later, an additional school was built and another one was built 5 years after that, in 1864. These rural schools averaged a student population between 20 and 30 in grades 1–8.

While Resputo Area Schools remained a fairly homogenous community in terms of race (primarily White) and class (working/middle) during most of the 20th century, by the 1990s the town/city experienced some shifts in demographics. These shifts included an increasing number of students of color—primarily African American and Hmong American—in addition to a growing student population whose families moved into several newly developed wealthy subdivisions in the area. According to two of the teachers (Zoë and Julia) in the study who had worked in the Resputo Area Schools for many years and a video created by the leader of a countywide student diversity program implemented at Resputo High School in the mid-1990s, these changes led to conflicts both among students and between students and faculty.

During my fieldwork, Julia pointed out that during the 1990s, the Resputo Area Schools redrew their district lines so that they would receive property taxes from several large retail stores that recently had opened in a nearby Lakeville community. When doing this, the district was required to service students who lived in the low-income housing and apartment complexes situated near the new retail area in Lakeville. Many of the students were students of color, qualified for free/reduced lunch, and were placed in the same school location. This became a concern because the district did not want all of the students from these communities attending the same school. While it was never explicitly explained to me why this was deemed a problem, on the basis of my conversations during fieldwork, I surmised that it may have been connected to funding concerns with Title I (i.e., a desire to spread money around to multiple school sites rather than concentrate it in one location) or with the perception that if all the students attended the same school, faculty at that school would face a challenge in trying to meet the needs of students who were perceived as academically deficient and needy. According to Julia, efforts were made to distribute these students across more schools. The school where I conducted fieldwork—Green Mounds Elementary—was one of the district schools that in the past 2 years had received this new population of students.

Green Mounds Elementary School

Green Mounds, a K–5 elementary school, opened in 1991. During the time of the study, Green Mounds had a student population of 586. Although the school originally opened in the old Resputo Middle School building, which had been converted to an elementary school, Green Mounds Elementary moved into a new building in 2000, where the study was conducted.

I found my way to Green Mounds in a serendipitous way that enabled me to recruit teachers using a modified snowball sampling technique (Cohen, Manion, & Morrison, 2000). Given the changing racial and socioeconomic makeup of students in the Resputo Area Schools, I was pointed to the district by an African American parent I met at a city-wide Black History luncheon. The parent was excited about my research on risk and suggested that I contact the superintendent of the Resputo Area Schools. This meeting led to a visit to Green Mounds Elementary, where I met with the principal who sought out teachers who might be interested in participating.

Green Mounds Elementary School was organized into four classroom clusters, or pods, designed to promote student interaction and sharing among teachers. Pods had a variety of movable walls, various large- and small-group instruction areas, as well as a technology center. Teachers in each pod also had direct involvement in budget development, hiring, planning, and governance for the entire school. While Green Mounds did not fall under the category of "Title I school" during the 2003–2004 school year, 20.5% of its student population qualified for free/reduced price lunch. As a result, Green Mounds received Title I funding and was considered a "targeted assistance school"—or Title I TAS. This meant that the school used its Title I money to fund programs directed specifically to targeted students, including those who qualified for free/reduced lunch and those who had low performance on statewide tests.

In the 2003–2004 school year, the annual report for the school highlighted that (NCLB) "encouraged schools to take a more in-depth look at their assessment data to determine if all students are making adequate gains." The report went on to say that while the overall scores for students on the State Knowledge and Concepts Examination had "increased every year for the past 3 years in reading, math and social studies (as well as science in the last year) . . . we still have an achievement gap when we examine how various subgroups of students perform compared to other groups." The subgroups that the report alluded to, but did not mention or provide the actual data for, fell into the following categories: gender, race/ethnicity, disability, economic status, English proficiency, and migrant status.

To get a clearer sense of the subgroups the report referred to as experiencing an achievement gap, I looked up the 4th-grade test data for Green Mounds Elementary for 2004, housed on its state department of instruction website.[1] For the purposes of this study, I looked at the disaggregated data for Green Mounds Elementary 4th-graders on the basis of economic status, English proficiency, and race/ethnicity—subcategories often talked about in relation to Title I status. I focused on the 4th-grade student results because they were the only group that was tested in 2004 that was relevant to this study.

When I looked at the breakdown in scores for those students who qualified for free/reduced lunch (i.e., economic status) and their peers who did not, I found there was a difference in (1) the percentage of students who received an advanced and/or proficient score (from here on referred to as a combined advanced or proficient level/score) and (2) the percentage of students who received an advanced score. For example, while 71.4% of the students who qualified for free/reduced lunch ($n = 13$) performed at the combined advanced + proficient level on the state reading test, 90.5% of students who did not qualify for free/reduced lunch ($n = 85$) scored in the same category. Among students who received an advanced score, only 23.8% of students who qualified for free/reduced lunch accomplished this task, as opposed to 58.1% of their nonqualifying peers. The results from the language arts, mathematics, science, and social studies portions of the state test revealed a similar pattern of gaps between students who qualified for free/reduced lunch and their peers who did not, with the better performances occurring across the board for those students who did not qualify for free/reduced lunch. Table 5.1 provides a detailed breakdown of the 4th-grade test result data for each of the above content areas according to economic status.

When I looked at the data on English proficiency, some interesting findings emerged between the performance of students designated as English language learners (ELL) ($n = 6$) and those who were not ($n=89$). While in some content areas (language arts, mathematics) lower percentages of

ELL versus non-ELL achieved at either the combined advanced + proficient level or the advanced level, this was exactly opposite the case in other content areas (reading, science, social studies), where higher percentages of ELL performed at the combined advanced/proficient level than did their non-ELL peers. Table 5.2 outlines the data for how 4th-grade ELL performed in relation to their non-ELL peers.

Table 5.1. Comparison of Green Mounds Elementary School 4th-Grade Test Result Data According to Socioeconomic Status

Subject	Advanced + Proficient	Advanced
Reading	(F/R) 71.4% vs. (NON) 90.5%	(F/R) 23.8% vs. (NON) 58.1%
Language arts	(F/R) 76.2% vs. (NON) 93.2%	(F/R) 23.8% vs. (NON) 52.7%
Mathematics	(F/R) 72.6% vs. (NON) 94.6%	(F/R) 28.6% vs. (NON) 55.4%
Science	(F/R) 76.2% vs. (NON) 89.2%	(F/R) 9.5% vs. (NON) 43.2%
Social studies	(F/R) 81% vs. (NON) 95.9%	(F/R) 42.9% vs. (NON) 81.1%

F/R – Students who qualified for free/reduced lunch (n = 13); NON – Students who did not qualify for free/reduced lunch (n = 85)

% more extreme lower # (handwritten annotation)

Deceptive (handwritten annotation, left margin)

Table 5.2. Comparison of Green Mounds School 4th-Grade Test Result Data According to Language Proficiency

Subject	Advanced + Proficient	Advanced
Reading	(ELL) 100% vs. (NON) 85.4%	(ELL) 16.7% vs. (NON) 52.8%
Language arts	(ELL) 66.7% vs. (NON) 91%	(ELL) 33.3% vs. (NON) 47.2%
Mathematics	(ELL) 83.3% vs. (NON) 91%	(ELL) 33.3% vs. (NON) 50.6%
Science	(ELL) 100% vs. (NON) 85.4%	(ELL) 16.7% vs. (NON) 37.1%
Social studies	(ELL) 100% vs. (NON) 92.1%	(ELL) 66.7% vs. (NON) 73%

ELL – English language learners (n = 6); NON – Non–English language learners (n = 89)

For instance, 100% of the ELL performed in the combined advanced + proficient level in reading, while only 85.4% of their counterparts scored in this range. Yet, only 16.7% of the ELL actually received an advanced score in reading, as opposed to 52.8% of non-ELL 4th-graders. A similar finding occurred with regard to performance on the science exam, where 100% of the ELL scored in the combined advanced and proficient category, with only 85.4% of the non-ELL falling in this group. Ironically, though, only 16.7% of the ELL received an advanced score on the science exam and 37.1% of the non-ELL performed at this high level. There was less of a gap in the performance between these two subgroups when I looked at the results of the social studies exam. There 100% of the ELL received a score situated in the combined advanced and proficient category, and 92.1% of their non-ELL counterparts fell in this category. Finally, in the areas of mathematics and language arts, 83.3% and 66.7% of the ELL, respectively, received a score in the combined advanced and proficient category. Their non-ELL peers scored in the same category at 91% in both language arts and mathematics, 91% and 91%, respectively. With regard to the percentage of ELL and non-ELL students who performed at the advanced level in language arts and mathematics, 33.3% of the ELL performed at the highest level in both of these content areas, while 47.2% of their non-ELL counterparts received an advanced score in language arts and 50.6% of these same students scored in the advanced level in mathematics.

Gaps in achievement on statewide exams also were noted when parsing the data out according to race/ethnicity. During the 2003–2004 school year, White and Black were the only race subgroups for which test data were disaggregated and reported at Green Mounds. This was due to the small number of student populations outside of these groups that were tested during that year (i.e., American Indian/Alaskan Native [$n = 2$]; Asian/Pacific Islander [$n = 4$]; Hispanic [$n = 1$]). However, in terms of differences in results on the basis of race, fairly large gaps were reported. Table 5.3 provides a breakdown of the 4th-grade test result data for each of the tested content areas according to race/ethnicity.

With regard to reading, 57.1% of Black students tested ($n = 7$) performed at the combined advanced or proficient level, while 88.9% of all White students tested ($n = 81$) performed at the same level. Further, although only 14.3% of all Black students tested at the advanced level, 56.8% of their White counterparts received an advanced score. Interestingly, while higher percentages of Black students performed at the combined advanced and proficient levels in language arts, mathematics, and social studies (71.4%, 85.7, 71.4%, respectively), there remained a gap between the Black students' performance and that of their White counterparts (91.4%, 92.6%, 95.1%, respectively). By far, however, Black students experienced the greatest gap in achievement and lowest scores at the

Table 5.3. Comparison of Green Mounds Elementary School 4th-Grade Test Result Data According to Race/Ethnicity

Subject	Advanced + Proficient	Advanced
Reading	(B) 57.1% vs. 88.9% (W)	(B) 14.3% vs. 56.8% (W)
Language arts	(B) 71.4% vs. 91.4% (W)	(B) 14.3% vs. 50.6% (W)
Mathematics	(B) 85.7% vs. 92.6% (W)	(B) 28.6% vs. 53.1% (W)
Science	(B) 42.9% vs. 90.1 % (W)	(B) 0% vs. 40.7% (W)
Social studies	(B) 71.4% vs. 95.1% (W)	(B) 28.6% vs. 76.5% (W)

B – Black students (n = 7); W – White students (n = 81)

combined advanced and proficient level in the science content area. Here, only 42.9% of Black students, versus 90.1% of White students, scored in the two highest levels of the statewide exam. As the table indicates, not one of the Black students received an advanced score.

In most cases, there was a large difference between the number of students who fell in a particular subgroup and those that did not fall in that subgroup across each of the categories discussed previously. What stands out is that students who qualified for free/reduced lunch and those who were Black performed at levels lower than their counterparts in each subgroup. I take caution in making this point because given the small and disparate sample sizes reflected in the data, coupled with the fact that I did not conduct any statistical procedures on these data, I cannot draw causal links or relationships between these achievement data. Rather, what I wish to convey is that differences existed in how 4th-grade student subgroups achieved during the 2003–2004 school year at Green Mounds. By admission of the stakeholders in the school and the district), these numbers stood as a stark reminder that teachers and staff were not meeting the academic and intellectual needs of all their students. This issue was not unique to Green Mounds. It was an issue that plagued schools across the United States.

Yet, in spite of these gaps in scores between targeted subgroups in the school, Green Mounds Elementary met adequate yearly progress (AYP) and was deemed satisfactory by its state department of instruction during the 2003–2004 school year.

WHO ARE THE INSERVICE TEACHERS?

To set the context for examining how the inservice teachers understood risk and the category and label of the at-risk student, I provide an overview of the teachers. The discussion that follows considers the factors that informed the teachers' entry into and outlook on teaching. My presentation of these data is designed to humanize the teachers by placing each one's perspectives and experiences in conversation with their practices. I also seek to avoid any essentialist read of the teachers because of their similar racial background—all of them were White—and choice to work in a suburban school. The teachers diverged in their positionalities, experiences, and approaches to teaching, even as they often converged in their knowledge around risk, the at-risk category and label, and their role in addressing these issues. Table 5.4 provides an overview of the background characteristics, teaching experiences, and purposes of schooling expressed by the inservice teachers in this study.

Dylan

Dylan is a White male who came from the Pacific Northwest region of the United States. Dylan taught 4th grade and was the only inservice teacher in the study who was not from the Midwest. Dylan received a BA degree in English and later, not finding work in the field of English, went back to school to complete a traditional master's degree program in education. While this was his first year at Green Mounds Elementary School, he was in his seventh year of teaching. Prior to coming to Green Mounds, Dylan worked as a 6th-grade computer teacher and technology integrator in a school district about 45 miles from Resputo. He did not like this job and missed working in the classroom. He decided to look for teaching positions in the Lakeville area and ended up in the Resputo Area Schools.

While Dylan wanted to become a teacher because he enjoyed working with children, he also suggested that his younger brother—who he said had "significant learning disabilities, cognition disabilities"—helped him become "attuned to the needs of students with learning needs that are particular to them" (Interview transcript, p. 1). He also admitted that he remains "a little bit of a kid at heart," as he said it was not uncommon for him to "go out and kick the ball with them [his students] at recess, when I am not too busy" (p. 1).

Dylan described his current class as "a good-natured group" who "get along well" (Interview transcript, p. 1). He was sensitive to identifying students who were leaders in the class, particularly if these individuals were negative in some way. He did not have a negative leader this year, but did feel that the class was academically low. He was referring to the fact that several students "are reading below their grade level" (Interview transcript, p. 2) and his ESL students—whose first languages range from Spanish to Russian—are far behind in their language skills. He also offered that his current class, while academically functioning at a lower level than the 4th-graders he taught in the Pacific Northwest, was "a lot more affluent than [the classes] I've taught before" (p. 2).

Table 5.4. Background Characteristics of and Beliefs Held About Schooling, Teaching, and Future Job Placement Among the Inservice Teachers

Teacher	Race, Gender, and Place of Origin	Teacher Education Program, Current Grade Teaching, and Total Years Teaching	Reason for Entering the Teaching Profession	Teaching Philosophy	Role and Responsibility of the Teacher	Beliefs About the Purpose of Schooling
Dylan	White male Pacific Northwest region of the United States	Traditional graduate-level teacher education program 4th grade 7 years	Enjoyed working with kids; inspired by younger brother who has significant learning disabilities	Passionate teacher; maintain a relaxed, loose classroom atmosphere that is focused on the student (student centered)	Serve as a role model for the students by showing how much she/he loves learning	Prepare students for what they will encounter after high school (e.g., 4-year university, apprenticeship, trade school)
Zoë	White female Midwestern region of the U.S. (right outside of Lakeville)	Traditional undergraduate teacher education program 4th grade 19 years	Inspired by two grandmothers, one of whom was a special education teacher and the other an informal teacher	Always provide students with what they need; find ways that will address the multiple needs of students and how they learn	Serve as a role model for the students by showing how much she/he loves learning; help students become independent learners	Help students find a love of learning
Isabelle	White female Midwestern region of the U.S.	Traditional undergraduate teacher education program 5th grade 1 year	Wanted to help out children from a positive side; both parents were teachers; always engulfed in the education system	Proactive; setting learning expectations early in the year; creating a relationship with the students	Provide students with opportunities to make choices and decisions about their own learning	Educate students to become participating adults in society (e.g., possess an all-around knowledge of the world to become independent and responsible)
Julia	White female Midwestern region of the U.S.	Traditional undergraduate teacher education program 5th grade 13 years	Wanted to since she was a little girl; played school with her best friend, whose mother was a teacher	Capture creativity and create a learning environment where students can be happy, healthy, and safe	n/a	Help students learn and discover how to become a lifelong learner

The reason Dylan's class was academically lower than previous class-es he taught may be attributable to the fact that Green Mounds orga-nizes classrooms in cluster groups. Dylan's class contained the cluster of students who had reading difficulties and those who qualified for ESL services. None of these students had identified special needs, as another 4th-grade teacher had the students in the special education cluster. Clus-tering, according to Dylan, was designed to provide additional support. In his case, a reading specialist was in his class during every reading period. He planned with her, appreciated her support, and felt that they worked well as a team (Interview transcript, p. 3).

Although Dylan described his approach to teaching as passionate, he viewed himself as "easy-going." "I like to have as loose, as relaxed a class as possible while maintaining some discipline" (Interview transcript, p. 3). It was not surprising that Dylan wanted his students to "feel comfortable" and that he "believe[d] strongly that the atmosphere needs to be safe, both emotionally and physically" (p. 3). He said:

> A lot of my management is based on mutual respect and a rapport that I build with the class and with the individual students. You know, that's why a couple of words to a student will go, for me . . . further than a big consequence because they care about what I think. And so in terms of my philosophy I am student centered . . . and I try to indi-vidualize my instruction. (Interview transcript, p. 3)

Dylan offered an example of how he understood "individualized in-struction," pointing out that "when you get 20-some kids, you know the levels for different subjects are going to be pretty varied" (Interview tran-script, p. 3). To address this variety, Dylan suggested that he must provide instruction and unit activities that allowed students at lower and high-er levels the ability to meet the requirements of the assignment, as well as room for higher level students to go beyond, exhibiting their unique self-expression.

Dylan felt the role of formal schooling was to prepare students for "what's to come, whether that be trade school or 4-year university or an apprenticeship" (Interview transcript, p. 3). This entailed more than "book knowledge," as it required "an interest in finding out more, that in-nate curiosity" (Interview transcript, p. 4). Teachers played an important role in helping students develop this, as Dylan pointed out that it was "the role of the teacher to model [innate curiosity of the world]. To be curious, to enjoy learning in and of itself. And to show the students the intrinsic value of learning, of doing your best. Rather than for rewards [like] good-ies and candies and stuff" (p. 4). He found that people often would say that elementary-grade students generally are focused on wants. He refused to dole out candy and other treats as incentives for student learning, as it was part of the "teacher's role to make kids want to do their best for the sake of doing their best" (p. 4).

When I asked Dylan whether he thought schools generally did a good job of helping students meet this goal, he said he was biased because he believed "elementary school teachers do a better job of that [than others]" (Interview transcript, p. 4). He offered that upper elementary grades increasingly were becoming a battleground for content and skills coverage, yet his experience teaching in middle school suggested that teachers in those grades "get mired in having to try and cover a lot of material" (Interview transcript, p. 5). He did not believe that simply covering material would help students develop a love of learning. He felt that standards push teachers to cover more and more material, without providing the space to really delve deeply into a topic of interest. He stated:

> What really shows a love of learning is when you study something in depth and get to know it well. And you know you really do some of that higher order thinking about your topic, about your subject. When you're in a race to cover everything, you are going to skip it, you're gonna just settle for knowledge, without going for any of the upper levels. So I think that kind of gets in the way. (Interview transcript, p. 5)

Zoë

Zoë is a White female who was born and raised in a small town that sits on the eastern outskirts of Lakeville. Zoë was the most veteran teacher in the study, having taught for 19 years. She taught 4th grade and often taught with a partner. She taught for 9 years in the Resputo Area School system (8 years as a permanent teacher and 1 year as a building substitute teacher). She taught for 10 years in a school district in the northeastern region of the United States, during which time she received a master's degree in general education plus an additional 30 credits. Zoë completed a traditional teacher certification program at one of the Midwest University system campuses housed about 180 miles northwest of Lakeville. Her certification was for grades 1–8 and she holds a minor in child psychology.

Zoë wanted to become a teacher because of the influence of her grandmothers. While her paternal grandmother was a special education teacher for over 40 years, her maternal grandmother

> never had a formal education but was a teacher . . . [who showed me] how to bake and cook and sew and knit. And she had this patience

about her and this helping kindness and love of humanity. She also influenced me that I wanted to be in a helping profession. (Interview transcript, p. 2)

Zoë loved reading and always loved school. She went to a parochial school that was very strict, but encountered "some wonderful, influential teachers" there who made her say, "I wanna do this" (Interview transcript, p. 2). Zoë believed by teaching she could "truly make a difference," yet she realized that her initial naïve belief that teaching was an apolitical field did not prepare her for finding out that "it's probably the most political profession out there" (Interview transcript, p. 2).

Zoë described her current class as "kind, loving children" (Interview transcript, p. 3). She quickly added, however:

Here's the but . . . I find that they have so many other things in their life that are inhibiting their learning. Poor family structure, not that I'm the one to judge their family structure, but things that are preventing them at times to be the best person they can be. They have low concept of self, they have low self-esteem. They don't trust their feelings first; they need reassurance constantly and I would say about 75% of the kids in my class right now are like that. They need, just this constant, "you can do it, you can do it, you can do it." And they don't believe in the talents that they have. And trying to help them believe that has been very difficult this year for me. Without stifling them and making them not want to be here at school. I don't want to say the word dysfunctional, but at times, just a whole bunch of kids that have a whole lot of needs. I don't feel that I'm meeting all their needs effectively. I'm trying everyday to bring in new stuff and new ideas. I don't know if it's the mix. I've never had a group of kids like this before. (Interview transcript, p. 3)

Zoë's assumption that the students in her current class suffered from a crippling form of insecurity and low self-esteem that impeded their achievement was echoed throughout my interactions with her. She also believed this distinguished her current class from classes she had taught before.

Zoë described her teaching philosophy as focused on "what kids need" according to the "objectives, the standards, and what the district has hired me to teach" (Interview transcript, p. 5). Zoë expressed some disagreement with what she was expected to teach, stating that some of it was "unnecessary . . . a waste of time." However, she also acknowledged that it was her job to do so because she "signed a contract and I have to be moral and ethical and follow what the standards state" (Interview transcript, p. 5). To offset some of these difficulties, Zoë offered that she "need[ed] to find ways that will address the needs of the kids and how they learn" (Interview transcript, p. 5). This desire was related to the fact that Zoë generally had classes where students ranged in their learning styles and needs. She worried that when students required diverse approaches to teaching and learning, she might fail to provide them exactly what they needed. She said:

> Am I doing the best for them [those students who have special needs]? I don't have all the training in special education and we're finding that with inclusion there's a lot of children with special education needs within our classroom. And that's something I need to work on because they are going to be there and they're a great addition to the class, but I question myself. Should I be making more modifications for them? Should I expect that they are going to do this? Or are my expectations too high? (Interview transcript, p. 6)

Similar to concerns raised by the preservice teachers interviewed in this study, Zoë, a 19 year veteran teacher, also found herself in an *ontological dilemma* around the existence of and resolution for learning difficulties.[2]

Like Dylan, Zoë believed that the purpose of formal schooling was to help students "find a love of learning" (Interview transcript, p. 6). This meant students "are independent enough to realize that—gosh, I'm a good person. I know how to make good decisions and I'm responsible and know how to build relationships" (Interview transcripts, p. 6). This was "not so much about knowing your math facts and knowing the 50 capitals and states," but rather finding fun in learning, or "wanting, being curious" (Interview transcript, p. 6). Zoë also pointed out that too many students, including her own son, had no idea why they were in school. It was important, for her, to realize that education necessarily meant something different for different students. This difference, according to Zoë, made it difficult to clearly define what the end goal of education is. Zoë stated:

> I don't know what [it means] to get an education because what I need for education is going to be different from what Johnny needs and someone else. And I think we put too much emphasis on higher education in the United States. We need to go back to there are some kids that will never go to college. And that's okay. They might learn how to do something else, but I think people need to find the meaning for them, what learning is for them. And I think it's stifled too much in formal education because we tell them what we think they should be learning. What we know is right, but until they internalize what

learning is, they're not gonna learn it, they're not going to have that love for it. (Interview transcript, p. 6)

To reach the goal of helping students to love learning, Zoë, like Dylan, believed that "the role of the teacher was, number one, to be that role model, to show how much he or she loves learning and to be authentic to them [the students]" (Interview transcript, p. 7). Here, the teacher's role was to serve as a guide, a mentor, or a coach.

Zoë did not believe schools generally did a good job of helping students meet the goal of becoming lovers of learning. She blamed "part of it [on] the standards" and "part of it [on] competition between other teachers"—particularly the common practice of teachers telling their colleagues, "I did this unit and I got it all done, and so and so did this" (Interview transcript, p. 7). Zoë also thought that parents impacted students' abilities to become lovers of learning because "parents are so into their kids learning what they [the parents] learned in school" (p. 7). Overall, Zoë assumed that society held certain assumptions about school that failed to acknowledge schools as or hold them accountable for being places where students have fun:

> We [society] look at school as a place that sometimes, it's not supposed to be fun. We are supposed to follow rules, we're supposed to do all that. But I think schools need to be more inviting. They need to be more exciting for kids. So they want to be here. They want to take an active part . . . I don't know how to change that 'cause I think there's a lot of people that go into teaching that should not be teachers because I don't think they love learning themselves. [They] think it's just a job. And this is not just a job. This is a life-changing business. We can make or break a child in what we do or say to them . . . you need to have passion in this job and if you don't—find another job. (Interview transcript, p. 7)

Isabelle

Isabelle is a White female who was completing her first full year of permanent teaching. Isabelle worked as a substitute teacher for 1 year in the Resputo Area Schools prior to receiving a permanent position at Green Mounds as a 5th-grade teacher. Both her parents were teachers. Her mom was a kindergarten teacher and her dad was a middle school math teacher. She always felt engulfed in the education system: "both the political side and the classroom side" (Interview transcript, p. 1). Interestingly, she was voted "Most Likely to Become a Teacher" during her senior year in high school, and that, she said, "kind of made me not want to do it, just because everybody thought I was going to." However, upon arriving at her university, one of the campuses in the Midwest University system, about 140 miles slightly northwest of Lakeville, she majored in child psychology. She "just kind of [got] overwhelmed with that and wanted a more positive side to help out children" (Interview transcript, p. 1). This led her to enroll in a traditional teacher education program. She loved the change to education, viewing this work as "very much my calling" (Interview transcript, p. 1). In the months following the conclusion of my fieldwork at Resputo, Isabelle would begin a master's program through the university where she completed her teacher certification. It is an ME (master educator) program where she will meet only one weekend a month for 2 years at alternate high schools sites in Lakeville. She described the program as a "comprehensive learning group where you are incorporating community . . . your action plan is actually something that combines the community with the school" (p. 1). She hoped to eventually get a districtwide professional development position.

Isabelle described her current class as "very diverse" (Interview transcript, p. 1). By this, she was referring to "their needs, their attitudes, and their backgrounds" (p. 1). She noted that the students come from

> a wide range of economic [backgrounds] from very low income, to average, to high. I have a special education group that gets services. I also have some low learners and very high learners. Racially diverse, not so much. I do have a few African American students and Asian students, but majority White students. (Interview transcript, p. 2)

Isabelle admitted that because she worked as a substitute teacher and a summer school teacher at her current school, she knew her class pretty well and was aware of some of the diversity before she was hired as a permanent teacher. However, she learned more about the economic diversity, and some of the learning-level diversity, along the way in her teaching. The diversity of her current class was similar to the students she taught during her student teaching. One difference, however, was that she was much more involved in getting to know the families and backgrounds of her students than she was during her internship and as a student teacher. She said, "Now I am fully immersed. So knowing everything and just communicating, I think that's a big key" (Interview transcript, p. 2).

Isabelle described her approach to teaching as "proactive," by which she meant "starting off the school year in an upbeat way but also setting the standards and setting where we want to go" (Interview transcript, p. 2). For her, this meant "letting the children know what I expect from them. Also telling them what I'm going to give them and if they have any other expectations for me, just letting them know it's a team relationship that we have" (p. 2). Isabelle pointed out that when she saw students getting restless, "I know it's time to change" (p. 2). One of the things that she really liked about teaching 5th grade was that "they really start understanding" how to recognize when "I'm not having the greatest day" (Interview transcript, p. 2). This was important to Isabelle because "this is a relationship that we're going through" (p. 2).

When I asked Isabelle what she believed was the purpose of formal education, she said, "to educate children throughout their years to become participating adults in society" (Interview transcript, p. 3). This meant that students should "have an all-around knowledge of the world and . . . be able to get out on their own, be independent, be responsible" (p. 3). Isabelle drew a parallel between her beliefs about formal education and her classroom philosophy, and the Green Mounds Elementary School philosophy, stating:

> the key things our school philosophy and our classroom philosophy deals with is independence, you know, you need to be an independent learner. Think for yourself. You need to be responsible—can you get your homework in? (Interview transcript, p. 3)

Isabelle believed the teacher had a role and responsibility to provide students with more choices and decision-making opportunities to facilitate the growth of independence. This meant that students learned how not only to do their own work independently, but also to gauge whether this work was indeed their best work. She did not say whether she believed schools in general did a good job of meeting this goal of facilitating independent learners. She felt, however, that Green Mounds was doing a better job of helping students reach this goal by placing it at the forefront of its teaching and learning agenda for 5th-graders.

Julia

Julia is a White female who taught 5th grade. Julia had been teaching for 13 years, 11 in the Resputo Area Schools, one in a 5th-grade classroom in a neighboring midwestern state, and one in a progressive charter school about 90 miles south of Resputo. She took pride in the fact that she had taught students between the ages of 7 and 12. Although Julia attended a traditional teacher certification program at a liberal arts college in the Midwest, she decided to go back to school to get her master's degree simultaneously with her first full year of teaching. Julia always wanted to become a teacher because "it's just part of who I am since I was a little person" (Interview transcript, p. 2). She said:

I always loved playing school. I'm going to give you the typical response of all teachers. I played school with my best friend everyday. Her mother was a teacher; my parents were not. But we had all of the teacher supplies in her basement. We had a chalkboard and we literally skilled and drilled ourselves everyday when we would come home from school. We loved school! It was just like part of who I was. So it wasn't like I was choosing to be, I think I was already a teacher when I was little. (Interview transcript, p. 2)

When describing her current class, she noted, "It is an unusual one" (Interview transcript, p. 2). This perspective made sense when she offered, "Last year my class was *fan-tastic*!" (Interview transcript, p. 2). For her "to go from a high year to a low year is very difficult" (p. 2). She attributed this change to many things. She said:

I took into consideration a lot of different factors of where these kids were coming from. Last year I had a class where almost all of my kids came from two-parent families and they had homes and parents that supported education. This year, I have out of 23 students, probably about 18 that are from divorced families or from where they may not even know one of their parents. But I also have homeless students this year, students with learning disabilities. And some that are on medication for their behavior. So I have quite a vast degree of emotional needs, I guess I would call that. But then on top of that I have, I think it's more like average ability. I don't have a lot of leaders this year that will step up. There are a lot of great kids and they're bright but they stay in this zone where they don't speak up, they don't raise their hands, they don't lead by example. They just are quiet and kind of stick to themselves. So that is what I'm dealing with this year, trying to help those kids come out of that shell and become leaders. (Interview transcript, p. 2)

Julia's concern that her students face problems external to school that lead to overall learning problems in the classroom was a recurring theme across my interactions with her. She viewed her role as a 5th-grade teacher as pivotal in helping students transition from acting like elementary school–aged students to students who have the independence necessary to succeed in middle school. One of the most important prerequisites for this to occur was that the students had a safe, supportive classroom environment. When asked about her approach to teaching, Julia immediately talked about creativity and the mood she tried to capture in the room. She noted:

As you can probably see, I try and capture creativity and so I try to make my room very homey and warm. That's why I have the little shelves and the lamps that kind of become their [the students'] own. And I bring my own artwork in the classroom and make it so it's cheerful. (Interview transcript, p. 3)

She thought this approach to teaching worked because "a lot of kids come in at the beginning of the year and say, 'I wanted to be in this room because I just love the colors and it's so bright and everything'" (Interview transcript, p. 3). Julia believed that these students, once getting settled in the room, "know that not only is it going to be happy, healthy, and safe in here but [that they] are going to be appreciated for who [they] are" (p. 3). In addition, she said that these students also know that they are going to be loved and "are going to experience the joy of learning," which, incidentally, Julia pointed out to me, is "close to our school mission statement" (Interview transcript, p. 3).

Julia told me that the purpose of formal schooling was to "help them [students] learn and to discover how to learn for themselves so that it becomes a lifelong skill for them. So that they're never stopping the learning process, they just continue it" (p. 3). The teacher's role in helping to meet this goal was similar to what her colleagues told me: a role model of a learner. Schools had a responsibility to help create children who one day would become a "contributing person to society and to the world in a positive way" (Interview transcript, p. 3). Julia did not believe that schools did as good a job meeting these goals in the present as they did in the past when she was in school. She based this on knowledge she garnered about her own students: where they ended up and what they accomplished (or failed to accomplish) after they left her class.

TALKING ABOUT RISK IN THE INSERVICE TEACHER SITE

Similar to the preservice teachers, the inservice teacher participants had much to say about risk and the category and label at-risk. Our discussion around these ideas highlighted four key themes that emerged across the findings: (1) engaging in risk discourse; (2) acknowledging *at-risk* as a familiar label for students; (3) recognizing the at-risk student as a real and viable category of person; and (4) risk related to family and student characteristics. Across these findings, risk was reflected in the danger *associated with failing to identify students who might face academic risk.*

Engaging in Risk Discourse

Similar to the preservice teachers, all of the inservice teachers believed it was necessary to engage in risk discourse, or the practice of identifying students who seemed less likely than their peers to experience academic success.

For example, Dylan not only believed it was necessary to identify these students, but also found it nearly impossible for this process not to occur in the classroom. He stated:

> Well . . . they're going to identify themselves . . . you know, certainly there are the kids who are going to try to fall through the cracks and not be noticed and I think it is a teacher's job to not let them fall through the cracks. But if you are keeping your eyes open it's pretty easy to tell who's needy and who's not. So yeah, I think it's important to identify that. (Interview transcript, p. 7)

Dylan was not the only inservice teacher who felt these students inevitably would "show themselves" to the teacher, especially when the teacher was experienced. For instance, Julia felt that experienced teachers not only recognized potentially low-achieving students, but also could anticipate the students that might fall in this category, within a short span of classroom interaction and teacher observation. Julia said:

> Yes, I think it is important to identify them but I pretty much have to be blind not to be able to see it at this point in my career. Because I can just see and I know where I am needed. I can pretty much anticipate a child's needs before it kind of even happens [the student display of behavior that indicates a child may be low achieving] sometimes. I can see a facial expression. Just little things that are—I need help—or whatever it is. So it is not necessarily me taking the time to identify. It's almost like at this, I can observe it myself at this point it's already there. (Interview transcript, p. 5)

Julia pointed out the importance of teachers identifying potentially low-achieving students because "there are some kids that have needs and if you do nothing they might not have the skills to help themselves" (p. 5). She noted that without teacher intervention, these students might just sit there quietly and continue on with their day pretending . . . that they're succeeding but not really learning anything. And that's pretty risky to have that happen for some kids" (p. 5).

Like her colleagues, Zoë also believed that teachers should identify those students who seemed more likely than their peers to experience academic success. She viewed this as a vital part of the teacher's role. This was not only an ethical or moral responsibility, but a professional one as well. Zoë stated:

> Yes, definitely. . . . They [the students] deserve it. They have that right. I mean, I work in a public place. I am paid through public money. It is my job to find a way to get those kids up to speed without making them feel frustrated. (Interview transcript, p. 9)

Zoë's concern that potentially low-achieving students had the right to receive special attention from their teacher was the precursor to her simultaneous belief that in meeting these students' needs, the teacher should not make the learning process more difficult for the students.

Isabelle also noted the importance of identifying students when she stated: "I think it's important just so that I can possibly give them extra help, extra attention" (Interview transcript, p. 45). But unlike her colleagues, Isabelle implied that some potential problems might exist in the risk identification process, particularly when other 5th-grade teachers asked her to identify potentially low-achieving students. This occurred in the context of "classroom switching" where students in Isabelle's classroom went to another 5th-grade teacher's classroom to receive instruction in a particular content area. All of the 5th-grade teachers switched classes, and, according to Isabelle, it was not uncommon for other teachers to ask about those students who were not doing well. She noted:

> When we do switching, they [students] might have another teacher in 5th grade teach them. I don't always necessarily identify my low learners as low learners unless they [the other 5th-grade teacher(s)] request it. If they come up to me a week later and say, "What about this person," then I can talk. But I don't like to necessarily identify them right away. I kind of want to see what they [the other 5th-grade teacher(s)] will come up with. Some teachers don't like that so I'll go with what they want. But I [usually like to handle this situation this way] because [the students who might be identified as low achieving] can achieve differently [in the other teacher's class]. (Interview transcript, p. 5)

What Isabelle illustrated was an underlying assumption that potential problems might exist when engaging in risk discourse, such as biasing the perspective other teachers hold about a given student's ability to achieve. Isabelle recognized that giving her opinion about the students she believed might have trouble in the class could close off other teachers' opportunity to effectively meet the students' needs. Isabelle was the only inservice teacher who expressed this concern. Interestingly, while Isabelle felt it was better to hold off on engaging in risk discourse during the initial meeting with the other 5th-grade teachers, she readily admitted that she would do this if asked. The extent to which Isabelle felt bound to the desires of other teachers, even at the exclusion of her own convictions, may have resulted from her standing as a first-year teacher, the youngest 5th-grade teacher at Green Mounds.

Acknowledging At Risk as a Familiar Label for Students

As with the preservice teachers (see Chapter 4), I asked the inservice teachers whether they were aware of the term *at-risk student* and how they understood its meaning.[3] While three of the four teachers said they heard the term used in school talk and practice, including referrals for special services or in calls for more instructional support, only one teacher said she heard the term used among parents and in university classes.

When discussing what he understood the term *at-risk* to refer to, Dylan offered that two definitions existed. The first was sanctioned and used by the school and district. Dylan asserted:

> You see it [the term *at-risk*] on a list of students who are at-risk for failure in certain areas [subject areas]. The students are identified as at-risk because of low test scores. At risk because of socioeconomic factors. Lots of different ways in which it is used depending on what the person wants to say. A student could be doing fine, but yet still come up on the at-risk list because of socioeconomic factors. (Interview transcript, p. 2)

In this case a student may receive at-risk status because of experiencing an unwanted outcome—for example, low test scores—or because of close proximity to conditions negatively (and often normatively) positioned as bad and risky. The second definition of at-risk that Dylan offered was the one that he used and that had more meaning for him. This perspective was couched in Dylan's belief that some students became at-risk because of their negative attitudes toward learning (e.g., "I find students who are at-risk tend to have more attitude issues than anything else") (Interview transcript, p. 2). Similar to previous statements made by Dylan that a correlation existed between low socioeconomic status and potential risk for low academic achievement, these were also the students likely to develop "a bad attitude" toward learning. For Dylan, the at-risk student was one "who is not able to achieve success. . . . Even after I've made modifications and done all I can [he/she] is still at-risk for failure" (Interview transcript, p. 3).

Julia also focused on internal student characteristics to identify students labeled and categorized as at-risk. She said:

I've heard it used so many different ways. I mean it could be a truancy at-risk student. It could be at-risk for not being a great reader, writer. They [the students] could be at-risk for dropping out later on. We've talked about that, different situations. At-risk for abuse, neglect, at-risk for falling through the cracks in the classroom, or in the grade level or in the school. (Interview transcript, p. 2)

What stood out in Julia's comments was how she carefully differentiated between different types of at-risk students. She implied that-riskiness was variable, playing out in a variety of ways that inevitably spoke to specific characteristics and circumstances that defined and marked these students. Concomitantly, Isabelle felt that at-risk referred to student-level characteristics that might or might not lead to low academic achievement. She said:

Sometimes it [the term *at-risk*] is used in paper referrals. If a student is at-risk . . . it might possibly be that they are in a broken home or that they are homeless. Might be that they do have special needs, possibly behavioral or academic. Those are the major terms that at-risk covers. (Interview transcript, p. 2)

What mattered most in Julia's definition of the term was that the student faced some extenuating factor in his or her life that made it more difficult and potentially problematic.

Recognizing the At-Risk Student as a Real and Viable Category of Person

All of the inservice teachers believed some students were at-risk. For these teachers, the category and label at-risk served as a red flag or warning signal that something might be amiss with a student. Julia noted that "at-risk . . . it's kind of like a red flag for us . . . a way of talking generally about a student that's a concern to us. And the concerns vary, it could be lots of different things" (Interview transcript, p. 2). In common with the preservice teachers, only Zoë among the inservice teachers expressed apprehension around using the term *at-risk* to label and categorize students. She suggested using the term *damaged* instead of *at-risk* because the former term indicated that the student "can . . . be fixed" (Interview transcript, p. 5). Ultimately, she still acknowledged that at-risk meant "that there's something wrong, something is not quite right" (Interview transcript, p. 5). She also pointed out, similar to Julia, that these students might face multiple problems "academically, socially, emotionally, psychologically . . . that truly interfere with their regular schooling day" (Interview transcript, p. 5).

Dylan also alluded to at-risk status as a marker for potential problems that manifested from external conditions, as well as from internal issues that students actually can control. In this regard, he told me that *at-risk*

> means students who have risk factors—you know, socioeconomic, language—on top of have shown weaknesses in particular areas. I find students who are at-risk tend to have more attitude issues than anything else . . . the ones who won't give a rat's ass. Or have a bad attitude and are putting up hindrances to success themselves. So to me, at-risk are kids who are putting up barriers to their own success. Because if a kid comes to me low achieving but working hard, to me, that's a good sign. (Interview transcript, p. 2)

Dylan clearly assumed that certain external factors, coupled with low achievement in some content areas, stood as a marker for at-riskness. He offered that these conditions often led students to sabotage their own learning. It was this attitude that created the "at-risk" student—one who did not respond to the very best that the teacher had to offer. The teacher, not pedagogy or the curriculum, was culpable. Dylan argued:

> What I consider at-risk is a student who is not able to achieve success in the classroom regardless of modifications . . . [and] experiences failure. To me a student who is at-risk for failure is one who, even after I've made modifications and done all I can, is still at-risk for failure. (Interview transcript, p. 3)

Interestingly, when I asked Dylan how he determined when he had done all that he could for a student, he was unable to provide a clear answer.

While Dylan's perspectives on the at-risk student were likely colored by his experiences with a specific student he believed was at-risk in his classroom, this was clearly the case with Isabelle. She identified a couple of the students in her class as at-risk. One was "going through a divorce so that's very hard on her [the student]," and another "who had been achieving all year and is still achieving . . . is moving across the country . . . and she's sick all the time" (Interview transcript, p. 2). Achievement or lack thereof, in this case, aligned with at-risk status. Isabelle acknowledged another student that "really has no guidance at home, [who] pretty much sets his own bedtime, going to bed at midnight and coming to school tired every day" as at-risk (p. 2). She also discussed a student who "has a background where her mother is from Russia, so translating and having the guidance at home where she doesn't really speak Russian [but understands it], it is hard for her to communicate" (p. 2). Finally, she highlighted the last kind of at-risk student: one "who live[s] with grandparents or an aunt or an uncle" (Interview transcript, p. 2). Isabelle did not provide any specific explanation for why she thought these students, across their current, varied situations, were at-risk. Yet her responses implied that certain conditions, regardless of the academic performance of students, led some students to be at-risk.

Risk Related to Family and Student Characteristics

Regarding the factors associated with at-risk students, the inservice teachers highlighted characteristics similar to those offered by the preservice teachers in Chapter 4.[4] In Isabelle's case, she highlighted parent/family characteristics as particularly influential in leading to at-risk status. In making this claim, she took care to justify why these characteristics emerged. Isabelle said:

> Okay. Some of it like just with research and schooling that I've had, they talk about if, with babies having the spoken word, having books read to them at 6 months of age, if you put it too far past that they're losing their vocabulary every day. So in households where there is not a lot of reading aloud or there is not a lot of print material, not a lot of varied language, those students already come to school in kindergarten a step behind. And it could be any household, you know, doctors' who are never home to read to their kids. Or it could also be the low economic families who don't have money for the books and mom is working 9–5. So, I mean it's varied. I don't think it necessarily goes to a specific group of children that would be low achieving. I think that the print material, the vocabulary, reading is pretty much the core of all education. Be it math, be it social studies, so I think that's sort of where you start lagging behind. (Interview transcript, p. 4)

Isabelle recognized the value placed on certain kinds of experience and knowledge that students brought to school. What she did not acknowledge was how this experience and knowledge were not valuable in themselves, but were viewed this way because of their alignment to and sanctioning by Whiteness. In those families where this experience and knowledge were not available, Isabelle felt students were likely to have low achievement.

Zoë, who also cited school, parent/family, and student-level factors, was the only inservice teacher who pointed to teacher-level factors as well. Below she is quoted at length:

> One thing is life experiences. I think some kids are exposed to different things in their lives that others aren't. I think other kids see advancements with some of the kids who have a lot and it doesn't

necessarily mean material things but they have a lot of things that they've done [and] bring [with them] into school. The other kids see that and feel—I'm never gonna be able to compete with that—so they psychologically kind of drop out because of the competitive nature of school. I think, I hate to say this, but I think a lot of educators have certain views of what a child should be like in their classroom and not all children fit that view mainly because of where they [the students] are from, maybe because of their background, of religions, cultural-ly, race. I think there is this inner prejudice at times where teachers don't expect certain populations of children to do well. So they don't because their [the teachers'] expectations aren't there. And I see that more often than it should be. I think a lot of educators blame parents for the ineptness of their students or children. But I don't believe that, I think parents do the best they can. And I think they [educators] have to stop being so judgmental, 'cause there's not a darn thing we can do about changing what the parents do so we need to change it here at school. So we have to stop that. Stop blaming parents as a reason for why their kids aren't successful 'cause we can't do that. We can't change their home life, we can't change their parents, that's what they're born into. As educators we need to stop doing that. I don't feel I do that, but I see it a lot. And it bothers me. (Interview transcript, p. 3)

Zoë acknowledged that a variety of factors, coupled with contextual factors associated with the teaching process and classroom dynamics, framed students who get identified as at-risk. Yet, even while Zoë was highly critical of both school-based factors (e.g., problematic classroom environment) and teachers, she began her comments by acknowledging that some students come to school having failed to receive exposure to highly valued knowledge that impacts their achievement. Zoë did not question the nature of this knowledge, as much as she critiqued the cul-ture of schools that fostered an unhealthy competition between students who came from unequal backgrounds. Additionally, Zoë recognized a White, economically privileged student in her class as at-risk. This was because Zoë assumed that the student should not be having problems due to her privileged position, as she had "every luxury in life. Every life experience possible, but there's something wrong. . . . And her parents won't believe it. They think she has a learning disability. [But] there's something that's causing her to be anxious" (Interview transcript, p. 5). Zoë continued in a related fashion, pointing out that some students are at-risk because of damage they incurred in the context of their families. She noted that families were no longer "normal," highlighting that only five families out of the total number of students in her classroom had a "natural mom and dad at home. The rest are either single [or] step-parents" (Interview transcript, p. 7). Factors that made these seemingly normal middle-class families not normal included divorce, where one parent was lenient and the other one strict, and a parenting style that adhered to a helicopter approach where children were not allowed to experience disappointment or failure (Interview transcript, pp. 6–7).

When I asked Dylan what factors characterized the at-risk student, he pointed to student-level characteristics he believed students could control. He stated, "Attitude, attitude, attitude. Yeah, I've found that the biggest hindrance to success is attitude. And how do you change a kid's attitude?" (Interview transcript, p. 4). Although Julia cited factors that emerged at two different levels (i.e., student characteristics, parent/family), she, similar to Dylan, drew a distinction between factors that she believed students could and could not control. For example, she felt that learning/cognitive disabilities "are the two main" factors and that these two issues "cannot be controlled" (Interview transcript, p. 3). She also noted that "there are some things that can be controlled that are used as excuses by teachers or parents or students as factors for not being successful in school," including homelessness, living in a shelter, and abuse (p. 3). In the case of these factors, Julia believed they were too often used as excuses for low student achievement.

LOCATING AND REMEDYING ACADEMIC RISK IN THE INSERVICE TEACHER SITE

In the section that follows, I discuss how the inservice teachers locate and address risk and the category and label of the at-risk student. I present the data in three sections that individually address the following themes that emerged from the data: (1) sliding scale definition of achievement; (2) judging achievement through informal assessments and unspecified grade-level expectations; and (3) family and student characteristics as key contributors to academic achievement. Across these findings, risk was reflected both in the danger *associated with failing to identify students who might face academic risk* and the danger of *students not performing where state, local, and/or personal criteria suggest they should be.*

Sliding Scale Definition of Achievement

Only one teacher, Julia, pointed out formal standards or goals as integral to the achievement process. Her colleagues conversely looked at and defined academic achievement in terms of individual student potential and performance. In the case of the latter, these teachers held that students achieved when they made progress toward meeting their individual learning potential. Similar to how some policymakers and preservice teachers positioned achievement as having a flexible nature, many of the inservice teachers approached achievement as variable, dependent on the individual student. In Chapter 4 I referred to this as a *sliding scale approach to achievement*. For example, Zoë noted:

> Academic achievement is that I am helping that child reach his or her potential, what I think they're capable of doing. It's going to be different for every student . . . we [schools and society] want all these cookie cutter kids. People aren't like that. We can't mold all these kids to look alike, act alike, have their papers alike. It's not realistic. Schools try to do that. Academic achievement for me is finding where that kid is, where can he or she go and get them there. (First interview, pp. 7–8)

Isabelle supported the idea that achievement was connected to students having their own unique capabilities that teachers identified and helped students to meet. She said:

> Academic achievement, I think is hard in this day and age, just with the many varied abilities. I feel that if anyone is achieving at a level —if they've made some strengths, made some distance in their level learning, that's achievement. It might not necessarily be at the grade-level achievement, but it's still their personal achievement. So I look at it in two ways: personal achievement and then to the grade-level or classroom achievement that we're kind of meeting . . . you have to diversify because they're diverse. (Interview transcript, p. 4)

Here, Isabelle made an interesting point: the idea that teachers must recognize and employ a perspective on academic achievement that takes into account variability because of the diversity found in contemporary classrooms. Isabelle did not elaborate on who or what constituted this new diversity, nor did she seem to know, as pointed out in Chapters 1 and 2, that concerns around the changing diversity of students have proliferated across education discourse since the early 20th century. She did imply that all students, for whatever reasons, cannot and, perhaps more important, should not be expected to achieve at the same levels.

Dylan also espoused the belief that achievement was variable across students and over time. He defined academic achievement as:

> . . . to do your best, almost all of the time. I don't expect for students to do their best with everything because everybody is going to have an off day or an assignment that didn't work out. Things happen but I

would say that academic achievement involves doing your best almost all of the time. (First interview, p. 5)

Like Zoë and Isabelle, Dylan acknowledged that teachers should not expect students to meet, or hold them accountable to, the same standards. This begged the question I asked in Chapter 4: How does a teacher decide what is best for one student and best for another? When I asked Dylan this very question, he stated:

Well, I have standards that the kids must meet. And yeah there's a little bit of give in terms of what will earn a three—which is good for one student. [But] what is a two for one student might be a three for another. But there's not that much give [in the assessment system] that I could give an advanced [score] to a student who is doing basic-level work just because that's their best. So there is a bit of rigidness in the way that we evaluate. (Interview transcript, pp. 5–6)

What Dylan illustrated here, rather than providing an answer to my question of *how* he decided what was the highest level any given student could achieve, was the role (albeit constrained) that teacher judgment played in decisions about achievement. What teachers believed about achievement and how they made sense of and read their own students' performance, or lack thereof, mattered a great deal.

Judging Achievement Through Informal Assessments and Unspecified Grade-Level Expectations

When considering the methods offered, specifically the tools employed to recognize a student as low achieving, the inservice teachers, like the preservice teachers, relied on the use of formal assessments such as tests and classroom performances. Only one teacher, Dylan, specifically mentioned the use of standards. Both Isabelle and Julia discussed using creative or alternative forms of assessment that they each thought corresponded to their students' unique learning preferences. All of the teachers cited their reliance on informal assessments, including talking to students and observing students, which was noted by all of the teachers. In the case of the latter, the teachers felt it was "important to keep an eye" on students (Interview transcript, p. 6) or "observ[ing] and keep[ing] track of notes in [her] head" (p. 4). Other teachers, like Isabelle, stated that they use "face to face" interaction with students to determine who is not doing well. Zoë said that teachers could tell which students needed help, as "it's just in their [the students'] body language" (Interview transcript, p. 9).

All of the inservice teachers cited making assessment decisions based on comparisons they made between a perceived low-achieving student and some general, unspecified grade-level expectation.[5] For instance, Dylan stated that he "put[s] up a red flag when . . . notic[ing] students who are easily distracted, who can't stick with the task, who can't stay on task without frequent reminders" (Interview transcript, p. 8). Zoë similarly pointed to unfocused, distracted students as indicative of low achievement. Additionally, both Isabelle and Julia highlighted their reliance on making comparisons between students and generalized, informal criteria when assessing academic achievement. They pointed to the importance of watching students and observing that students who seemed less likely than their peers to experience academic achievement often engaged in specific types of behaviors.

In terms of the support the inservice teachers provided their low-achieving students, these teachers used strategies that spanned three distinct areas: (1) modifying lessons; (2) working with students; and (3) working with other teachers and/or support staff. While two teachers (Dylan and Julia) highlighted approaches connected with the actual lesson-making and presentation process, most of the teachers spoke of working with students directly and working with other teachers and staff to meet these students' needs. For instance, three teachers (Zoë, Isabelle, Julia) discussed the usefulness of other staff to assist in them in teaching their low-achieving students. These individuals included parent volunteers, special education/resource teachers, as well as other students in the class. In the case of Julia, she also recognized the importance of "get[ting] the ball rolling on testing and going through the appropriate channels." She was concerned about this process because it can "take a long time," leaving considerable room for the teacher to "flounder" with the students (Interview transcript, p. 8). Outside of Zoë's practice of asking parent volunteers to help in class, Julia was the only inservice teacher who suggested calling parents as one of the strategies she used. Finally, in terms of the strategies offered that related to working with students, all of the inservice teachers engaged in this practice. The teachers overwhelmingly cited providing additional instructional time to individual students with specific learning needs.

Family and Student Characteristics as Key Contributors to Academic Achievement

Most of the inservice teachers pointed to student-level factors and/or factors related to parents/family as key indicators for potentially low-achieving students. Only in the case of one teacher, Zoë, were school-level factors (specifically towards teacher practices) cited. No one pointed to issues related to societal factors.

For example, Isabelle highlighted students who "may be a little bit more quiet and not as willing to participate," yet immediately followed by saying that while "that's one key thing, sometimes it just depends . . . [because] I also have very high achievers who just don't participate either" (Interview transcript, p. 5). This complex rendering of "sometimes, but not always" signaled the variability Isabelle recognized as existing in accounting for low academic achievement. By way of her experience, Zoë also recognized that low student self-esteem was an important factor facing students who seemed less likely to attain academic success:

> It's been my experience [that] low self-concept, not believing in self—which is low self-concept, lack of confidence [is to blame]. A lot of them [students likely to experience low achievement] do not take [learning] risks, and have a fear of failure. Somewhere, and I don't know where, whether it's parents, peers, or previous teachers, someone has told them they are not smart and they are starting to believe that. And something that I heard at a workshop is that kids psychologically drop out of school in kindergarten. (Interview transcript, p. 10)

Julia, more than any other inservice teacher, had a lengthy—and, by her own admission, incomplete—list of factors related to students who seem more likely than their peers to experience low achievement. Below I included her entire response to clearly and explicitly illustrate the comprehensive nature of her answer, and the depth to which she factors in very particular kinds of issues around achievement. Julia stated:

> Well, okay, some of the things that trigger my concerns would be: truancy, frequently absent from school. And it might fit a pattern like I've noticed in my own career that for some students, Mondays and Fridays are hard. And when you maybe say—where were you? Were you sick? [the potentially at-risk students say] no not sick just couldn't get out of bed, or didn't catch the bus. School wasn't a priority that day. So that tells me if school's not a priority, why not? Why isn't it a priority that morning?
>
> Where I look at it from my point of view, I loved school. I was looking forward to Monday morning. So that's one indication, frequent truancy. Also being late to school, not catching the bus, not being able to get here on time frequently. That kind of sends up a red flag to me as well. Then I think also, I could go on forever on this one, when they get to school sometimes it's where they are. Like are they milling around outside the classroom or are they in the classroom. I have students who in the past have had difficulties in school, that hang out in the bathroom or eat breakfast real slowly in the cafeteria and the last thing they want to do is get to class. Or they maybe go and

visit other teachers or find somebody that they can talk to—a friend in the hallway—and they're socializing someplace. But the getting to class and wanting to be here on time and get their materials organized doesn't happen right away [for these students].

[And] while I've had students that are not achieving that are organized and some that are not achieving that are very disorganized, I think that more times than not students that are not achieving are not organized or lack organization skills. Putting things in folders, wanting to keep the desk neat, wanting to keep their materials together. Which kind of leads to bringing things home, bringing things back, and I think that can be a struggle in many different ways. I have kids who will leave things at school and then tell parents one story but they purposefully left it at school. Or they leave it at home and they tell me, "I'm not quite finished," but they really forgot it at home. So little things like that would be a red flag to me about achieving.

Also I would say, one of the things I have noticed is we have a daily planner, and sometimes the kids that aren't achieving don't fill out their planner, they don't take their homework home and they don't get their planner signed by a parent. There's [also] communication. I write a note home; it doesn't get to the parents that day. It might get there 2 weeks from then. Little things like that. Also like during the day, I have witnessed things like physically hiding their body behind another student so you don't call on them, maybe hiding someplace in the room so you don't know they're there and . . . it might be 15 minutes before you notice they are missing. Leaving and taking bathroom breaks when you start a lesson, or when you pass out the assignment: "Oh I've got to go to the bathroom" and leave.

I think too, when you're working in groups, like small groups, the kids have a task to do, they might kind of be on the fringe of the group, letting somebody else take charge—listening, but not really contributing. They might be gaining information and actually learning but they're not a contributing member of that group. Let's see what else . . . I would say probably not being able to read or write as well or compute for math. I mean those are pretty big indicators for a teacher. And language can be a barrier if they are kind of between speaking one language at home and speaking another language at school so they don't really have a language that is their core language. That can be a barrier. I don't know, there are so many things. It can even be something as, like they can't achieve because there is a lack of sleep.

I've had students where I was—okay you're not giving it your best effort today, you know, how come you're not doing so well? "I didn't get any sleep last night" and it can be because they don't have a bed or they don't have sheets or a blanket. I've had that happen where a student had no blankets and it is the middle of winter and they're cold. Or you know they're hungry. You know they come to school very hungry sometimes and those students don't achieve as well on those days. I've also had students who completely zone out and you get to the bottom of it and it turns out that they're being abused physically or sexually. Or that they have too many responsibilities for other siblings and they're taking care of everybody else but they can't, they're exhausted and can't take of their own learning at school. There's just so many factors, I mean outside the classroom but inside the classroom, I mean I just see so many things that—shutting down, putting their head on their desks, sleeping, pretending like they're asleep. Being silly, acting out, being rough, being mean to other kids sometimes. I mean it can be shown in so many different ways. Maybe being born with a disability. I would say there's probably economic factors, parent factors, friend factors.

Like I said there is just a lot of different circumstances that kids go through when they're growing up that their life might change from second to second or minute to minute that affect their ability to learn. It could be a teacher factor, that they don't gel with the teacher. Divorce issues. I think sometimes there's even cultural things that happen. I think here I notice that sometimes kids feel different with their friends. Where they feel different because their skin is a different color or they're from a different country and they are first generation. And a lot of times it is because their families celebrate different holidays or they have a different religion. I think, too, one of the characteristics of these students is the way the community treats each other from one side of town to the other. And what parents say at home when you think your kids aren't listening, they are listening and they actually come to school and they repeat those things. (Interview transcript, pp. 5–7)

It is clear from this lengthy passage that Julia believed many kinds of factors aligned with those students she saw as more likely than their peers to experience low academic achievement. These factors spanned across issues related to student characteristics (e.g., disability, peer relations, cultural conflict between students) and those found at the level of the parent/family (e.g., not providing support), while also acknowledging issues found at the level of the teacher and her/his practice (e.g., dislike of teacher) and economic factors (e.g., homeless). What stood out to me was the comprehensive nature of the list, particularly when noting that she based this knowledge on her personal experience as a teacher for 13 years. It is also interesting to note how Julia made judgments about students, using the lens of her own experience as a student. This was a recurring idea that came up in Julia's talk with me—her love of learning as a student and her assumption that "good students" would share this trait.

Dylan did not go into as much depth as Julia when addressing the factors he related to students positioned as more likely than their peers to experience low academic achievement. He simply pointed to "kids of lower socioeconomic status where reading is not a priority, where kids don't see their parents doing a whole lot of reading" as a key factor. He went on to assert that in these homes "where education is not valued, I find more at-risk kids coming from situations like that than I do from situations where students see their parents reading" (Interview transcript, p. 8). Similar to some of the preservice teachers in the study, Dylan did not categorically blame these families or position them as uncaring. Rather, he justified his statement in a larger argument around the social and economic barriers that hindered families from providing adequate support. For example, he followed his earlier comments with this statement:

> And you know sometimes there's nothing that the parents can do anything about [in terms of providing more support]. I mean if a child is being raised by his mom alone and she's got to work two jobs to support the family that doesn't provide much time for reading. I mean you get home and you're tired. It's nice to just sit and watch TV and just relax. (Interview transcript, p. 8)

Dylan accounted for low academic achievement by focusing on what the parent was not providing her son, presumably because of the larger socioeconomic conditions that made it difficult for her to meet these needs.[6] Regardless of this nuanced perspective, this explanation implicated the parent as a single, working mother who did not value education or provide a home environment that supported or even possessed literacy that was of worth.

BRIDGING REMARKS: INSERVICE TEACHERS, RISK, AND THE CATEGORY OF THE AT-RISK STUDENT

In this chapter, I explored how the inservice teachers in the study talked about, located, and remedied risk. This discussion highlighted how risk and the category and label of the at-risk student emerged and exerted influence on concerns with academic achievement. I would argue that-risk, as a guiding principle, helped to frame how the inservice teachers thought about their role and responsibility in the classroom, as well as how they approached the work of educating students. In this way, similar to the preservice teachers, risk mattered.

When considering the background and teaching perspectives for the inservice teachers, they possessed divergent experiences and approaches toward their work. These differences disrupted any simplistic, essentialist view of the teachers as the same simply because of their shared racial identity or their working in a similar school context. They were not carbon copies of one another, even though they were all White and taught at the same midwestern, suburban elementary school. Instead, as the data clearly illustrated, the inservice teachers diverged from one another with respect to their backgrounds, years of teaching experience and perspectives on education and the role of teaching. They held different approaches to teaching, as well as different philosophies, aspirations for their students, and even fears about their practice.

In acknowledging this, it was also clear that in spite of the differences in the inservice teachers' years of teaching experience, place of origin, and perspectives on teaching and education, they shared understandings and ways of thinking about and acting in their work as educators. This was perhaps most evident in how the teachers defined the fundamental purpose of schooling and the responsibility teachers had in helping students reach these goals. Each teacher highlighted the need to help students become independent learners, capable of contributing positively to the larger society. To reach this goal, they overwhelmingly felt that teachers should serve as role models of lifelong, continuous learners.

Yet these data tell us much more than simply this. They also point out what the inservice teachers valued most about teaching, what they believed about schooling and schools, and what they felt students should strive to achieve. Becoming a good citizen, one who was independent and capable of positively participating in society, was of supreme importance.

It was evident that what the teachers did in the classroom was associated to how they thought about their students and their students' learning (or lack thereof). The inservice teachers were concerned about meeting their students' needs. This concern was fundamental, speaking, in part, to the most important role of the teacher: figuring out what students needed in order to provide them with a quality education. Like the preservice teachers, all of the inservice teachers believed it was necessary to engage in *risk discourse*, as it allowed them to meet the needs of all of their students. This was recognized as the responsibility of the teacher and, I would argue, informed their view that potential academic risk was something that a teacher had to recognize and then figure out how to address.

Unlike the preservice teachers, however, the inservice teachers—with the notable exception of the first-year teacher Isabelle—did not highlight any potential risks involved with engaging in risk discourse. The inservice teachers had little, if any, anxiety about engaging in this process. In many cases they felt that their years of experience as a teacher made them uniquely qualified to ascertain quickly which students were at-risk. Skiba, Simmons, Ritter, Kohler, Henderson and Wu (2006) noted a similar pattern among the inservice teachers in their study regarding the special education referral process. These inservice teachers, as well as those in my study, did not harbor the concerns my preservice teacher participants expressed that in identifying students presumed more likely than their peers to experience low academic achievement, the teacher might close off rather than open up the possibility of providing all students an equitable education. This focus on risk identification and management points to a *technico-scientific* orientation to risk (Lupton, 1999a, 1999b).

This chapter also highlighted that the inservice teachers acknowledged the existence of at-risk students. The category and label at-risk continued to play a functional role in the context of school and district practices, as well as in the talk of other education stakeholders concerned with academic achievement (e.g., parents). At-risk served primarily as a "red flag" or warning that certain students might not achieve and required special assistance. Only one teacher, Zoë, expressed displeasure with and concern around the use of the label *at-risk*. She did not question the larger category of at-risk as a viable way to refer to students. Rather, she worried that the term *at-risk* did not go far enough in acknowledging that at-risk, "broken students could be fixed," a perspective she thought good teachers should hold.

Additionally, all of the inservice teachers drew from popular definitions of the category and label *at-risk*, pointing to the fact that at-risk students possessed certain factors in their lives that made it more difficult for them to experience academic success. At the same time, the teachers offered a different take on what the term specifically meant to them. For example, Dylan believed that two definitions existed, one of which was a formal category used in school and district talk, and the other was connected to his personal beliefs about what made a student at-risk. The at-risk student was defined in ways that drew from normative, stereotypical constructions of risk that were raced, classed, and gendered (Swadener, 1995). Yet teachers also recognized students who did not meet these normative criteria as at-risk. Students who lived in economically wealthy homes, but lacked attention from their busy, working parents, along with those whose parents were divorced or too hovering, also were viewed by some of the inservice teachers as at-risk. This finding illustrates how the inservice teachers converged and diverged around meanings of at-riskness.

Fundamentally, the point of positioning certain students as at-risk was related to the fear that these students might fail to achieve academically. For this reason, it was important to consider how the inservice teachers defined, accounted for, and acted in response to academic achievement. For example, all of the inservice teachers were drawn to strategies that relied on teacher observation and required direct work between the teacher and the student. None of the teachers believed that the support they provided could effectively address the needs of their low-achieving students. Three highlighted strategies that required the assistance of people other than themselves. In the end, more so than the preservice teachers, the inservice teachers did not believe these strategies were enough. This suggested, at least from the perspective of the inservice teachers in this study, that they felt they could provide only a limited amount of assistance to academically struggling, at-risk students. They did not view this challenge as connected to the larger structures and normative expectations and practices that defined how schooling was expected to occur. They simply felt that some students had needs that exceeded their ability to function as effective pedagogues in the classroom. What, then, does this imply about the role and responsibility of the teacher in actually meeting the needs of all students?

The inservice teachers generally understood academic achievement in relation to variable notions of achievement that moved across students. I refer to this as a *sliding scale of achievement,* and it was an approach to which both the inservice teachers and the preservice teachers overwhelmingly adhered. For the inservice teachers, achievement was measured in relation to student mastery of nonspecified, grade-level learning goals, mainly determined by the teacher. This often equated to assessing students with regard to whether they were "achieving at their personal best." Yet it was simultaneously uncertain *how* the teachers actually decided what constituted a student's "personal best." The inservice teachers, more so than the preservice teachers, suggested this was indicative of academic achievement. When asked to explain this, the inservice teachers often were unable to provide an explanation for how this process actually took place. This lack of clarity was also present in how teachers (e.g., Dylan) determined when they had done all they could do for a student and consequently recognized the student as at-risk.

None of the inservice teachers suggested that low academic achievement was connected to factors related to societal/structural concerns. Only one cited school-level concerns leveled specifically at teacher practices. Student- and parent/family-level factors were overwhelmingly cited as contributing to low academic achievement. Interestingly, in those instances where the teachers pointed to societal/structural factors like low socioeconomic status, it was offered as a justification for why the students' parent/family provided an inadequate, academically risky environment. With regard to the factors attributed to students classified as at-risk, the inservice teachers similarly pointed to issues connected to student characteristics and the parent/family.

I would argue that across the teachers' responses, they drew from *cultural deficit* explanations. In a more complicated way, they also drew from a *structural/institutional inequalities perspective* to account for low academic achievement, with these responses offered to justify explanations that placed blame on parents and families. Two of the teachers, Zoë and Julia, offered a *cultural difference* argument when discussing how incongruent interactions between teachers and students or among students might impact students' learning. Two teachers also implicated genetic factors as having an impact on low academic achievement (e.g., gender, cognitive/learning disability). In the case of Julia, she distinguished between factors that can and cannot be controlled, citing learning disabilities as falling in the latter category. However, regarding Dylan, who pointed out that boys seemed to be more at-risk than girls, it was not clear whether he attributed this distinction to biological differences between males and females or to cultural norms that dictated what and how gendered ways of being were valued and rewarded in the classroom.

Risk as both a necessary and dangerous discourse was present in how the inservice teachers understood and addressed risk. Across the inservice teachers, this particular risk was reflected in the danger *associated with failing to identify students who might face academic risk.*

Looking at the data from the school, it was clear that differential achievement was found between students of color, particularly Black students, and those from low-income backgrounds, and their White, middle-class peers. There was a necessary equity imperative to figure out what was going on in order to better meet students' needs. Similar to the preservice teachers, this necessity led the inservice teachers to seek out methods—whether successful or not—to locate potentially at-risk students and specific methods to intervene in possible academic risk. The inservice teachers viewed this as an important and necessary activity. Only one recognized that engaging in *risk discourse* was potentially dangerous itself. Another expressed frustration when teachers placed blame on students and their families for low achievement and then used this as an excuse to not meet these students' needs. She viewed the term *at-risk* as a cop-out and barrier to better intervening on real student academic risk. The danger that some students were academically at-risk and in need of intervention was in part related to another danger: that of *students not performing where state, local, and/or personal criteria suggest they should be.* The primary way teachers addressed this issue was in the context of teacher judgment. Across the board, the inservice teachers viewed themselves as experienced educators and fully confident in their ability to accurately judge students who were academically at-risk.

With this insight in mind, in the final chapter I consider what these findings, along with those illuminated in both the federal policy and the preservice teacher site (Chapters 3 and 4, respectively), tell us about risk and the at-risk category and label.

TOOLS FOR CRITICAL REFLECTION AND PRACTICE

Key Terms to Consider

- Essentializing
- Sliding scale of achievement
- Normalizing judgment

Questions

1. Why do you think it is popular practice to place blame on the parent/family for difficulties students experience in school? What are the implications of this practice for the work of schools and teachers?

2. What do you think is the role and responsibility of teachers in the classroom regarding student academic achievement? How might teachers approach this topic in a way that is concerned with equity but that does not position students as deficient and disadvantaged?

Extended Activity

Identify two or three teachers. Interview each teacher about the role that teacher judgment plays in the everyday work of teaching. What are the kinds of judgments that teachers make every day in their classroom practice? Do they ever struggle with uncertainty or confusion when making judgments? What supports do they draw from to assist in making judgments? Create a list for how teacher judgment informs the everyday practices of teachers. What are the implications of these judgments for the everyday work of teachers and student achievement?

CHAPTER 6

After the "At-Risk" Label

Toward a Critical Standpoint of Risk and a Critical Reorientation to Risk in Education Policy and Practice

In education there is contention around the use and utility of the at-risk label and category (Gadsden et al., 2009; Swadener, 1995). This disagreement reflects a general pulse in conversations around the term and its recognition as either a necessary or a dangerous construct for use. When viewed as a necessity, it is deployed as a legitimate category of person in need of targeted or specialized treatment. An example of this kind of usage is found in official education policy at the federal, state, and district levels. Another example is the ad hoc and popular uses of the term. This is often found in the talk of educators and laypersons when discussing children or young people that are viewed as outside of the normal and likely to experience unintended outcomes. The fact that presumably at-risk students exist in schools points directly to the belief that some action is needed. Identifying at-risk students—those who seem more likely than their peers to face an unwanted consequence—becomes necessary in order to meet students' needs.

Yet, at the same time, the term *at-risk*, along with the alternative monikers used to denote a similar category of student, is also recognized as dangerous. These dangers point to the situated and contextual way that at-riskness is constructed in the confines of normative Whiteness that define societal values. To be sure, historically and in the present, the students viewed as at-risk, disadvantaged, deprived, problematic, or backward were those with bodies, knowledge, experiences, standpoints, dispositions, and comportments delegitimized by dominant societal expectations. Questions of ontological, or real, at-riskness become exceedingly difficult to evaluate in a context where from the onset one's very being must be parallel to a valuation system (Locke, 1989) that maintains the status quo. I find useful the philosopher Alain Locke's conception of *value theory*, because it elaborates on the way "values" are systematically normalized. In this sense, the assessment of risk is constituted by hierarchical meanings of social and educational value that reproduce durable educational inequities.

These questions around risk and the at-risk category and label implicate important concerns with educational equity. These commonly are
recognized as opportunities to learn (Milner, 2012). Gadsden et al. (2009)
argued that the contemporary context of schooling has intensified expectations for schools and teachers. Standardized testing, and the practices
of surveillance and accompanying constriction of the curriculum it engen-
ders, make schooling a risky enterprise. This compromises the ability of
schools to equitably meet students' needs. The socially constructed nature
of risk, then, makes it both a potentially useful and yet a precarious idea.

In presenting the findings from my study that examined risk and the
at-risk category and label, I have taken seriously the contentious nature
of risk in education. I did this by attending closely to the sociocultural
knowledge of risk that emerged across three key education sites—federal
policy, preservice teachers, and inservice teachers. Like the history of the
risk construct discussed in Chapter 2, each of these sites held a vested
role and interest in academic achievement. Akin to the permanent place
that race and racism hold in our modernist, Western society (Bell, 1992;
Ladson-Billings & Tate, 1995), risk too is an enduring construct in U.S.
schooling and social relations. As the study illustrated, risk as a construct
and *at-risk* as a category and label occupy a lingering place in education
policy and practice. This place is grounded in history, while also informing
the present.

RISK AND THE AT-RISK CATEGORY AND LABEL
ACROSS A MULTISITED EDUCATION CONTEXT

Across the multisited education context I explored, risk most often operated as a mechanism to identify, target, and remediate potential unwanted
outcomes. This signaled a *technico-scientific* orientation (Lupton, 1999a,
1999b). For example, federal policies overwhelmingly recognized risk in
the context of national vitality and global competition. The strength of the
nation was couched in economic and political terms, indicating the important role that education played in preparing a citizenry that would maintain the country's international economic and political dominance. These
concerns also speak to a *risk society* orientation (Lupton, 1999a, 1999b)
with the focus on intensified risks emerging in late modernity, figuring out
how to manage these risks remained salient in policy. Indeed, this need provided the rationale for the policy itself, consequently placing attention on
detecting students who were at-risk for not achieving, and hence placing
the larger nation at-risk. The risk identification process was not particularly complicated. Historically, those students living in poverty or who were
of color generally were viewed as at-risk for low academic achievement.
Similarly, the factors associated with low achievement often were related

to family demographics, primarily socioeconomic status and racial identity. This was likely connected to the extensive corpus of research connecting the two, as well as the tradition in scholarly, policy, and popular discourses of positioning living in the condition of poverty as maladaptive and deficient (O'Connor, 2001). Increasingly, this focus in federal policy expanded to targeting school systems and teachers as sources of risk. These schools, not surprisingly, often served students who were of color and/or living in low-income families. Thus, while the emphasis shifted from placing risk squarely on students of color and those living in working-class and impoverished families to placing it on the schools they attended, the underlying premise remained the same. Risk can be aligned with the race and social class background from which one came, with these identities discursively constructed as non-normative and outside of the mainstream.

In the case of the preservice teachers, risk occupied a place in how achievement was understood and approached. The preservice teachers came from different backgrounds and experiences, yet held similarly aligned beliefs about the purposes of schooling, the role and responsibility of teachers, and the issue of risk and achievement. They also expressed the important role that their teacher education program played in their development as teachers, with one, Noah, discussing specific content knowledge he gained around achievement from his coursework.

All of the preservice teachers were familiar with the term *at-risk student*, while few were familiar with or knew the definitions for more recent terms such as *resilient*, *at-promise*, or *placed at-risk*. All of them recognized the necessity for teachers to *engage in risk discourse*—the practice of identifying those students who seem more likely than their peers to experience low academic achievement. They all also believed that some students were at-risk for low academic achievement, yet most of them simultaneously recognized the dangers related to engaging in risk discourse. This created an *ontological dilemma* for the preservice teachers, where they struggled with their own abilities to discern risk when it truly existed. The risk that they felt insecure about identifying was risk located at the level of the student or the student's family. These factors were the ones most commonly cited by the preservice teachers as associated with low academic achievement. Interestingly, the preservice teachers' insecurity around engaging in risk discourse was linked to the knowledge they held about academic risk and achievement. This knowledge likely was gained in their teacher education program, which highlighted how discourses of risk and at-riskness can operate in ways that implicate racialized, classed, and gendered stereotypes and biases (Fine, 1993; Swadener, 1995). In this way, the preservice teachers drew from both *technico-scientific* and *cultural symbolic* orientations to risk (Lupton, 1999a, 1999b). They also subscribed to *cultural difference* explanations and a complicated mix of *cultural deficit* and *structural/institutional* explanations when accounting for students' low academic achievement. When *structural/institutional* approaches were invoked, they were used to justify why certain families failed to offer students the support they presumably needed to achieve.

The preservice teachers' concomitant perspectives on academic achievement complicated their knowledge about risk. Overwhelmingly, the preservice teachers held what I call a *sliding scale view of achievement*. Here, they felt that students experienced academic achievement when they progressed from where they previously were in their understanding or performance. This, coupled with the uncertainty the preservice teachers felt about assessing whether students were really at-risk (or not), shed light on the murkiness of teaching and the important role that teacher judgment and decisionmaking had on students' opportunities to learn.

Similarly, the inservice teachers came from different backgrounds, held varying levels of teaching experience, and approached teaching in diverse ways. All of the inservice teachers acknowledged familiarity with the term *at-risk* and felt that some students were at-risk for low academic achievement. Similar to the preservice teachers, all of the inservice teachers believed it was necessary to engage in risk discourse. What was different, however, was the fact that only one—the novice, first-year teacher Isabelle—recognized any danger in this practice. The inservice teachers did not harbor anxiety about their ability to correctly identify students who were at-risk for low academic achievement. Similar to findings in previous research (Skiba et al., 2006) overwhelmingly the inservice teachers recognized their years of experience as instrumental in allowing them to make accurate assessments about students' academic risk. Interestingly, when identifying students who were at-risk, the inservice teachers drew from normative, stereotypical constructions of risk that were raced, classed, and gendered. These students were often of color and/or came from low-income households. The inservice teachers, however, also recognized students that did not align with these categories when identifying students as at-risk. Students who came from families with economic affluence, but were not given attention from their busy, working parents, who were living in divorced homes, or who had parents that were too hovering also were recognized as at-risk. Like the preservice teachers, the inservice teachers drew from a complex mix of *cultural deficit* and *structural/institutional* explanations to account for academic achievement. The latter were offered when attempting to explain why a low-achieving student from a low-income background had a parent or family that was unable to provide needed academic support. Only two of the teachers, Zoë and Julia, advanced a *cultural difference* argument when discussing how the incongruence among teachers and students can impact students' learning in the classroom.

The inservice teachers also drew from a *sliding scale of achievement* in their perspectives that students achieved when they made some progress in their learning. Here, growth in achievement is what mattered. The inservice teachers generally recognized achievement in the context of nonspecified, grade-level learning goals that the teacher determined. Interestingly, it was not clear how teachers made a judgment as to when students were performing at their personal best. This was important, however, because teachers used this as a barometer to make decisions about when a student was at-risk and required additional support.

Across all of the sites examined, key dangers related to risk emerged, many of which cut across the sites. For instance, federal policies were particularly concerned about the danger of losing future social, economic, and/or political national influence/competitiveness. They were also concerned with the danger of encountering social problems that threaten the well-being of both the "risky" individual and the larger society, and inadequately meeting the "risky" individual's academic needs. The preservice teacher site illuminated a clear danger related to misidentifying, failing to identify, and/or holding low learning expectations for students who might face academic difficulty. A second, related danger was the belief that students were not performing where state, local, and/or personal criteria suggested they should be. The inservice teachers expressed dangers similar to those communicated by the preservice teachers around risk. These included students not performing in relation to where state, local, and/or personal criteria suggested they should be and failing to identify students who might face academic risk. While both the preservice and inservice teachers expressed anxiety around students not experiencing academic achievement and around failing to identify potentially low-achieving students that needed additional support, only the preservice teachers and one first-year inservice teacher, Isabelle, worried about misidentifying students. Most of the preservice teachers expressed some concern about possibly holding low learning expectations when making judgments about low-achieving students. Zoë, a notable exception, was the only inservice teacher who expressed this concern.

FROM NECESSARY AND DANGEROUS
TO A *CRITICAL REORIENTATION TO RISK*

Findings from the study point to the complex and contradictory knowledge that informs how risk is understood and approached across education. This knowledge recognizes risk as a necessary and dangerous idea in the context of academic achievement. The previous discussion outlined how the sites examined in the study acknowledged risk as both necessary and dangerous, with these issues speaking directly to how education stakeholders imagined best meeting the needs of students. At the root of discussions around risk resides a fundamental assumption about the reality of risk and, in this case, academic risk. Academic risk is recognized as a real and objective concern and possibility. As it goes, risk is best managed when it is identified as such and then remediated, either through direct intervention or by protective supports that buffer the factors that potentially lead to unintended outcomes. As noted in Chapter 2, this approach to risk was an invention of modernity. It involved the creation of mathematical laws, expanded forms and disciplines of knowledge, and shifts in how people viewed their power to intervene in, rather than solely exist as hapless victims of, the uncertainties of life. The layering of these technologies, knowledge, practices, and orientations to self and the world opened new vistas in which to order reality. Risk made sense because of its utility in bringing a semblance of stability to an indeterminate world steeped in potential, unknown dangers.

Across all of the sites, risk was reflected in the necessary impetus to identify and mitigate potential academic loss, or underachievement. This necessity led to efforts to locate where risk resided regarding achievement, with the end goal of better remediating or buffering the actual end result of risk. This was the rationale for federal policy and the explanation given for why both the preservice teachers and inservice teachers thought it necessary and a part of their role as teacher to engage in risk discourse—even as the preservice teachers and the first-year inservice teacher, Isabelle, recognized the dangers in engaging in this process.

This study brings to light the challenges wrought by risk as a construct and subsequent category and label of student. Regardless of intentionality, risk is tricky. It is real, yet illusive because of its possibility, rather than certainty, of occurrence. It also is fully grounded in the conditions that established and continue to maintain inequitable societal relations based on race, class, and gender in the United States. As the federal policies and preservice teacher and inservice teacher participants in this study indicated, people positioned as risky continue to be those also viewed as deprived and deficient because their bodies and ways of being and knowing do not align with White, normative valuation systems (Grant et al., 2016). These circumstances are not simply happenstance. They exist in a cultural logic (Goldsby, 2006) and set of institutionalized practices that historically have reinforced White superiority—politically, socially, economically, and culturally. Power, in its most overt and subtle forms, sits at the center of conditions of risk.

As a result, risk in practice operates like a two-edged sword. It is problematic in its normative deployment around concerns with academic achievement, while also offering a way to denote possible dangers, some of which received little, if any, attention in the discussions of risk and the at-risk category and label in this study. These dangers, while speaking to the possibility of academic loss or underachievement, require turning our eyes away from viewing already marginalized people and groups as at-risk, and toward considering how larger institutionalized practices and structures create the conditions of risk in the first place. For example, while the preservice teachers in the study expressed anxiety when making judgments about whether students faced academic risk, the seduction of experience (Britzman, 2003) allowed most of the inservice teachers to feel comfortable deciding what makes a student at-risk for low achievement. Here, there was no regard for the longstanding institutional histories and practices that normatively place certain raced, classed, and gendered bodies as risky. Outside of one teacher, Zoë, not much thought was given to how the institutional practices of school operated in risk discourse. Neither was there consideration of how the history of normative societal construction of risk also might play a role.

At the same time, however, another interesting finding emerged, indicating that each of the three sites recognized and cited multiple explanations for why some students experienced low academic achievement. This is an important consideration, as much of the debate in conversations on academic achievement focuses on this very question: Why do some students fail to achieve academically? And in the case of teacher education, there is an assumption that it matters how preservice teachers, in particular, account for low academic achievement because these perspectives guide how they will later respond (or not) to their students.

Across each of the sites an interesting mix of explanations were offered to account for low achievement, including both society- and school-level *structural/institutional* explanations, *cultural difference* explanations, and *cultural deficit* explanations. What made this mix interesting was not so much *which* explanations were used (or not) to account for low academic achievement, but rather *how* one made sense of the explanation(s) chosen. Looking closely at how explanations were deployed provides a deeper, more meaningful analysis of how policies and participants made sense of low academic achievement; and, perhaps even more importantly, of how teachers might choose to respond (or not) to students. An example of this was noted earlier when participants drew from structural/institutional explanations—perspectives often positioned as more sensitive to issues of societal power and oppression—as well as cultural deficit explanations that placed blame for low achievement on the lack of support provided by parents and families. What did this mean? Were these individuals engaging in deficit thinking (Valencia, 2010)? Were they attempting to lessen the emphasis and responsibility placed on them as policymakers or teachers? Or were they trying to account for multiple forms of knowledge they had acquired regarding the role played by institutional factors and the parent/family as important in the academic life of the student?

Without looking closely, then, at *how* these explanations were used, one might view the respondents as well-informed and thoughtful regarding the various contextual factors that may lead some students to face low academic achievement. Others, however, might suggest the respondents were simply confused. And still others might offer that the respondents were uncaring, or at worst racist and simply looking for an excuse not to take responsibility for addressing low achievement in the classroom. While each of these analyses may accurately explain what is going on in this situation, when we closely examine *how* this explanation for low academic achievement was used and the context in which it was given, rather than simply *what* explanations were offered to explain this phenomenon, something telling emerges.

For example, across all of the sites, society-level structural/institutional explanations, like the one above, were offered for low academic achievement only when respondents were trying to rationalize or justify the simultaneous deployment of cultural deficit explanations that placed blame on parents/families for failing to provide support to their children. Clearly, there were many potential reasons for why these respondents used society-level structural/institutional explanations in this manner, including some that may indicate respondents simply held problematic perspectives about students and their families. For instance, perhaps respondents did not see society-level structural/institutional explanations as viable in and of themselves, or wanted to acknowledge the important role parents/families play in the learning process. Another option is that the respondents believed families did not care about education and therefore did not support their children's learning at home. All of these are possibilities and require further consideration in order to make any clear statement on intentionality. Yet regardless of why the participants accounted for low achievement in the ways they did, their explanations aligned with long-standing tropes of cultural deficiency that are both raced and classed, and often gendered.

The fact that these explanations were offered in the first place points to the necessity to examine more deeply why the participants expressed these ideas. This is particularly the case for the preservice teachers. I would argue there was enough evidence across the interview data to suggest that, in general, they did not want to actively engage in deficit thinking (i.e., based on their feelings about engaging in risk discourse and their trepidation around the specific use of the term *at-risk*). Yet they often found themselves doing just this when they were unable to address the contextual factors they believed were related to low academic achievement (based on knowledge gained in their programs) without resorting to deficit explanations themselves. This study illuminates clearly why we need to know more about what informs the knowledge base from which the participants, particularly the preservice teachers and the inservice teachers, pulled their ideas about risk and achievement.

The complex, yet still myopic, knowledge underlying how risk and achievement were understood across the sites illuminates why we likely will not do away with the construct of risk anytime soon but must reorient it for more critical use. The construct of risk has been with us for a long time. Risk thinking is deeply embedded in the foundational logic of modernist, Western ways of organizing thought and action, and implicated in the work of schooling. Without a paradigmatic transformation in dominant ways of looking at, reading, and acting on the social world, risk is unlikely to disappear anytime soon. As similarly pointed out by critical race theory scholars regarding the permanence of race, perhaps one of the most contentious and endemic social constructs in modern Western history (Bell, 1992) and in education (Ladson-Billings & Tate, 1995) in the world we currently inhabit, risk occupies an enduring place.

Further, schooling itself is a risky enterprise for reasons not actually acknowledged by the participants in this study. These unacknowledged risks are not located "inside" students or their families. Nor are they associated with common terms, like *poverty, low income,* or *language learner,* used to describe students and the communities and cultural groups from which they come. The risks to which I refer are those that bring meaning to the construct of risk, both contextualizing and defining it. They are invested in structures and institutional practices that, while historically grounded, remain impactful in the present. Below, I discuss four such risks in more detail.

First, it is true that with regard to standard measures of academic success, many students are not doing well in school. Students of color, those from low-income backgrounds, those whose first language is not English, and those identified as having special learning needs often underperform their peers on statewide standardized exams and in high school graduation rates. This is a real danger that warrants critical, serious inquiry.

Second, deep and durable inequities exist in schooling that impact student achievement. Both underachievement and the inequities connected to it are linked to structures, organizations, and practices found both in schools as well as in the sociohistorical patterns of inequity located outside of school (Ladson-Billings, 2006). Concentrated poverty, and the accompanying patterns of economic divestment associated with it, creates neighborhoods with limited access to goods, services, and even human capital valued in the larger mainstream society (Noguera, 2003).

Schools themselves continue to have inequitable funding (Biddle & Berliner, 2003) and reflect disparities in student achievement (Ladson-Billings, 2006), disciplinary referrals (Skiba, Michael, Nardo, & Peterson, 2002), and identification in special education (Artiles, Kozleski, Trent, Osher, & Ortiz, 2010; Artiles & Trent, 1994; Blanchett, 2006) that relate to the race, gender, and socioeconomic characteristics of students. These conditions warrant serious consideration because of their longevity and reproduction.

Third, public schools and the teachers in them are facing increasingly aggressive scrutiny and political attack for perceived ineffectiveness. Similar to students categorized and labeled as at-risk, schools and teachers are stigmatized. These are most often the schools and teachers that serve student populations that are of color, live in families and communities that are low income, and/or are second language learners. The risk traditionally placed on students from particular raced, classed, and linguistic backgrounds has shifted to these students' schools and teachers (Gadsden et al., 2009).

Fourth, schools and teachers engage in important, life-impacting work that relies on personal judgment. These judgments make it possible for students to become categorized and labeled as risky and in need of intervention. These decisions are important as they make certain options available to students, while diminishing the likelihood of others. Here, the stigma associated with labeling practices operates in deleterious ways (Bruce & Phelan, 2001). This is particularly troubling because too often students labeled and tracked as having learning or behavioral issues become locked in an identity as learning or behaviorally challenged. In this case, as pointed out by sociologist Charles Tilly (1998), categories matter. They reflect boundaries that demarcate and distinguish. They also become subject to narratives held and told about people.

In the case of schooling, the social identifications that come as a result of the categories where students are placed impact the kinds of learning they can access and acquire. For example, Wortham (2006) examined the construction of two students' identities in the classroom. The author illustrated how entrenched sociohistorical models of identity (often stereotypes) get enacted locally, by way of teacher–student interactions in the classroom. The everyday practices of teaching and learning aided in the formation of student identities—or categories of students—that drew from longstanding stereotypical tropes, but that were unique in their local instantiation. These constructions were more than simply a "label" to describe students. Rather, these identifying boundary markers had profound implications on how students were positioned as learners, as well as the subject matter learned.

AN ORIENTATION TO PRACTICE:
TOWARD A *CRITICAL STANDPOINT OF RISK*

Given the endemic way that-risk operates in how we read and act on the world, along with the challenges it presents to education and the fact that most underserved communities encounter pervasive, yet unacknowledged risks deeply connected to societal structures and institutional practices, can we reimagine a different, more viable approach to risk in schooling?

I would argue that this is both a necessity and a possibility. This means, however, that-risk cannot continue to operate in the deeply problematic ways that normatively invoke race, social class, and gender inequities in education. Nor can it serve as an easy indicator to mark who or what is considered normal (or not), even as it has since the beginnings of compulsory public schooling in the United States. Risk as a construct is concerned with calculability, probability, and possibility. And it is grounded in Western rules of rationality. Yet, this tool, like all societal inventions, reflects the societal context in which it was created and enacted. Thus, regardless of one's stance on the value and usefulness of the risk construct, in the context of a society characterized by inequitable power relations, any usefulness is compromised by the potential danger in its application. This space of danger, as part of the pervasive risk knowledge reflected in education policy and practice, highlights the importance of this study. How might illuminating the complexities around the knowledge about risk and the at-risk category and label allow us to disrupt its normative application, while also transforming it for more equitable use?

The findings from this study point to why we need a critical approach to risk that can attend to concerns around academic risk and the challenges it presents as a social construct. These concerns acknowledge that-risk and the at-risk category and label exist in a social context imbued with power, historically fashioning people in culturally normative ways that implicate specifically race, social class, and gender. In discussions of risk, the issue of race (often in concert with social class and gender) is a curious one that requires particular attention, as the history of schooling is replete with the practice of connecting degeneracy, disadvantage, and subpar intelligence to race identity. These practices were rampant during the early 20th century and continue to manifest well into the 21st, as discussed in Chapter 2. Racial difference (often in connection to social class) has served as the fundamental and enduring axis upon which to distinguish intellectual capacity going back to the 18th century in the United States. It was expressed by scholars—both leading natural scientists and social scientists—as well as key U.S. figures and politicians, including Benjamin Franklin, Thomas Jefferson, and Abraham Lincoln (Gould, 1996). As Gould argued, beliefs about race and ability were not established initially as a result of empirical science. Rather, the science reflected already-held assumptions about race, intelligence, and identity. These *a priori* perspectives, then, effectively framed what empirical questions were possible to ask regarding the racial ranking of intelligence. As the pursuit for evidence to support these assumptions mounted, not surprisingly, data were produced to support the claims that the sociopolitical discourse of the time already presumed. These data emerged concomitantly with the development and growth of statistical methods, an approach whose history played an integral role in lending scientific support for innate racial differences across groups.

For example, Zuberi (2000) outlined the coterminous relationship between the development of statistics and efforts to scientifically link racial differences to intelligence. This history abounds with myopic understandings of how race operates as a social category that shifts both temporally and spatially. This complexity of race in statistical data is of particular concern because it often is not fully accounted for in data when deployed as a variable. Not surprisingly, Zuberi (2000) also argued that scientists often are unable to address and account for the fundamental social meaning they ascribe to race when deploying it in statistical studies. This challenge is grounded in the recognition that one can understand race only in relation to the historical and social context that defines its meaning. These meanings historically have shifted over time and space, with one salient example being how a person's race could change in the United States simply according to the state in which she/he resided. Thus, as Bonilla-Silva and Zuberi (2008) stated:

> It is not a question of how a person's race causes disadvantage and discrimination. The real issue is the way the society responds to an individual's racial identification. The question has more to do with society itself, not the innate makeup of individual characteristics. Race is not about an individual's skin color. Race is about an individual's relationship to other people within society. While racial identification may be internalized and appear to be the result of self-designation, it is, in fact, a result of the merging of self-imposed choice within an externally imposed context. When we forget or make slight of this point, social science becomes the justification for racial stratification. (p. 7)

What the history of race and science tells us is that no social space, including the field of science, statistics, and the calculability of risk, operates outside of the larger racist histories, knowledge, and practices that define it and bring it meaning. Context matters. In the case of the construct of risk, its contours and enactment—particularly around race—make questionable the possible utility of the idea itself.

Given the sociocultural landscape of schools and the deep inequities that mark longstanding social arrangements in U.S. society, three orientations to risk are needed in order to engage a *critical reoriented risk construct* in a more useful way. These include approaching risk as (1) a social construction; (2) a warning sign of possible danger, individually, institutionally, and structurally and (3) critical and fluid. These orientations allow one to approach a critical reoriented concept of risk in a reflexive way that I call a *critical risk standpoint*. This reflects a particular standpoint and set of knowledge needed to talk about and act on risk in a more fruitful, yet critical way. A critical risk standpoint recognizes how structural and local factors, as well as historical and contemporary social arrangements and relationships, inform how educational risk is fundamentally understood. This knowledge is connected to what I previously have called a *critical humanizing sociocultural knowledge* (Brown, 2012) about the racial, social, political, and economic histories that have framed and shaped social and schooling relations in the United States and beyond. This knowledge is vitally important but generally is not considered integral to what preservice or inservice teachers are expected to know as classroom teachers.

A critical risk standpoint, then, is a personal orientation taken by an education stakeholder when approaching risk from a critical, reoriented perspective. Here risk is approached self-reflexively and without any attempt to essentialize who or what constitutes risk. It attends to risk as individual and institutional, while also deeply contextual, expansive, and fluid in application and use. Here, risk moves from being something that resides in people or for the sake of efficiency is placed wholesale on entire groups of individuals because of their identity or membership in a particular group positioned as more likely than others to experience an unintended outcome (e.g., at-risk students). Risk is understood only in relation to the historical practices and contexts that have come to define it. As a result, risk is also not a condition of totality, defining one's entire life condition or being. It can and does shift across different spaces and times. A critical risk standpoint also recognizes risk as a warning sign that something is going awry, signaling that more critical, reflexive consideration is needed to assess why this is the case. Table 6.1 provides an outline of a critical risk standpoint.

Out of this consideration, taking up a critical reoriented concept of risk would require that one critically appraise how those systems (i.e., schools, policy, etc.), including the people associated with them that seek to remedy the risk, may themselves be complicit in perpetuating, exacerbating, or even creating conditions that lead to risk.

Table 6.1. Characteristics of a Critical Risk Standpoint

Recognizes risk is complex	• Understands that-risk reflects structural, institutional, and local factors, as well as historical and contemporary social arrangements and relationships
Approaches risk self-reflexively	• Makes judgments about risk critically and consciously; continually self-reflective about personal assessments of academic risk
Views risk from a nonessentialist perspective	• Realizes that-risk is not categorically placed on a person because of generalized assumptions (often made through statistical calculations) about a person's or thing's presumed proximity to certain risk factors
Situates risk contextually and recognizes its reach is expansive	• Recognizes risk as related to historical practices and contexts that have come to define risk, both for the individual making the decision and in the larger societal context in which it is made
Reads risk as a fluid idea that can shift over time	• Acknowledges that-risk can and does shift across different spaces and times • Accepts that-risk does not define one's entire life condition or being

TO REIMAGINE RISK: ENVISIONING A *CRITICAL REORIENTATION TO RISK* FOR EDUCATION POLICY AND PRACTICE

I would argue that if one adopts a critical risk standpoint that allows for a more critical, reflexive, and flexible practice around academic risk, a critical reoriented construct of risk becomes both viable and possible. This reoriented construct draws from and links together important elements from the orientations to risk outlined by Lupton (1999a, 1999b). These include the technico-scientific orientation, with an acknowledgment of the reality of risk and the need to address identify and address it; the cultural symbolic orientation, in light of the boundary-marking, socially constructed nature of risk; and the governmentality orientation, because it recognizes risk as a material artifice manufactured in relations of power and discourse. This reoriented construct of risk would align with three key assumptions about risk that disrupt how the federal policy and the participants in the study talked about and engaged risk in their practices. First, a critical reoriented construct of risk must account for the socially constructed nature of risk. Second, a critical reoriented construct of risk serves as a warning sign that something might possibly go awry, but not because of a preconceived set of conditions or set of data that generalizes whole populations of people or things as more risky without cause. Third, when making judgments about risk, a critical reoriented construct of risk should allow one to view risk critically, but with an open mind that continuously questions what and who reflects risk. As a result, the critical reoriented construct of risk acknowledges the historical, institutional, and structural factors that normatively position some people, things, and activities as at-risk *prima facie*.

Risk as a Social Construction

From the onset, a critical reoriented construct of risk must account for the socially constructed nature of risk. What and who is recognized as risky operates in a constellation of relationships rooted in history, social context, practices, and meaning-making. Societal discourses and practices shape the contours of risk. What is viewed as risky practice in one space is not necessarily in another. Consider the example of allowing preschool-aged children to use a knife in their classroom environment. Most traditional preschool classrooms do not have or allow children to use knives because they are recognized as potentially dangerous to the well-being of children who are not yet mature enough to use them. However, in many Montessori classroom environments, knives are present in the classroom and young children use them daily as part of the early childhood curriculum. Risk is not fully objective. It is subjective, both socially situated and dependent on the dominant values and norms held by the community making the judgment about potential risk.

Risk as a Warning Sign of Possible Danger, Individually, Institutionally, and Structurally

The findings from this study point out that the construct of risk serves as a warning sign that something, in this case academic achievement, might possibly go awry. A critical reoriented construct of risk would recognize this, yet remain skeptical about assigning risk to a person or thing simply because of some preconceived assumption or generalized body of data about a person's proximity to factors causing risk. A critical reoriented risk construct does not recognize risk as real simply on the basis of calculated probabilities that fail to account for the raced, classed, and gendered ways that-risk has historically operated in these contexts (Zuberi, 2001). Rather, risk is recognized through observation and continuous critical questioning whether something is possibly awry and might continue off course without thoughtful, reflexive intervention. This might involve a particular student or group of students, as well as a set of educators, a school, or a school system. Risk does not operate at only the individual level, nor is it located in particular people or bodies. Risk is complex in its application to both people and systems.

Risk as Critical and Fluid

This risk would come as a result of direct observation, gathered in the everyday work of schooling, of a possible problem. Examples might include a student who is not meeting expected learning outcomes, a student who is not attending class or school, or a student who is struggling to keep up with work in class. First, the teacher must recognize the normative nature of her/his judgments about students, as well as the overarching goals with respect to which teachers are expected to make judgments. These might include formal objectives outlined at the state, district, or school level, and, as the data from this study indicate, they often are objectives held by the teacher. Whether officially sanctioned or aligned with one's personal commitments, all of these objectives are contextual and normative. This space alone should ask that teacher always, regardless of experience or knowledge, take pause when passing judgment. This is not meant to undermine the experiential and professional knowledge that surely comes over time as educators mature in their practice (Lunenberg & Korthagen, 2009; Verloop, Van Driel, & Meijer, 2001). What it does recognize, however, is that risk, like other important elements in the schooling process, including curriculum and pedagogy, is not neutral. It is vested in social relations characterized by power and inequitable access.

Given the problematic contexts in which risk and schooling reside, teachers and all education stakeholders should always approach making judgments about student risk and potential from a place of critical, yet tentative consideration and openness. Equally important, this approach allows for a critical reoriented risk construct that appreciates a critical appraisal of how systems (i.e., schools, policy, etc.), and the individuals working within them—including teachers and other education stakeholders—that seek to remedy risk, are, advertently or inadvertently, complicit in perpetuating, exacerbating, or recreating conditions that themselves re-inscribe the conditions of risk. See Table 6.2 for an overview of a critical reoriented risk construct.

TAKING UP A *CRITICAL RISK STANDPOINT* IN EDUCATION POLICY AND PRACTICE

It is clear that a reoriented stance toward risk—what I call a critical risk standpoint—makes it possible to view risk differently and more critically.

Table 6.2. Characteristics of a Critical Reoriented Construct of Risk

Risk as a social construction	• Recognizes risk as constructed through social relations, both historically and in the present, that make it possible to view specific people or things as a risk • Understands that who and what count as risky shifts over time and space • Judgments about risk align with the value system held by the individual making the judgment and/or the dominant societal perspectives about risk found in the larger society
Risk as a warning sign of possible danger individually, institutionally, structurally	• Recognizes academic risk through an initial observation that something might go awry without intervention • Does not presume possible academic risk on the basis of a preconceived set of conditions or set of (statistical) data that generalize whole populations of people or things as more/less risky • Acknowledges that academic risk comes as a result of individual, institutional, and/or structural conditions • Is cognizant of how those making assessments about or working to remedy possible risk may create or exacerbate the condition of risk
Risk as critical and fluid	• Makes judgments about academic risk from a critical perspective that acknowledges how society and schooling exist in power relations that have operated in inequitable ways • Presumes risk is a fluid construct, dependent on context and not reflective of a person's or thing's entirety

The critical reoriented construct of risk I propose recognizes the socially constructed, normative nature of risk that is rooted in both personally held and socially transmitted values about what constitutes legitimate risk. It also recognizes risk as a warning that something may be amiss. This is judged through direct observation of a problem that is itself normatively valued (e.g., performance on a standardized test; meeting an expectation held by a teacher, school, or district). A critical reoriented risk construct further acknowledges the linkages historically made between race, social class, and gender identities, and their taken-for-granted assignment to deficiency and risk. It asks that we reflect on how structural and institutional contexts, including the primary one tasked with addressing academic risk, the school, enables risk to exist and flourish.

As pointed out previously, a critical risk standpoint requires one take up a critical reoriented construct of risk. This standpoint eschews essentialism, with its attention to both the individual and the institutional. It is also critically self-reflexive, while deeply contextual, expansive, and fluid in application and use. How might educators cultivate such a positionality in light of the pervasiveness of risk in policy and practice? What would it look like in education practice? In the discussion that follows I consider these questions in the context of both education policy and teacher education and teaching.

Education Policy

Education policy helps to shape the education agenda and, in the case of federal policy, it has become increasingly important and controversial since the passage of NCLB in 2001. This policy cemented an already growing argument for the creation and use of content learning standards and standardized measures of assessment to evaluate the extent to which students were successfully meeting these learning goals. Criticism soared, with families opting their children out of testing, and schools, under the gun to show students across all subgroups were achieving, began to constrict curriculum, course offerings, and related teacher decisionmaking. Risk resided at the heart of these conditions.

Risk in policy is complicated, focusing at once on risk as a systemic threat undermining the wealth and security of the nation, and also on meeting the needs of specific populations already positioned as risky. The challenge, then, with invoking a critical risk orientation in policy is that it moves away from the presumption that certain raced, classed, and gendered populations face academic risk that requires remediation. This means that when approaching policy, from whatever vantage point one might take, one must make an effort to intentionally and critically read how risk and achievement are invoked. Doing this means analyzing what constitutes risk and how it, along with achievement, is accounted for in the policy. Key questions to consider include: What is risk? How is it conceptualized? What are the implications of this conceptualization for how specific students and communities are positioned? It is also important that when reading policy, one takes note of where risk is located. Is it placed primarily at the level of the individual or is it connected to larger histories and institutional practices that play out both in structures and in the everyday, local context of classroom and schools?

One of the ways that policy might adopt a more robust, critical reorientation to risk is to consider the static and essentialized ways in which risk is placed on people, as well as the institutions associated with them. For example, since federal education policy comes from a history of using education as a tool to alleviate poverty, it is not surprising that every policy passed since ESEA 1965 has recognized poverty as a condition of risk. This positioning of poverty constructs it as fully a problematic condition in need of remedy, but also as outside of the larger historical practices that made these conditions of poverty possible in the first place. Poverty, then, is an institution that is both total and fully bad. Yet in policy, the condition of poverty, integrally connected to housing patterns and generational wealth, often is addressed as disconnected from the societal practices and histories that, ironically, made it possible. Redress is not considered in the context of a radical redistribution of economic, political, and social resources. Rather, it is limited to the allotment of monies used to compensate for and add to existing educational programming. Understanding this complicated, yet historically situated condition is key to addressing policy from a critical risk orientation and a critical reoriented construct of risk. Without this knowledge, one might uncritically accept an essentialized knowledge about what and who constitutes risk, with this calculus of risk presenting as more static than fluid and ultimately unable to account for the socially constructed nature of risk itself.

Teacher Education and Teaching

As noted in Chapter 1, teacher education programs are concerned with knowledge. This is why teacher education programs invest in organizing the specific kinds of content and experiences preservice teachers need in order to successfully become teachers. Classroom instruction, field-based studies, and classroom observational and apprenticeship experiences constitute the traditional teacher education curriculum. These experiences account for multiple kinds of knowledge, including *institutional/professional knowledge*, *cultural/societal knowledge*, and *background and experiential knowledge*. These reflect some of the most important forms of knowledge in the preparation and ongoing work of teaching. What can they tell us regarding the transmission of knowledge around risk and achievement in teacher education and teaching?

Preparing teachers to work effectively with all students is of particular concern in teacher education. Teacher education is an important space in which to take up this challenge—particularly those programs similar to the one that the preservice teachers in this study completed, which hold commitments such as multicultural education and teacher reflection. This point is supported by existing literature (Cochran-Smith & Zeichner, 2005; Darling-Hammond & Bransford, 2005) and by the findings of this study in two ways. First, findings from the preservice teacher site illuminated how the teacher candidates attributed their knowledge base about academic achievement and risk to the coursework they experienced in their teacher education program. Second, the preservice teachers held key commitments and goals identified in the literature as important for teachers to possess in order to teach all students well. These include the beliefs that: (1) teachers need to reflect on their teaching practice (Zeichner & Liston, 2014); (2) teacher positionality (Ladson-Billings, 2009) and cultural mismatch can adversely affect teacher effectiveness (Irvine, 2003); (3) school organization and school practices function in ways that disadvantage certain students (Oakes, 2005); (4) stereotypical and/or racist thinking can lead teachers to inappropriately label and hold low learning expectations for some students (Sleeter & Grant, 2006; Solórzano & Yosso, 2001); and finally (5) families play an important role in the schooling of students (Hattie, 2008), but may have experiences and perspectives that differ from those valued by teachers and schools (Valdes, 1996; Valenzuela, 1999).

This suggests that the content and experiences provided for teacher candidates in teacher education programs play a vital role in the knowledge base held by these individuals. This knowledge reflects what I call *institutional/professional knowledge*. It is based on the formal knowledge teacher candidates and existing teachers get exposed to in university coursework or in professional learning opportunities. This knowledge comprises: (1) theoretical knowledge gained during coursework and/or professional learning that is based primarily on readings and/or non-K–12 school-based field activities (e.g., pre-education course requirements, foundation courses, subject matter/methods courses), and/or (2) school-based field knowledge gained on site in schools under the supervision of existing classroom teachers and/or university-based faculty/staff (e.g., practicum, student teaching). This type of knowledge was recognized as important across each of the three sites examined in this study. Examples include federal policies that argued for improving the content of teacher education and professional learning, and the preservice teachers and inservice teachers who cited the useful knowledge they gained in formal learning environments.

Given the extent to which university-based programs, in both teacher education and professional learning, rely on formalized knowledge, these are prime locations for examining what this knowledge conveys about risk and achievement. In the case of teacher education programs, this would include looking closely at coursework situated inside and outside of schools/colleges of education, as students generally take those courses prior to beginning their education courses. These intellectual spaces can provide important perspectives about the knowledge preservice teachers bring to their teacher education programs regarding race, social class, gender, institutional inequality, and various cultural groups in the United States.

While institutional/professional knowledge plays an important role in the life of teachers, this is not the only kind of knowledge that impacts their practice and that is implicated by the findings of this study. For example, all teachers get exposed to cultural/societal knowledge. This knowledge is based on what people know about schooling and students. It is connected to the norms, expectations, and discourses found in society by way of textual documents (e.g., federal policies, policy reports, research briefs, books, newspapers), popular discourses (e.g., media reports), and the ways of knowing and being legitimated by societal practices.

Teachers also hold knowledge gained through two kinds of "personal" experiences.[1] The first, background knowledge, is based on the understandings and experiences a teacher candidate had prior to beginning a teacher education program. In this study, background knowledge was captured in the narrative, biographical data that opened Chapters 4 and 5. Both preservice and inservice teachers drew from this repository of knowledge in their (proposed) teaching practice. The second kind of personal knowledge drawn upon by teachers is experiential knowledge. This is gained from one's teaching work in the classroom, either as an apprentice or as the classroom teacher. It generally is understood as a teacher's "experience." As indicated across the inservice teacher data in Chapter 5, "experience" often served to justify these teachers' perspectives and subsequent actions. Experiential knowledge was highly valued and frequently referred to by inservice teachers.

In the case of both background knowledge and experiential knowledge, the focus is on knowledge directly experienced by the individual. While the former speaks to the life experiences people bring with them to their teacher education programs, the latter speaks to knowledge gained in teacher preparation. Both types of knowledge embody how students understand and "know" the world, education, and the practices of teaching. While in the extant literature preservice teachers overwhelmingly cite knowledge gained from direct, personal experiences as key in their development as teachers (Britzman, 2003), teacher educators find the background knowledge of preservice teachers particularly salient and difficult to disrupt (Lortie, 2002). The power and drawback of both kinds of knowledge is that because of its intimate, close proximity to individuals, it is deeply held, yet often underexamined for its limitations and partiality (Scott, 1992).

For this reason, teacher education programs advance the need for personal reflection—another unique kind of experiential knowledge (Zeichner & Liston, 2014) that bridges all of the other forms of knowledge. Through personal reflection people identify the perspectives and assumptions they bring to their programs that stand to impact how they look at self, others, and teaching. Reflection can focus on one's personal experiences as a learner and as a classroom practitioner. It also can target experiences related to sociopolitical and cultural issues such as personal identity (e.g., race, socioeconomic status, gender, disability, language, sexuality, ethnicity, geographic location) and structural/institutional power. It is fairly common for teacher education programs and professional learning opportunities, including the teacher preparation program attended by the preservice teachers in this study, to incorporate elements of personal reflection in coursework. The processes for reflection can vary. When employed in intentional, critical ways, these methods can help home in on problematic perspectives about risk and achievement.

For example, programs can offer teacher candidates and teachers the opportunity to critically reflect on their understanding of academic achievement and academic risk. Specifically, they can ponder what these ideas mean to them, from where they acquired these ideas, the degree to which their ideas fit within or challenge dominant perspectives, and whether any contradictions exist between them. Examples of possible questions include: What is academic achievement? What is academic risk? From where did these ideas come? What are the histories, practices, and discourses in society that inform these belief systems? What kinds of knowledge about academic risk have I gained in my personal experiences as a learner? What knowledge have I learned about academic risk and achievement from my coursework? What, if any, contradictions exist in this knowledge? How do these perspectives speak to my role and work in the classroom with teachers? In what ways are students provided greater opportunities to learn (or not) with regard to my perspectives on academic risk? Table 6.3 presents a complete list of possible reflection questions to consider at different times across a teacher education program. Allowing teachers the opportunity to sit with these questions will provide space to critically reflect on how various kinds of knowledge inform their thinking about both academic risk and achievement.

Additionally, programs can ask individuals to examine how existing societal knowledge—for example, federal educational policies, popular media representations, trade book publications, and everyday discourse—approaches achievement and risk. This encourages preservice and inservice teachers to consider their perspectives on risk and achievement, by interrogating the knowledge they hold and draw from that comes from taken-for-granted societal discourses, practices, and norms. Here, preservice and inservice teachers can consider: What are popularly held beliefs about what constitutes academic risk and achievement? How does history shape these perspectives?

Critical reflection work is not only for preservice and inservice teachers. Teacher educators also can engage in this process, particularly at the level of courses and coursework. For example, when looking at the classes

Table 6.3. Examples of Questions for Critically Reflecting on Academic Risk and Achievement

	Preservice or Inservice Teacher
Institutional/ Professional Knowledge	• What is academic achievement? • What is academic risk? • What knowledge have I learned about academic risk and achievement from my coursework? What, if any, contradictions exist in this knowledge? • How do these perspectives speak to my role and work in the classroom with teachers? • In what ways are students provided greater opportunities to learn (or not) with regard to my perspectives on academic risk?
Cultural/ Societal Knowledge	• What are popularly held beliefs about what constitutes academic risk? Academic achievement? • Where are these ideas found in societal discourse? • What are the histories, practices, and discourses in society that inform these belief systems?
Background/ Experiential Knowledge	• What are the assumptions that inform my perspectives on academic risk? • From where did these ideas come? • What kinds of knowledge about academic risk have I gained in my personal experiences as a learner? • Are these salient only in my personal experience or do they have wider appeal and relevance?

students take in their program, either an individual course instructor or a program coordinator might reflect on the following questions: How, and to what degree, do course materials and class discussions—both those inside and outside of schools of education—address issues of risk and academic achievement? To what extent are course instructors aware of how these kinds of knowledge explicitly and (perhaps more important) implicitly emerge in classroom materials and learning activities?

While critical reflection on knowledge about risk and academic achievement is important, preservice and inservice teachers can benefit from engaging in in-depth critical inquiry around these ideas in the context of their everyday work in the classroom. As an example of an activity, preservice or inservice teachers could be asked to choose one or two students whom they have identified or who have been identified for them as struggling academically. Over a period of time—possibly a month or a semester—the teacher would create a portfolio of work samples and reflective memos that illustrated what the student was doing well and areas

Table 6.3. Examples of Questions for Critically Reflecting on Academic Risk and Achievement (continued)

Teacher Educator

Institutional/ Professional Knowledge	• How, and to what degree, do course materials and class discussions—both those inside and outside of schools of education—address issues of risk and academic achievement? • To what extent are course instructors aware of how these kinds of knowledge explicitly and implicitly emerge in classroom materials and learning activities? • What are the assumptions about academic achievement and potential academic risk that undergird course materials, class discussions, and assignments? • What are the implications of these perspectives for how teacher candidates and teachers view their role and responsibility as teacher? • How is academic achievement defined for students? Is it a goal that varies in relation to individual students? Or is it a fixed set of goals held for all students to meet? • What are the implications of holding a particular definition or perspective about academic achievement for the learning potential of one's students? • How is academic achievement discussed and accounted for in course materials and in class discussions? • Do teacher candidates or teachers get exposed to multiple perspectives about why students experience academic difficulty? If so, how do the teacher candidates or teachers reconcile these differences? Do they integrate these ideas in ways that increase or potentially decrease the likelihood of providing their students with an equitable learning experience?

of challenge; and a log/journal of the teacher's and others' pedagogical interactions with the student and how the student interacted with other students in the class.

This critical observation study also would include work samples and reflections from the teacher about her/his perspectives on and work with the student. Included too would be examples of the student's self-created drawings or writings or self-collected artifacts that collectively reflected important aspects of the student's identity. These might speak to what the student felt she/he did well. In beginning this work, the teacher would adopt a critical risk standpoint that asked her/him to reflect on the difficult issues discussed previously in this chapter. The teacher also would draw from a critical reoriented construct of risk using the description provided earlier.

The goal of this assignment is to see how intentionality and critical reflective attention to risk and achievement possibly impact how a teacher reads and works with a student potentially positioned as experiencing academic risk. See Table 6.4 for an overview of this activity and key questions to critically consider.

SO WHAT COMES AFTER THE "AT-RISK" LABEL?

The findings from this study suggest that, for better or worse, talk and action about risk are, on the one hand, pervasive and slow to change; yet, on the other hand, paradoxically productive, sometimes flexible, and potentially hazardous over time and across education sites. This is a mouthful but points to what I hope comes through in the study—that-risk indeed reflects an endemic, complicated, and contextual body of knowledge. In this study, I recognized risk and the category and label of the at-risk student as a cultural phenomenon that was worthy of close examination (McDermott et al., 2006). I attended closely to knowledge production (Foucault, 1983; Hacking, 2002; Popkewitz, 1998; Wynter, 2005) by interrogating the knowledge that framed how federal policy, preservice teachers, and inservice teachers understood risk. I acknowledged how this process operated in power and inequitable sociopolitical and economic relations (Apple, 2014), uniquely implicated by race (Bell, 1992; Ladson-Billings & Tate, 1995). It also was linked to histories, social practices, and valuation systems (Grant, Brown, & Brown, 2016; Locke, 1989) that operated in taken-for-granted, normative ways.

Is there a life after the "at-risk" label? I think there is, but not nearly one as optimistically and critically transformative as we might hope. As noted in Chapter 2, "at-risk student" is just one of many monikers used across the 20th century to demarcate students' academic potential. As one term was criticized, another emerged to take its place. The quest to find a better, more useful, and less problematic term is a legacy that continues to haunt us (Martinez & Rury, 2012). It is for sure that when (not if) the label "at-risk student" falls out of favor, like the phoenix, another will rise in replacement. The problem, then, with the at-risk label is not the term itself, but rather the fundamental idea and category that it signifies, regardless of verbiage or where it locates risk. It points to a person who is always potentially at-risk. In this case, what is needed, and what I have argued for in this chapter, is a reoriented way to think about and enact risk as a construct. This informs and grounds the specific label used to describe students recognized as more likely than their peers to experience underachievement. If we reorient how the endemic construct of risk is understood and used in practice, the actual term used, whatever it may be, loses significance.

Let me state emphatically: I do not advocate continuing to use the "at-risk" label to categorize and name students perceived as potentially underachieving. The use of any term necessarily invokes essentialist thinking and a static construction of risk that I seek to disrupt. I do not use the term *at-risk* in my own research, teaching, or everyday talk. I do not see its usefulness or the need for others to use it and would like to see it erased from education discourse. Yet, in saying this, I worry about the value of creating another replacement term. What is sorely needed, much more than simply a name change, is a more critical way to address the very risks that accompany the deep cleavages of inequality found in society and schools. As an enduring organizing logic of Western thought, risk occupies an entrenched place. It is with us. And it begs that we acknowledge it for what it is and has been, and then use it to transform our work and, ultimately, the worlds in which we live.

While I was finishing this book, the United States bore witness to several inescapable risks, captured by the #BlackLivesMatter movement, that punctuate the everyday realities of some of its most maligned citizens. The unrelenting assault against Black people, characterized by police killings, racist vigilante violence, and the blatant disregard of state officials to provide even the most basic and important necessity for life—safe drinking water—brings into relief the utility of risk. The traditional construct of risk makes it possible to see these conditions for what they are and engender: possible danger to the Black body. Yet a critical reoriented construct of risk allows us to connect this danger to a longer legacy of dehumanizing, anti-Black practices that justify the fear Black people feel, literally for their own and their communities' lives. These fears are real and justified given the historical and social context in which they sit. In this way, a critical reoriented construct of risk makes it possible to address this risk as part of a longer, existential reality of being Black in America.

This is what a critical reoriented construct of risk offers us: a way to understand risk as socially constructed, historically constituted, and fully invested in power. When left unfettered and unexamined, traditional risk knowledge can stigmatize, malign, and stymie efforts at creating a more socially just world. But when engaged critically, there is an inspired, yet unguaranteed hope (Bell, 1992; Hall, 1996) that it also can offer an entry

Table 6.4. Outline of Example of Critical Inquiry Project Around Risk and Achievement

Select a student whom you or someone else identified as struggling academically. Over the course of a (semester, month, etc.) you will create a portfolio of work samples and reflective memos that includes work samples that illustrate what the student is doing well and areas of challenge; and a log/journal of your own and others' pedagogical interactions with the student and how the student interacts with other students in the class. You also will include drawings, writings, and other artifacts created by the student that reflect her/his personal views of self as a learner and any other identity that is important to her/him.

Keep a log/journal (daily, weekly) of your pedagogical interactions with the student, as well as how others interact pedagogically with the student. Make note of the kind of interactions, including how the person interacted with the student and how the student responded to the interactions.

Keep a log/journal of how the student interacts with other students in the class. Make a note of the kind and quality of interactions, as well as how the students respond to one another.

Personal Reflection Questions for the Teacher: Critically reflect on and respond to the following questions at the beginning of the project. Come back to these questions as you complete the project.

- Why is this student positioned as at-risk for low achievement? On what evidence was this decision made? Do I agree or disagree with this perspective?
- What are the larger historical, structural, and institutional contexts that surround this student and her/his placement in a category of potential academic risk?
- What role does the student play in this process?
- In what areas is the student exhibiting academic, social, and/ or personal achievement/success/growth?
- What role and responsibility do I hold as the teacher to address the issues presented by the student?
- Is the support needed for the student outside of my capacity as a teacher (candidate) to fulfill?
- How will I enact a critical risk standpoint in this project?
- How will I approach risk from a reoriented perspective?
- How did my responses to these questions impact my view about or work with the student?

Table 6.4. Outline of Example of Critical Inquiry Project Around Risk and Achievement (continued)

Ask the student to write an essay about or draw a picture of things she/he can do well. Across the (month, semester) have the student submit additional writings, drawings, or other artifacts that self-reflect important aspects of her/his identity.

Final Reflection for the Teacher: At the end of the project reflect on your experiences doing this project, including what you learned; whether/how your ideas about risk, achievement, or the student changed; and whether/how the student changed across the time of your work together. Also reflect on how you both adopted a critical risk standpoint and drew from a reoriented construct of risk in the project. What, if anything, did these ideas make possible in your work with the student?

point to a fuller, more complex understanding of the worlds in which we live, and the ones that we ultimately wish to inhabit. The question we are left to ask is: How can we reimagine an education that acknowledges a sociocultural knowledge of risk but that does not label, categorize, or stigmatize students, much like the example of the teacher Jesus and the Samaritan woman that I introduced in the opening chapter? Is this possible? I believe that it is. But putting this into action will require a transformation in our knowledge, standpoint, and practices regarding risk. If this is to occur, we must take knowledge of risk, and in this case the sociocultural knowledge of risk, as a serious matter. I have taken an initial step in this direction by offering up this work. How, then, will you take up this charge?

TOOLS FOR CRITICAL REFLECTION AND PRACTICE

Key Terms

- Critical standpoint of risk
- Critical reorientation to risk
- Types of knowledge informing teacher education and teaching
  - ✓ institutional/professional knowledge
  - ✓ cultural/societal knowledge
  - ✓ background and experiential knowledge

Questions

1. Discuss each of the three broad kinds of knowledge that operate in teacher preparation programs and impact the construction of the teacher. Which of these kinds of knowledge do you think has a powerful impact?

Which of these do you think is less impactful? If you are or are becoming a teacher, which ones resonate with you?

2. Describe how you imagine a teacher might draw from a *critical risk standpoint* in the context of teaching and making judgments about student achievement. What makes this a viable approach for effective teaching? What are the challenges associated with this approach?

3. What are your perspectives on the idea that the construct of risk has an enduring role in how thought and action are organized within the U.S. (Western) world context? What does this mean? What are the implications of this for education policy and practice?

Extended Activity

This chapter introduced several practical ways that teacher education programs and practicing teachers could draw from a *critical risk standpoint* and a *critical reoriented construct of risk*. One way to extend the ideas presented in this chapter is to engage with these activities. See Table 6.3 for a set of reflection questions to use with preservice teachers, inservice teachers, and/or teacher educators. See Table 6.4 for a detailed description of the critical observation study of a student.

Notes

Chapter 1

1. See Chapter 2 for more discussion on the global impact of risk studies in the fields of education and child/youth welfare.

2. *Modernism* refers to a particular temporal context in which specific assumptions about the world, the person, society, and knowledge operate. The belief that the natural world, and later the social world, operated according to patterned and fully knowable laws characterized thinking during this time (Hacking, 1990). Coinciding with the emergence of the social sciences, one of the hallmarks of this episteme (Foucault, 1994; Wynter, 1995) was the belief that social progress was an eventual outcome when using rational thinking and the application of scientific methods to study the problems of society. See Rose (1999) for more discussion on this topic.

Chapter 2

1. The idea of identifying and addressing such factors informs the concept of risk prevention. Risk prevention is a field of study often found in educational psychology and focuses on locating, ameliorating, and/or buffering potential risk factors (Pianta & Walsh, 2013).

2. Lupton (1999a) suggests that Beck "somewhat confusingly sees risk as simultaneously reinforcing positions of inequity and as democratizing, creating a global citizenship" (p. 68).

3. While this research pointed to the presumed low expectations held for student learning by teachers, some of this work has received critique for its own deficit framing of Black teachers as unconcerned about Black students (e.g., see M. Foster's [1993] critique of Rist [1970]).

Chapter 3

1. This conception seems to draw from a Bourdieuian perspective that recognizes a limited form of human agency that exists only in the midst of a larger discursive system that constrains human thought, movement, and possibility. See Bourdieu (1984) for more on this topic.

2. See Snyder et al. (2004) for a detailed, yet selective outline of the history of federal education activities in the United States from 1787 to 2003.

3. Cross (2004) astutely pointed out that even though "the Smith–Hughes Act is considered a landmark as it was the first legislation to provide direct federal program support for schools," the financial investment of this act was "negligible" (p. 2). Cross further stated: "Three years after the Congress enacted Smith–Hughes, the federal government was providing only .3% of support to elementary and secondary education; more than 83% was provided by local funding, the remainder by the states" (p. 2).

4. During the early stages of the Johnson Administration (1964–1968) there was a perception that the United States had experienced "the greatest upward surge of economic well-being in the history of any nation" (Committee on Labor and Public Welfare, 1965, p. 4). According to the State of the Union Address delivered by President Lyndon Johnson on January 4, 1965, the Great Society programs were needed to ensure that all Americans had the opportunity to live in abundance (Committee on Labor and Public Welfare, 1965, p. 5). This was in response to a seeming lack of "public consciousness" concerning "widespread poverty, especially among ethnic minorities in large cities" (Mirón, 1996, p. 28). Mirón suggested one of the primary strategies in designing the Great Society programs was to combine teaching, learning, and legislation to ensure all students had equal educational opportunities. This, it was felt, benefited the students, their families, and the national economy as well.

5. Based on the initial goals developed by U.S. governors at the 1989 Education Summit, the emphasis on standards, achievement, and accountability became intimately connected with and fully integrated into federal policy during the Clinton Administration. Interestingly, Clinton took a lead role in the development of these goals during his tenure as governor of Arkansas (Vinovskis, 1999).

6. This statement is not meant to suggest that the idea of education standards is novel and first emerged during the late 20th century in U.S. federal education policy. Clearly, recommendations for set learning expectations were a part of conversations during the late 19th and early 20th centuries around secondary schooling in the United States (e.g., Committee of Ten, Cardinal Principles of Education). See Tyack & Cuban (1995) for more discussion on this topic.

Chapter 4

1. Pseudonyms were used for the names of participants, locales, schools/institutions and programs to maintain anonymity.

2. I do not provide the citation for this material in order to maintain the anonymity of the participants.

3. Millside is a large city that sits 72 miles east of Lakeville. Millside has the largest population in its state—554,965. According to the 2000 Census (Demographic Services Center, n.d.), 37.34% of the population is African American, and, among some, it has been dubbed "the most segregated city in America" (I do not provide the citation in order to protect the anonymity of the participants).

4. Here, Marisol was referring to schools located in suburban areas as well as those that are technically deemed urban but that do not have the kinds of challenges typically associated with urban schools. Marisol believed that Lakeville schools fell in the latter of these two categories.

5. Here I think Samantha was indirectly letting me know that she did not want to work in the Millside Public Schools, an urban school context very close to her home neighborhood. It is not uncommon for student teachers (both those placed in Millside and those who are not) to criticize the district's use of Direct Instruction—an instructional program that relies on highly scripted lessons.

6. Risk is discussed in at least two other ways, both of which refer to student-initiated behaviors. The first way is a positive attribute—one that is necessary in order to progress academically. It refers to the belief that students must be academic "risk takers" in order to push their learning to the highest capacity (Ramos & Lambating, 1996). The second way the signifier of risk is discussed is as a social problem, one that very often is related to low academic achievement, but that could feasibly exist in spite of academic success. This type of risk falls in the category of risky or negative risk-taking behaviors presumed to have an adverse effect on students, such as drug and alcohol abuse and sexual promiscuity (Dryfoos, 1990; Raffaelli & Crockett, 2003; Rolison & Scherman, 2002). In this study, I focused on the signifier of risk (and the category of the at-risk student) as related to concerns with academic achievement and student learning.

7. These data were generated from questions that examined the characteristics and circumstances the preservice teachers thought made some students at-risk for low academic achievement. I recognized the controversial nature of the term *at-risk* and I wanted to get at the underlying signifier of risk that undergirded (and historically has undergirded) educational concerns around low academic achievement in the United States. To do this, I asked two different questions. One, I asked early in the interview, did not use the term risk. The second came later in the interview after I had first asked the respondents whether they were familiar with the term *at-risk*. Both questions were similar in nature, focusing on whether the participant believed that some students were (1) at-risk for low achievement (a question

directly using the term at-risk) or (2) more likely than their peers to experience low achievement (a question that asked about at-riskness without using the specific term). By taking this approach, I was able to explore not only how the preservice teachers thought about the signifier of risk (which is embedded in concerns with and approaches to low academic achievement), but also how they understood the category of the at-risk student, and to distinguish between candidates' responses.

8. When using the phrase "nonspecified, generalized grade-level expectations," I am referring to the expectations that the preservice teachers held that were not associated with formal learning standards sanctioned by the school, district, or state. The candidates discussed these expectations as if they were commonly held knowledge that was fully recognizable by others and thus did not require any explanation or justification on their part.

Chapter 5

1. I looked at the reported data for 2004 because it corresponded with the testing period immediately following my fieldwork in the school (Spring 2004). Note that all of the information I present about student performance data at Green Mounds Elementary was either summarized or directly quoted from published materials provided by the school in its annual report or housed on its state department of instruction website. In order to protect the anonymity of the school, district, and participants, I have not included citation or reference material that would identify the location of the state, district, or school.

2. See Chapter 4 for a discussion of Janice's "ontological dilemma" related to academic achievement issues and potential teacher bias and mismatch.

3. When discussing the findings in this section, I am referring to the responses provided by Dylan, Isabelle, and Julia. Due to the semi-structured nature of the interview protocol, I realized after looking at the interview transcripts that I did not ask Zoë whether she recognized the term *at-risk*. She did, however, talk about the at-risk student at other points in the interview. I also did not ask Dylan, Zoë, or Julia about the two other popular terms used to refer to what some consider "at-risk" students, including *at-promise* and *resilient*.

4. As with data presented in Chapter 4 on the preservice teachers, these data were generated from questions that examined the characteristics and circumstances the inservice teachers thought made some students at-risk for low academic achievement. Prior to asking these questions, I asked whether they were aware of the term *at-risk* and if they believed that some students were in fact at-risk.

5. As pointed out in Chapter 4, I used the phrase "nonspecified, generalized grade-level expectations" to refer to expectations that the preservice teachers held that were not associated with formal learning standards sanctioned by the school, district, or state. Similar to the preservice teacher candidates, the inservice teachers discussed these expectations as if they were commonly held knowledge that was fully recognizable by others and thus did not require any explanation or justification.

6. While it is not clear whether Dylan was correct in his assessment of what actually was going on in the home of this student, what is interesting is the way he read the situation and then accounted for why the student was not successful.

Chapter 6

1. The term *personal* is a bit misleading in that it gives the impression that what a "person" experiences is separate and distinct from what another "person" experiences. Indeed, how people make sense of what they go through and feel about a situation is situated in larger societal frames of reference that assist people in reading and, later, responding to the events of their life. See Scott (1992) for more on this perspective of experience.

References

Addams, J. (1911). *Twenty years at Hull-House*. New York, NY: Macmillan.

Anthony, E. J., & Cohler, B. J. (Eds.). (1987). *The invulnerable child*. New York, NY: Guilford Press.

Anyon, J. (1980). Social class and the hidden curriculum of work. *Journal of Education, 162*(1), 67–92.

Apple, M. W. (2004). *Ideology and curriculum* (2nd ed.). New York, NY: Routledge.

Apple, M. W. (2014). *Official knowledge: Democratic education in a conservative age* (3rd ed.). New York, NY: Routledge.

Artiles, A. J., Kozleski, E. B., Trent, S. C., Osher, D., & Ortiz, A. (2010). Justifying and explaining disproportionality, 1968–2008: A critique of underlying views of culture. *Exceptional Children, 76*(3), 279–299.

Artiles, A. J., & Trent, S. C. (1994). Overrepresentation of minority students in special education: A continuing debate. *The Journal of Special Education, 27*(4), 410–437.

Ayers, W. (2001). *To teach: The journey of a teacher* (2nd ed.). New York, NY: Teachers College Press.

Baldridge, B. J. (2014). Relocating the deficit: Reimagining Black youth in neoliberal times. *American Educational Research Journal, 51*(3), 440-472. doi:0002831214532514

Ball, S. J. (1993). What is policy? Texts, trajectories and toolboxes. *Discourse, 13*(2), 10–17.

Banks, C., & Banks, J. (1995). Equity pedagogy: An essential component of multicultural education. *Theory Into Practice, 34*(3), 152–158.

Banks, J. A. (1988). Ethnicity, class, cognitive, and motivational styles: Research and teaching implications. *Journal of Negro Education, 57*(4), 452–466.

Banks, J. A. (1993). Multicultural education: Historical development, dimensions, and practice. *Review of Research in Education, 19*, 3–49.

Banks, J. A. (2004). Multicultural education: Historical development, dimensions, and practice. In J. A. Banks & C. M. Banks (Eds.), *Handbook of research on multicultural education* (2nd ed., pp. 3–29). San Francisco, CA: Jossey-Bass.

Baratz, S. S., & Baratz, J. C. (1970). Early childhood intervention: The social science base of institutional racism. *Harvard Educational Review, 40*, 29–50.

Barnes, C. B. (2003). Managing risks in schools. *Independent Schools, 62*(3), 82–93.

Bell, D. A. (1979). *Brown v. Board of Education* and the interest-convergence dilemma. *Harvard Law Review, 93*, 518–533.

Bell, D. A. (1992). Faces at the bottom of the well: The permanence of racism. New York, NY: Basic Books.

Bermak, F., Chung, R. C., & Siroskey-Sabdo, L. A. (2005). Empowerment groups for academic success: An innovative approach to prevent high school failure for at-risk, urban African Americans. *Professional School Counseling, 8*(5), 377–389.

Betz, T. (2014). Risks in early childhood: Reconstructing notions of risk in political reports on children and childhood in Germany. *Child Indicators Research, 7*(4), 769–786.

Bialostok, S. (2012). "Have a go at it": Embracing risks and teaching in late modern capitalism. In S. Bialostok, R. L. Whitman, & W. S. Bradley (Eds.), *Education in the risk society: Theories, discourse and risk identities in education contexts* (pp. 75–96). Rotterdam, Netherlands: Sense Publishers.

Bialostok, S., & Whitman, R. L. (2012). Education and the risk society: An introduction. In S. Bialostok, R. L. Whitman, & W. S. Bradley (Eds.), *Education in the risk society: Theories, discourse and risk identities in education contexts* (pp. 1–34). Rotterdam, Netherlands: Sense Publishers.

Biddle, B. J., & Berliner, D. C. (2003). *What research says about unequal funding for schools in America.* San Francisco, CA: WestEd.

Blanchett, W. J. (2006). Disproportionate representation of African American students in special education: Acknowledging the role of White privilege and racism. *Educational Researcher, 35*(6), 24–28.

Blascoer, F. (1915). *Colored school children in New York.* New York, NY: Public Education Association of the City of New York.

Bonilla-Silva, E., & Zuberi, T. (2008). Toward a definition of White logic and White methods. In T. Zuberi & E. Bonilla-Silva (Eds.), *White logic, White methods: Racism and methodology* (pp. 3–27). Lanham, MD: Rowman & Littlefield.

Bourdieu, P. (1977). *Outline of a theory of practice.* New York, NY: Cambridge University Press.

Bourdieu, P. (1984). *Distinction: A social critique of the judgment of taste* (P. Nice, Trans.). London, UK: Routledge & Kegan Paul.

Bourdieu, P. (1986). The forms of capital. In J. G. Richardson (Ed.), *Handbook of theory and research for the sociology of education* (pp. 241–258). New York, NY: Greenwood.

Bourdieu, P., & Passeron, J. (1977). *Reproduction in education, society and culture.* Beverley Hills, CA: Sage.

Bowles, S., & Gintis, H. (1976). *Schooling in capitalist America: Educational reform and the contradictions of economic life.* New York, NY: Basic Books.

Boykin, A. W. (1978). Psychological/behavioral verve in academic/task performance: Pre-theoretical considerations. *Journal of Negro Education, 47*(4), 343–354.

Boykin, A. W. (2000). The talent development model of schooling: Placing students at-promise for academic success. *Journal of Education for Students Placed At Risk, 5,* 3–25.

Britzman, D. (2003). *Practice makes practice: A critical study of learning to teach.* Albany, NY: State University of New York Press.

Brown, K. D. (2012). Trouble on my mind: Toward a framework of humanizing critical sociocultural knowledge for teaching and teacher education. *Race, Ethnicity and Education, 16*(3), 316–338.

Brown, K. D., & Goldstein, L. (2013). Preservice teachers' understandings of competing notions of academic achievement co-existing in post-NCLB public schools. *Teachers College Record, 115*(1), 1–37.

Bruce, G., & Phelan, J. C. (2001). Conceptualizing stigma. *Annual Review of Sociology, 27*(1), 363–385.

Burbules, N. (2004). Jesus as teacher. In H. Alexander (Ed.), *Spirituality and ethics in education: Philosophical, theological, and radical perspectives* (pp. 7–20). Brighton, UK: Sussex Academic Press.

Burke, K. J., & Segall, A. (2015). Teaching as Jesus making: The hidden curriculum of Christ in schooling. *Teachers College Record, 117*(3), 1–27.

Carey, R. L. (2014). A cultural analysis of the achievement gap discourse challenging the language and labels used in the work of school reform. *Urban Education, 49*(4), 440–468.

Carter, P. L. (2006). Straddling boundaries: Identity, culture, and school. *Sociology of Education, 79*(4), 304–328.

Casanova, U. (1990). Rashomon in the classroom: Multiple perspectives of teachers, parents, and students. In A. Barona & E. Garcia (Eds.), *Children at-risk: Poverty, minority status, and other issues in educational equity* (pp. 135–149). Washington, DC: National Association of School Psychologists.

Cicchetti, D. (1990). A historical perspective on the discipline of developmental psychopathology. In J. Rolf, A. S. Masten, D. Cicchetti, K. H. Nuechterlein, & S. Weintraub (Eds.), *Risk and protective factors in the development of psychopathology* (pp. 2–28). Cambridge, UK: Cambridge University Press.

Clark, D. L., & Astuto, T. A. (1986). The significance and permanence of changes in federal education policy. *Educational Researcher, 15*(8), 4–13.

Clark, K. (1965). *Dark ghetto: Dilemmas of social power.* Hanover, NH: University Press of New England.

Clark, K. B., Deutsch, M., Gartner, A., Keppel, F., Lewis, H., Pettigrew, . . . Riessman, F. (1972). *The educationally deprived: The potential for change.* New York, NY: Metropolitan Applied Research Center.

Clark, K. B., & Plotkin, L. (1972). A review of the issues and literature of cultural deprivation theory. In K. B. Clark, M. Deutsch, A. Gartner, F. Keppel,

H. Lewis, T. Pettigrew, . . . F. Riessman (Eds.), *The educationally deprived: The potential for change* (pp. 47–73). New York, NY: Metropolitan Applied Research Center.

Cochran-Smith, M., & Zeichner, K. (Eds.). (2005). *Studying teacher education.* Mahwah, NJ: Erlbaum.

Cohen, L., Manion, L. & Morrison, K. (2000). *Research methods in education* (5th ed.). London, UK: Routledge Falmer.

Committee on Labor and Public Welfare. (1965). *Elementary and Secondary Education Act of 1965.* Washington, DC: U.S. Government Printing Office.

Cross, C. (2004). *Political education: National policy comes of age.* New York, NY: Teachers College Press.

Cuban, L. (1989). The "at-risk" label and the problem of urban school reform. *Phi Delta Kappan, 70*(10), 780–784, 799–801.

Darling-Hammond, L., & Bransford, J. (Eds.). (2005). *Preparing teachers for a changing world: What teachers should learn and be able to do.* San Francisco, CA: Jossey-Bass.

DeBray, E. H. (2006). *Politics, ideology, and education: Federal policy during the Clinton and Bush administrations.* New York, NY: Teachers College Press.

Degler, C. N. (1991). *In search of human nature: The decline and revival of Darwinism in American social thought.* New York, NY: Oxford University Press.

Dekker, J. J. (2009). Children at-risk in history: A story of expansion. *Paedagogica Historica, 45*(1–2), 17–36.

Delpit, L., & Dowdy, J. K. (Eds.). (2002). *The skin that we speak.* New York, NY: The New Press.

Demographic Services Center (n.d.). Available at http://www.doa.state.wi.us/demographic/mcdonly.asp

Derrida, J. (1976). *Of grammatology.* G. C. Spivak (Trans.). Baltimore, MD & London, UK: Johns Hopkins University Press.

Deschenes, S., Tyack, D., & Cuban, L. (2001). Mismatch: Historical perspectives on schools and students who don't fit them. *Teachers College Record, 103*(4), 525–547.

Deutsch, M. (1967). Some psychosocial aspects of learning in the disadvantaged. In M. Deutsch (Ed.), *The disadvantaged child* (pp. 31–38). New York, NY: Basic Books.

Dixson, A. D., & Rousseau, C. K. (2006). *Critical race theory in education: All God's children got a song.* New York, NY: Routledge.

Donnor, J. K. (2005). African-American football student athletes in major college sports. *Race, Ethnicity and Education, 8*(1), 45–67.

Dryfoos, J. (1990). *Adolescents at-risk: Prevalence and prevention.* New York, NY: Oxford University Press.

Du Bois, W.E.B. (1994). *The souls of Black folk*. New York, NY: Dover.

Dumas, M. J. (2015). Against the dark: Antiblackness in education policy and discourse. *Theory Into Practice, 55,* 1–10.

Duncan-Andrade, J.M.R., & Morrell, E. (2008). *The art of critical pedagogy: Possibilities for moving from theory to practice in urban schools*. New York, NY: Peter Lang.

Edwards, P. A., Danridge, J. C., & Pleasants, H. M. (2000). *Exploring urban teachers' and administrators' conceptions of at-riskness* (Ciera Report No. 2-010). Ann Arbor, MI: Center for the Improvement of Early Reading Achievement.

Elmore, R. F., & McLaughlin, M. W. (1983). The federal role in education: Learning from experience. *Education and Urban Society, 15*(3), 309–330.

Emoungu, P. A. (1979). Socioeducational ideologies of black education. *Journal of Negro Education, 48*(1), 43–56

Ewald, F. (1991). Insurance and risk. In G. Burchell, C. Gordon, & P. Miller (Eds.), *The Foucault effect: Studies in governmentality* (pp. 197–210). Chicago, IL: University of Chicago Press.

Executive Office of the President. (2015). *Every Student Succeeds Act: A Progress Report on Elementary and Secondary Education*. Available at www.whitehouse.gov/sites/whitehouse.gov/files/documents/ESSA_Progress_Report.pdf

Fanon, F. (2007). *The wretched of the earth*. New York, NY: Grove Press.

Ferguson, A. A. (2001). *Bad boys: Public schools in the making of Black masculinity*. Ann Arbor: University of Michigan Press.

Fine, M. (1993). Making controversy: Who's "at-risk"? In R. L. Wollons (Ed.), *Children at Risk in America* (pp. 91–110). Albany, NY: State University of New York Press.

Fordham, S., & Ogbu, J. U. (1986). Black students' school success: Coping with the "burden of 'acting white.'" *The Urban Review, 18*(3), 176–206.

Foster, K. M. (2004). Coming to terms: A discussion of John Ogbu's cultural-ecological theory of minority academic achievement. *Intercultural Education, 15*(4), 369–384.

Foster, M. (1993). Educating for competence in community and culture: Exploring the views of exemplary African-American teachers. *Urban Education, 27*(4), 370–394.

Foucault, M. (1980). *The history of sexuality: Vol. 1. An introduction*. New York, NY: Vintage Books.

Foucault, M. (1983). Afterword: The subject and power. In H. L. Dreyfus & P. Rabinow (Eds.), *Michel Foucault: Beyond structuralism and hermeneutics* (2nd ed., pp. 208–226). Chicago, IL: University of Chicago Press.

Foucault, M. (1991). Governmentality. In G. Burchell, C. Gordon, & P. Miller (Eds.), *The Foucault effect: Studies in governmentality* (pp. 87–104). Chicago, IL: University of Chicago Press.

Foucault, M. (1994). *The order of things: An archaeology of the human sciences*. New York, NY: Vintage Books.

Fox, N. J. (1999). Postmodern reflections on "risk", "hazards" and life choices. In D. Lupton (Ed.), *Risk and sociocultural theory: New directions and perspectives* (pp. 12–33). Cambridge, UK: Cambridge University Press.

Franklin, B. M. (1994). *From "backwardness" to "at-risk": Childhood learning difficulties and the contradictions of school reform*. Albany: State University of New York Press.

Freire, P. (2000). *Pedagogy of the oppressed* (M. B. Ramos, Trans.). New York, NY: Bloomsbury.

Frost, L. (1994). At risk statutes—defining deviance and suppressing difference in the public schools. *Journal of Law & Education, 23*(2), 123–165.

Fryer Jr,, R. G., & Levitt, S. D. (2004). Understanding the black–white test score gap in the first two years of school. *Review of Economics and Statistics, 86*(2), 447–464.

Fryer, R. G. & Torelli, P. (2010). An empirical analysis of "acting white'. *Journal of Public Economics, 94*(5), 380–396.

Frymier, J., & Gansneder, B. (1989). The Phi Delta Kappa study of students at-risk. *Phi Delta Kappan, 71*(2), 142–151.

Gadsden, V. L., Davis, J. E., & Artiles, A. (2009). Risk, schooling, and equity. *Review of Research in Education, 33*.

Garmezy, N. (1983). Stressors of childhood. In N. Garmezy & M. Rutter (Eds.), *Stress, coping, and development in children* (pp. 43–84). Baltimore, MD: Johns Hopkins University Press.

Gay, G. (1979). On behalf of children: A curriculum design for multicultural education in the elementary school. *Journal of Negro Education, 48*(3), 324–340.

Gay, G. (2010). *Culturally responsive teaching: Theory, research, and practice* (2nd ed.). New York, NY: Teachers College Press.

Geertz, C. (1973). *The interpretation of cultures*. New York, NY: Basic Books.

Gershon, W. S. (2012). Troubling notions of risk: Dissensus, dissonance, and making sense of students and learning. *Critical Studies in Education, 53*(3), 361–373.

Ginsberg, A. E. (2012). *Embracing risk in urban education: Curiosity, creativity, and courage in the era of "no excuses" and relay race reform*. Lanham, MD: Rowman & Littlefield.

Gleason, P., & Dynarski, M. (2002). Do we know whom to serve? Issues in using risk factors to identify dropouts. *Journal of Education for Students Placed at Risk, 7*(1), 25–41.

Goals 2000: Educate America Act, Sec. 2, Purpose. (1994). Available at www2. ed.gov/legislation/GOALS2000/TheAct/index.html

Goals 2000: Educate America Act, National Education Goals, Sec. 102 (1994). Available at http://www.ed.gov/legislation/GOALS2000/TheAct/sec102. html

Goldsby, J. (2006). *A spectacular secret: Lynching in American life and literature*. Chicago, IL: University of Chicago Press.

Gonzáles, G. G. (1999). Segregation and the education of Mexican children, 1900-1940. In J. F. Moreno (Ed.), *The elusive quest for equality: 150 years of Chicano/Chicana education*. (pp. 53–76). Cambridge, MA: Harvard Educational Review.

Gordon, L. (2006). African-American philosophy, race, and the geography of reason. In L. Gordon and J.A. Gordon (Eds.), *Not only the master's tools: African-American studies in theory and practice*. Philadelphia, PA: Temple University Press.

Gould, S. J. (1996). *The mismeasure of man*. New York, NY: Norton.

Gouldner, H. (1978). *Teachers' pets, troublemakers, and nobodies: Black children in elementary school*. Westport, CT: Greenwood.

Grant, C. A. (1979). Education that is multicultural as a change agent: Organizing for effectiveness. *Journal of Negro Education, 48*(3), 431–446.

Grant, C. A., Brown, K. D., & Brown, A. L. (2016). *Black intellectual thought in education: The missing traditions of Anna Julia Cooper, Carter G. Woodson, and Alain LeRoy Locke*. New York, NY: Routledge.

Grant, C. A., & Sleeter, C. A. (1986). Educational equity: Education that is multicultural and social reconstructionist. *Journal of Equity and Leadership, 6*(2), 106–124.

Green, J. (2009). Is it time for the sociology of health to abandon "risk"? *Health, Risk and Society, 11*(6), 493–508.

Hacking, I. (1990). *The taming of chance*. Cambridge, UK: Cambridge University Press.

Hacking, I. (2002). *Historical ontology*. Cambridge, MA: Harvard University Press.

Hackman, D. A., Farah, M. J., & Meaney, M. J. (2010). Socioeconomic status and the brain: Mechanistic insights from human and animal research. *Nature Reviews: Neuroscience, 11*(9), 651–659.

Hale-Benson, J. (1982) *Black children: Their roots, culture, and learning styles*. Baltimore, MD: John Hopkins University Press.

Hall, S. (1996). The problem of ideology: Marxism without guarantees. In D. Morley & K. Chen (Eds.), *Stuart Hall: Critical dialogues in cultural studies* (pp. 223–237). New York, NY: Routledge.

Harris, C. I. (1993). Whiteness as property. *Harvard Law Review, 106*(8), 1710–1791.

Hattie, J. (2008). *Visible learning: A synthesis of over 800 meta-analyses relating to achievement*. New York, NY: Routledge.

Haycock, K. (2001). Helping all students achieve: Closing the achievement gap. *Educational Leadership, 58*(6), 6–11.

Heath, S. B. (1983). *Ways with words: Language, life, and work in communities and classrooms*. New York, NY: Cambridge University Press.

Herrnstein, R. J., & Murray, C. (1994). *The bell curve: Intelligence and class structure in America.* New York, NY: Free Press.

Howard, S., Dryden, J., & Johnson, B. (1999). Childhood resilience: Review and critique of literature. *Oxford Review of Education, 25*(3), 307–323.

Howard, S., & Johnson, B. (2000). What makes the difference? Children and teachers talk about resilient outcomes for children "at-risk." *Educational Studies, 26*(3), 321–337.

Hughes, N. (2011). Young people 'as risk' or young people 'at-risk': Comparing discourses of anti-social behaviour in England and Victoria. *Critical Social Policy, 31*(3), 388–409.

Irvine, J. J. (1990). *Black students and school failure: Policies, practices, and prescriptions.* New York, NY: Greenwood Press.

Irvine, J. J. (2003). *Educating teachers for diversity: Seeing with a cultural eye.* New York, NY: Teachers College Press.

Jagers, R. J., & Carroll, G. (2002). Issues in educating African American children and youth. In S. Stringfield & D. Land (Eds.), *Educating at-risk students: One hundred-first yearbook of the National Society for the Study of Education, Part II* (pp. 49–65). Chicago, IL: University of Chicago Press.

James, C. E. (2011). Students "at-risk": Stereotypes and the schooling of Black boys. *Urban Education, 47*(2), 464–494.

Janda, K. (n.d.). Politxt: State of the union addresses.

Jensen, A. R. (1969). How much can we boost IQ and scholastic achievement? *Harvard Educational Review, 39*(1), 112–123.

Kaestle, C. F. (1973). *The evolution of an urban school system: New York City, 1750–1850.* Cambridge, MA: Harvard University Press.

Kaestle, C. F., & Smith, M. S. (1982). The federal role in elementary and secondary education, 1940–1980. *Harvard Educational Review, 52*(4), 384–418.

Kagan, J. (1998). Biology and the child. In W. Damon & N. Eisenberg (Eds.), *Handbook of child psychology: Vol. 3. Social, emotional, and personality development* (5th ed., pp. 177–235). New York, NY: Wiley.

Kantor, H., & Brenzel, B. (1992). Urban education and the "truly disadvantaged": The historical roots of the contemporary crisis, 1945–1990. *Teachers College Record, 94*(2), 278–314.

Kaplan, S. (2006). *The pedagogical state: Education and the politics of national culture in post-1980 Turkey.* Palo Alto, CA: Stanford University Press.

Keller, M. N. (1998). Jesus the teacher. *Journal of Research on Christian Education, 7*(1), 19–36.

Ladson-Billings, G. (2006). From the achievement gap to the education debt: Understanding achievement in U.S. schools. *Educational Researcher, 35*(7), 3–12.

Ladson-Billings, G. (2009). *The dreamkeepers: Successful teachers of African-American children* (2nd ed.). San Francisco, CA: Jossey-Bass.

Ladson-Billings, G., & Tate, W. F., IV. (1995). Toward a critical race theory of education. *Teachers College Record, 97*(1), 47–68.

Lagemann, E. C. (2000). *An elusive science: The troubling history of education research*. Chicago, IL: University of Chicago Press.

Land, D., & Legters, N. (2002). The extent and consequences of risk in U.S. education. In S. Stringfield & D. Land (Eds.), *Educating at-risk students: One hundred-first yearbook of the National Society for the Study of Education, Part II* (pp.1–28). Chicago, IL: University of Chicago Press.

Lewis, O. (1963). The culture of poverty. *trans-action, 1*(1), 17–19.

Lipman, P. (1995). "Bringing out the best in them": The contribution of culturally relevant teachers to educational reform. *Theory Into Practice, 34*(3), 202–208.

Lipman, P. (2011). *The new political economy of urban education: Neoliberalism, race, and the right to the city*. New York, NY: Routledge.

Locke, A. (1989). Cultural relativism and ideological peace. In L. Harris (Ed.), *The philosophy of Alain Locke: Harlem Renaissance and beyond* (pp. 69–78). Philadelphia, PA: Temple University Press.

Lohmann, I., & Mayer, C. (2009). Lessons from the history of education for a "century of the child at-risk." *Paedagogica Historica, 45*(1–2), 1–16.

Loretan, J. O., & Umans, S. (1966). *Teaching the disadvantaged: New curriculum approaches*. New York, NY: Teachers College Press.

Lortie, D. J. (2002). *Schoolteacher: A sociological analysis* (2nd ed.). Chicago, IL: University of Chicago Press.

Lubeck, S., & Garrett, P. (1990). The social construction of the 'at-risk' child. *British Journal of Sociology of Education, 11*(3), 327–341.

Luhmann, N. (1993). *Risk: A sociological theory* (R. Barrett, Trans.). Berlin, Germany: Walter de Gruyter. (Original work published 1991)

Lunenberg, M., & Korthagen, F. (2009). Experience, theory, and practical wisdom in teaching and teacher education. *Teachers and Teaching: Theory and Practice, 15*(2), 225–240.

Lupton, D. (Ed.). (1999a). *Risk*. London, UK: Routledge.

Lupton, D. (Ed.). (1999b). *Risk and sociocultural theory*. Cambridge, UK: Cambridge University Press.

Lupton, D., & Tulloch, J. (2002). "Risk is part of your life": Risk epistemologies among a group of Australians. *Sociology, 36*(2), 317–334.

Luthar, S. S., Cicchetti, D., & Becker, B. (2000). The construct of resilience: A critical evaluation and guidelines for future work. *Child Development, 71*(3), 543–562.

Marable, M. (2000). *How capitalism underdeveloped Black America: Problems in race, political economy, and society*. New York, NY: South End Press.

Marcus, G. E. (1995). Ethnography in/of the world system: The emergence of multi-site ethnography. *Annual Review of Anthropology, 24*, 95–117.

Martinez, S., & Rury, J. L. (2012). From "culturally deprived" to "at-risk": The politics of popular expression and educational inequality in the United States, 1960–1985. *Teachers College Record, 114*(6), 1–31.

McDermott, R., Goldman, S., & Varenne, H. (2006). The cultural work of learning disabilities. *Educational Researcher, 35*(6), 12–17.

McDonnell, L. M. (2005). No Child Left Behind and the federal role in education: Evolution or revolution? *Peabody Journal of Education, 80*(2), 19–38.

McGee, E. O. (2013). Threatened and placed at-risk: High achieving African American males in urban high schools. *The Urban Review, 45*(4), 448–471.

McWhirter, J., McWhirter, B., McWhirter, E., & McWhirter, R. (2012). *At risk youth*. New York, NY: Cengage Learning.

Menchaca, M. (1997). Early racist discourses: Roots of deficit thinking. In R. R. Valencia (Ed.), *The evolution of deficit thinking: Educational thought and practice* (pp. 13–40). London, UK: Falmer.

Milner, H. R. (2003). Reflection, racial competence, and critical pedagogy: How do we prepare preservice teachers to pose tough questions? *Race, Ethnicity, and Education, 6*(2), 193–208.

Milner, H. R. (2010). What does teaching education have to do with teaching? Implications for diversity studies. *Journal of Teacher Education, 61*(1–2), 118–131.

Milner, H. R. (2012). Beyond a test score: Explaining opportunity gaps in educational practice. *Journal of Black Studies*. doi:0021934712442539

Mirón, L. (1996). *The social construction of urban schooling: Situating the crisis*. Cresskill, NJ: Hampton Press.

Moll, L. C., Armanti, C., Neff, D., & Gonzalez, N. (1992). Funds of knowledge for teaching: Using a qualitative approach to connect homes and classrooms. *Theory Into Practice, 31*(2), 132–141.

Mueller, J., & O'Connor, C. (2008). Telling and retelling about self and "others": How preservice teachers (re)interpret privilege and disadvantage in one college classroom. *Teaching and Teacher Education, 23*(6), 840–856.

Musick, J. S., Stott, F. M., Spencer, K. K., Goldman, J., & Cohler, B. J. (1987). Maternal factors related to vulnerability and resiliency in young children at-risk. In E. J. Anthony & B. J. Cohler (Eds.), *The invulnerable child* (pp. 229–252). New York, NY: Guilford Press.

A Nation at Risk. (1983). Available at www.ed.gov/pubs/NatAtRisk/risk.html

Natriello, G., McDill, E. L., & Pallas, A. M. (1990). *Schooling disadvantaged children: Racing against catastrophe*. New York, NY: Teachers College Press.

Nespor, J. (1997). *Tangled up in school: Politics, space, bodies, and signs in the educational process*. Mahwah, NJ: Erlbaum.

Nettles, S. M., & Robinson, F. P. (1998). *Exploring the dynamics of resilience in an elementary school* (Rep. No. 26). Baltimore, MD: Johns Hopkins University, Center for Research on the Education of Students Placed At Risk.

Noguera, P. (2003). *City schools and the American dream: Reclaiming the promise of public education*. New York, NY: Teachers College Press.

Oakes, J. (2005). *Keeping track: How schools structure inequality* (2nd ed.). New Haven, CT: Yale University Press.

O'Connor, A. (2001). *Poverty knowledge: Social science, social policy, and the poor in twentieth-century U.S. history*. Princeton, NJ: Princeton University Press.

Ogbu, J. (1978). *Minority education and caste: The American educational system in cross-cultural perspective*. New York, NY: Academic Press.

Osgood, R. L. (1997). Undermining the common school ideal: Intermediate schools and ungraded classes in Boston, 1838–1900. *History of Education Quarterly, 37*(4), 375–398.

Parsons, W. (1895). The story of the Fresh Air Fund. In R. Woods (Ed.), *Poverty U.S.A.: The historical record* (pp. 131–150). New York, NY: Arno Press.

Pearl, A. (1997). Cultural and accumulated environmental deficit models. In R. R. Valencia (Ed.), *The evolution of deficit thinking: Educational thought and practice* (pp. 132–159). London, UK: Falmer.

Perry, I. (2011). *More beautiful and more terrible: The embrace and transcendence of racial inequality in the United States*. New York, NY: New York University Press.

Perry, M. (1914, May). Retardation in the public schools. *The School Journal, 7*, 211–213.

Pianta, R. C., & Walsh, D. J. (1996). *High-risk children in schools: Constructing sustaining relationships*. New York, NY: Routledge.

Picower, B. (2012). *Practice what you teach: Social justice education in the classroom and the streets*. New York, NY: Routledge.

Placier, M. L. (1993). The semantics of state policy making: The case of "at-risk." *Educational Evaluation and Policy Analysis, 15*(4), 380–395.

Placier, M. (1996). The cycle of student labels in education: The cases of culturally deprived/disadvantaged and at-risk. *Education Administration Quarterly, 32*(2), 236–256.

Plomin, R. (1989). Environment and genes: Determinants of behavior. *American Psychologist, 44*(2), 105–111.

Plomin, R., DeFries, J. C., Knopik, V. S., & Neiderheiser, J. (2013). *Behavioral genetics*. New York, NY: Palgrave Macmillan.

Plomin, R., & Rutter, M. (1998). Child development, molecular genetics, and what to do with genes once they are found. *Child Development, 69*(4), 1223–1242.

Pollock, M. (2008). From shallow to deep: Toward a thorough cultural analysis of school achievement patterns. *Anthropology & Education Quarterly, 39*(4), 369–380.

Pollock, M. (2009). *Colormute: Race talk dilemmas in an American school*. Princeton, NJ: Princeton University Press.

Popkewitz, T. (1998). *Struggling for the soul: The politics of schooling and the construction of the teacher*. New York, NY: Teachers College Press.

Presseisen, B. (1988). Teaching, thinking, and at-risk students: Defining a population. In B. Presseisen (Ed.), *At-risk students and thinking: Perspectives from research* (pp. 19–37). Washington, DC: National Education Association.

Raffaelli, M., & Crockett, J. (2003). Sexual risk taking in adolescence: The role of self-regulation and attraction to risk. *Developmental Psychology, 39*(6), 1036–1046.

Ramos, I., & Lambating, J. (1996). Risk taking: Gender differences and educational opportunity. *School Science and Mathematics, 96,* 94–98.

Richardson, V., Casanova, U., Placier, P., & Guilfoyle, K. (1989). *School children at-risk*. London, UK: Falmer.

Richman, J. (1906). The incorrigible child. *Educational Review, 31,* 484–506.

Riele, K. T. (2006). Youth "at-risk": Further marginalizing the marginalized? *Journal of Education Policy, 21*(2), 129–145.

Riessman, F. (1962). *The culturally deprived child.* New York, NY: Harper & Row.

Riis, J. (1895). The children of the poor. In R. Woods (Ed.), *Poverty U.S.A.: The historical record* (pp.86–130). New York, NY: Arno Press.

Rist, R. (1970). Student social class and teacher expectations: The self-fulfilling prophecy in ghetto education. *Harvard Educational Review, 40*(3), 411–442.

Roets, G., Rutten, K., Roose, R., Vandekinderen, C., & Soetaert, R. (2015). Constructing the "child at-risk" in social work reports: A way of seeing is a way of not seeing. *Children & Society, 29*(3), 198–208.

Rolison, M. R., & Scherman, A. (2002). Factors influencing adolescents' decisions to engage in risk-taking behavior. *Adolescence, 37,* 585–596.

Rose, N. (1999). *Powers of freedom: Reframing political thought.* Cambridge, UK: Cambridge University Press.

Rouse, J. (1984). The legacy of community organizing: Lugenia Burns Hope and the Neighborhood Union. *Journal of Negro Education, 69*(3/4), 114–133.

Rousmaniere, K. (1997). *City teachers: Teaching and school reform in historical perspective.* New York, NY: Teachers College Press.

Rutter, M. (1979). Protective factors in children's responses to stress and disadvantage. In M. W. Kent & J. E. Rolf (Eds.), *Primary prevention of psychopathology* (pp. 49–74). Hanover, NH: University Press of New England.

Rutter, M. (1987). Psychosocial resilience and protective mechanisms. *American Journal of Orthopsychiatry, 57*(3), 316–331.

Sameroff, A. J., Seifer, R., Baldwin, A., & Baldwin, C. (1993). Stability of intelligence from preschool to adolescence: The influence of social and family risk factors. *Child Development, 64*(1), 80–97.

San Miguel, G. S., Jr., & Valencia, R. (1998). From the Treaty of Guadalupe Hidalgo to Hopwood: The educational plight and struggle of Mexican Americans in the Southwest. *Harvard Educational Review, 68*(3), 353–413.

Sarsour, K., Sheridan, M., Jutte, D., Nuru-Jeter, A., Hinshaw, S., & Boyce, W. T. (2011). Family socioeconomic status and child executive functions: The roles of language, home environment, and single parenthood. *Journal of the International Neuropsychological Society, 17*(01), 120–132.

Savage, R., & Carless, S. (2005). Learning support assistants can deliver effective reading interventions for "at-risk" children. *Educational Research, 47*(1), 45–61.

Scott, J. W. (1992). "Experience." In J. Butler & J. W. Scott (Eds.), *Feminists theorize the political* (pp. 22–40). New York, NY: Routledge.

Shade, B. J. (1982). Afro-American cognitive style: A variable in school success? *Review of Educational Research, 52,* 219–244.

Shuey, A. M. (1966). *The testing of Negro intelligence* (2nd ed.). New York, NY: Social Science Press.

Simon, J. (2002). Taking risks: Extreme sports and the embrace of risk in advanced liberal societies. In T. Baker & J. Simon (Eds.), *Embracing risk: The changing culture of insurance and responsibility* (pp. 177–208). Chicago, IL: University of Chicago.

Skiba, R. J., Michael, R. S., Nardo, A. C., & Peterson, R. L. (2002). The color of discipline: Sources of racial and gender disproportionality in school punishment. *The Urban Review, 34*(4), 317–342.

Skiba, R., Simmons, A., Ritter, S., Kohler, K., Henderson, M., & Wu, T. (2006). The context of minority disproportionality: Practitioner perspectives on special education referral. *The Teachers College Record, 108*(7), 1424–1459.

Slavin, R., Madden, N. A., Dolan, L. J., Wasik, B. A., Ross, S., Smith, L., & Dianda, M. (1996). Success for all: A summary of research. *Journal of Education for Students Placed At Risk, 1*(1), 41–76.

Sleeter, C. E. (2008). Preparing White teachers for diverse students. In M. Cochran-Smith, S. Feiman-Nemser, & D. J. McIntyre (Eds.), *Handbook of research on teacher education* (3rd ed., pp. 559–582). New York, NY: Routledge/Taylor & Francis and the Association of Teacher Educators.

Sleeter, C. E., & Grant, C. A. (2006). *Making choices for multicultural education: Five approaches to race, class and gender* (5th ed.). New York, NY: Wiley.

Smith, C., & Carlson, B. E. (1997). Stress, coping, and resilience in children and youth. *Social Service Review, 71*(2), 231–256.

Smitherman, G. (1977). *Talking and testifying: The language of Black America.* Boston, MA: Houghton Mifflin.

Smokowski, P. R. (1998). Prevention and intervention strategies for promoting resilience in disadvantaged children. *Social Service Review, 72*(3), 337–364.

Snyder, T. D., Tan, A., & Hoffman, C. M. (2004). *Digest of education statistics, 2003* (NCES 2005-025). U.S. Department of Education, National Center for Education Statistics. (pp. 424–433). Washington, DC: U.S. Department of Education, National Center for Education Statistics

Solórzano, D. G., & Yosso, T. J. (2001). From racial stereotyping and deficit discourse toward a critical race theory in teacher education. *Multicultural Education, 9*(1), 2.

Spradley, J. P. (1979). *The ethnographic interview.* New York: Holt, Rinehart and Winston.

Stake, R. E. (1995). *The art of case study research.* Thousand Oaks, CA: Sage.

Steele, C. (2011). *Whistling Vivaldi: And other clues to how stereotypes affect us.* New York, NY: Norton.

Stringfield, S., & Land, D. (Eds.). (2002). *Educating at-risk students: One hundred-first yearbook of the National Society for the Study of Education, Part II.* Chicago, IL: University of Chicago Press.

Swadener, B. B. (1995). Children and families "at-promise": Deconstructing the discourse of risk. In B. B. Swadener & S. Lubeck (Eds.), *Children and families "at-promise": Deconstructing the discourse of risk* (pp. 17–49). Albany: State University of New York Press.

Swadener, B. B., & Lubeck, S. (Eds.). (1995). *Children and families "at-promise": Deconstructing the discourse of risk.* Albany: State University of New York Press.

Tilly, C. (1998). *Durable inequality.* Berkeley: University of California Press.

Tuck, E., & Yang, K. W. (2012). Decolonization is not a metaphor. *Decolonization: Indigeneity, Education & Society, 1*(1), 1–40.

Turnbull, G., & Spence, J. (2011). What's at-risk? The proliferation of risk across child and youth policy in England. *Journal of Youth Studies, 14*(8), 939–959.

Tyack, D. B. (1974). *The one best system: A history of American urban education.* Cambridge, MA: Harvard University Press.

Tyack, D., & Berkowitz, M. (1977). The man nobody liked: Toward a social history of the truant officer, 1840–1940. *American Quarterly, 29*(1), 31–54.

Tyack, D., & Cuban, L. (1995). *Tinkering toward utopia: A century of public school reform.* Cambridge, MA: Harvard University Press.

Ungar, M. (2011). The social ecology of resilience: Addressing contextual and cultural ambiguity of a nascent construct. *American Journal of Orthopsychiatry, 81*(1), 1–17.

United States National Advisory Commission on Civil Disorders, & Kerner, O. (1968). *Report of the National Advisory Commission on Civil Disorders, March 1, 1968.* U.S. Government Printing Office.

U.S. Department of Education. (1991). *America 2000: An education strategy.* Washington, DC: Author.

U.S. Department of Education. (2009). Race to the Top program: Executive summary. Available at www2.ed.gov/programs/racetothetop/executive-summary.pdf

U.S. Department of Education, Office of Elementary and Secondary Education.

(2002). *No Child Left Behind: A desktop reference.* Available at www2. ed.gov/admins/lead/account/nclbreference/reference.pdf

Vacha, E. F., & McLaughlin, T. F. (1992). The social structural, family, school, and personal characteristics of at-risk students: Policy recommendations for school personnel. *Journal of Education, 174,* 9–24.

Valdes, G. (1996). *Con respecto.* New York, NY: Teachers College Press.

Valencia, R. R. (1997). Genetic pathology model of deficit thinking. In R. R. Valencia (Ed.), *The evolution of deficit thinking: Educational thought and practice* (pp. 41–112). London, UK: Falmer.

Valencia, R. R. (2010). *Dismantling contemporary deficit thinking: Educational thought and practice.* New York, NY: Routledge.

Valenzuela, A. (1999). *Subtractive schooling: U.S.-Mexican youth and the politics of caring.* Albany: State University of New York Press.

Verloop, N., Van Driel, J., & Meijer, P. (2001). Teacher knowledge and the knowledge base of teaching. *International Journal of Educational Research, 35*(5), 441–461.

Villegas, A. M. (1991). *Culturally relevant pedagogy for the 1990s and beyond.* Washington, DC: ERIC Clearinghouse on Teacher Education & American Association of Colleges for Teacher Education.

Villegas, A. M., & Lucas, T. (2001). *Preparing culturally responsive teachers: A coherent approach.* Albany: State University of New York Press.

Villenas, S. A. (2012). Ethnographies de lucha (of struggle) in Latino education: Toward social movement. *Anthropology & Education Quarterly, 43*(1), 13–19.

Vinovskis, M. (1999). *Federal compensatory policies from Ronald Reagan to George W. Bush.* Available at nationalhistorycenter.org/wp-content/uploads/2008/10/vinovskislecture21.pdf

Waxman, H. C., Gray, J. P., & Padrón, Y. N. (2002). Resiliency among students at-risk of academic failure. In S. Stringfield & D. Land (Eds.), *Educating at-risk students: One hundred-first yearbook of the National Society for the Study of Education, Part II* (pp. 29–48). Chicago, IL: University of Chicago.

Wendell, E. J. (1895). Boys' clubs in New York. In R. Woods (Ed.), *Poverty U.S.A.: The historical record* (pp. 151–176). New York, NY: Arno Press.

Werner, E., & Smith, R. (1982). *Vulnerable but invincible: A study of resilient children.* New York, NY: McGraw-Hill.

Werner, E. E., & Smith, R. S. (1992). *Vulnerable but invincible: A longitudinal study of resilient children and youth.* New York, NY: McGraw-Hill.

Wortham, S. (2006). *Learning identity: The joint emergence of social identification and academic learning.* Cambridge, MA: Cambridge University Press.

Wynter, S. (1995). 1492: A new world view. In V. Lawrence Hyatt & R. Nettleford (Eds.), *Race, discourse, and the origin of the Americas: A new world view.* Washington, D.C.: Smithsonian Institute Press.

Wynter, S. (2005). On how we mistook the map for the territory, and re-imprisoned ourselves in our unbearable wrongness of being, of Désêtre. In L. Gordon & J. A. Gordon (Eds.), *Not only the master's tools: African American studies in theory and practice* (pp. 107–169). Boulder, CO: Paradigm.

Yosso, T. (2005). Whose culture has capital? A critical race theory discussion of community cultural wealth. *Race, Ethnicity and Education, 8*(1), 69–91.

Zeichner, K. M., & Liston, D. P. (2014). *Reflective teaching: An introduction.* (2nd edition). New York, NY: Routledge.

Zuberi, T. (2000). Deracializing social statistics: Problems in the quantification of race. *Annals of the American Academy of Political and Social Science, 568*, 172–185.

Index

About the Author

Keffrelyn D. Brown, PhD, is associate professor of cultural studies in education in the Department of Curriculum and Instruction at The University of Texas at Austin in Austin, TX. She is a former K–12 teacher, school administrator and curriculum consultant whose research focuses on teaching, curriculum, Black education and the sociocultural knowledge of race and culture in schooling.